TRENDS
& ISSUES

IN ELEMENTARY LANGUAGE ARTS

2000 EDITION

NATIONAL COUNCIL OF TEACHERS OF ENGLISH
1111 W. KENYON ROAD, URBANA, ILLINOIS 61801-1096

Staff Editor: Bonny Graham
Interior Design: Tom Kovacs for TGK Design; Carlton Bruett
Cover Design: Carlton Bruett

NCTE Stock Number: 55138-3050
ISSN 1527-4233

TRENDS AND ISSUES

Keeping track of the myriad issues in education can be a daunting task for those educators already stretched to fit thirty hours into a twenty-four-hour day. In an effort to inform and support English educators, the National Council of Teachers of English annually offers this volume featuring current trends and issues deemed vital to the professional conversation by our membership at large. Whether specialists or generalists, teachers know that no single "trend" or "issue" could touch the interests and concerns of all members of NCTE; with these books—one for each section of the Council: Elementary, Secondary, Postsecondary—we aim to chronicle developments in the teaching and learning of English language arts.

The wealth of NCTE publications from which to draw the materials for *Trends and Issues* proves a double-edged sword. Publishing thirteen journals (bimonthly and quarterly) and twenty to twenty-five books annually provides ample content, yet what to include and what not? Of course, timeliness and pertinence to the issues of the day help shape the book, and, more important, we aim to meet our primary goal: to answer the question, Is this valuable to our members? This edition of *Trends and Issues* offers readers a seat at the table, a chance to join the discussion. At the postsecondary level, the trends and issues cited for this year are "Race/Class/Gender Positions," "Technology," and "Writing Assessment." At the secondary level, members cited "The World Wide Web in the Classroom," "The Reemergence of Critical Literacy," and "Aesthetic Appreciation versus Critical Interrogation" as those topics of current relevance to them as English language arts professionals. At the elementary level, the trends and issues encompass "Writing and a Move to New Literacies," "Critical Literacy," and "Taking New Action."

We hope that you'll find this collection a valuable resource to be returned to often, one that facilitates professional development and reminds us that we all have a stake in the language arts profession.

NCTE invites you to send us those trends and issues in the English language arts that you feel are the most relevant to your teaching. Send your comments either to our Web site at www.ncte.org or e-mail directly to Kathryn Egawa at kegawa@ncte.org.

Kathryn A. Egawa
Associate Executive Director

CONTENTS

III. Taking New Action

INTRODUCTION

This volume is the second in a series that identifies trends and issues from among the wide scope of NCTE activities and publications. The selections here, culled from dozens of articles and book chapters, represent a glimpse into the lives of our nation's English/language arts teachers at the end of the twentieth century. These issues are further supported by the work of NCTE's many commissions and committees, and by the resolutions brought forth by the membership each November. We hope you will find the issue a valuable resource.

Our membership continually requests that we keep writing at the forefront of literacy education, especially at a time when the reading abilities of the nation's students are under scrutiny. Most language educators understand the integral role of writing to the process of reading and of reading to the process of writing. Thirty years of pedagogy focused on process and product have served our members well; you'll find that evidence here.

Further, writing serves a greater end: to name and to transform the communities in which we live and work. NCTE members are providing curricular shape to the critical literacy challenges of the past decade while simultaneously broadening our definitions of literacy. We invite you to use the lenses offered here to view these authors' teaching stories, as well as those from your own communities.

This volume focuses on topics addressed primarily by NCTE's elementary leadership. You may also want to peruse the complementary secondary and postsecondary volumes. The trends and issues identified for secondary educators include The World Wide Web in the Classroom, The Reemergence of Critical Literacy, and Aesthetic Appreciation versus Critical Interrogation; for postsecondary educators, the trends and issues are Race/Class/Gender Positions, Assessment, and Technology.

I Writing and a Move to New Literacies

The major findings of the National Assessment of Educational Progress (NAEP) 1998 Writing Report Card are clear: students experienced in writing more than one draft of a paper and students whose writing was saved in folders or portfolios achieved higher average scores than their peers who did not write multiple drafts or save their writing (see http://nces.ed.gov/nationsreportcard/writing). While long-term trend data are currently unavailable, educators recognize the increased profile that the actual *teaching* of writing plays in today's classrooms. The work that Janet Emig and Donald Graves launched almost thirty years ago continues to affect teachers and students, and now NAEP scores. Their research has been reworked and refined in the hands of capable teachers across the country. It's no surprise, then, that many NCTE authors have focused on writing and that each continues to push our thinking about this activity that is so central to our field.

Many teachers have transformed the writing practices they themselves experienced: topics chosen without writer input, focus on a final product, evaluation after the assignment has been completed, or competition among classmates. But authors Brenda Power and Susan Ohanian warn us that the worst enemy of teachers who hope to improve their writing programs is complacency. It is entirely possible to replace one set of entrenched practices with another. These educators' comments leave few pedagogical stones unturned, and you may laugh at your own teaching along the way.

It is also possible to neglect a balance between process and product, narrative and nonfiction, or to celebrate authorship at the expense of truly engaging the often long and hard work that quality writing demands. A trio of capable teachers, JoAnn Portalupi, Pat McClure, and Linda Rief, work us through such sensitive territory. Where are we headed? These teachers express a new recognition of the significant role that drawing plays in

1

shaping thought and writing, of the important role of strong mentors/authors, and of the challenge to conduct effective writing conferences. One could spend a career living up to Tom Romano's observation that effective evaluation keeps the writer writing.

And then we ask the important question: *writing about what?* The final piece in this section illustrates the role of writing that is embedded within day-to-day curriculum experiences—and within experiences of value to a distinct cultural community. Machan Elementary School in Phoenix is acknowledged for the strength of its support of bilingual learners. Students are engaged as Spanish- and English-language learners simultaneously with exploring significant content. Teachers Cecilia M. Espinosa and Karen J. Moore prompt their students to ask questions—such as Who is telling this story?, What kinds of stories would we write about ourselves?, Why would anyone want to make such a general statement about a group of people?— as they consider how texts work ideologically and how those texts operate as part of larger social practices. "Speech, voice, language, and word—are all ways of being in the world" (Nourbese Philip 1989, 16), and they all reflect a range of literacies.

Work Cited

Nourbese Philip, Marlene. 1989. *She Tries Her Tongue.* Charlottetown, P.E.I., Canada: Ragwood Press.

1 Sacred Cows: Questioning Assumptions in Elementary Writing Programs

Brenda Power and Susan Ohanian

This essay began as a series of e-mail conversations between the two authors. We are not close friends, but professional acquaintances who share a love of good stories and tough talk about teaching writing. We decided to use the e-mail exchanges as a way to reconsider some of the "sacred cows" in elementary writing programs that are rarely questioned. The four questions we chose were:

Do teachers need to be writers?

Do students need to keep journals?

Is writing a political act?

Do students need to publish their work?

Even though the format of a debate is artificial, it was a helpful way to keep ourselves honest in discussing these issues. We decided who would be "pro" and "con" in the discussions by flipping a coin, and then each of us did our best to defend whatever position was assigned to each of us. We found as we were writing that we often agreed with each others' points. Because this is a debate, not a typical scholarly essay, we overstate our views at times. We expect some of the ideas here will make readers laugh, get angry, or shake their heads in bafflement. Our goal is to provoke a response.

Reprinted from *Language Arts*, January 1999.

While we disagree about some critical issues in writing programs, we agree
on one point: the worst enemy of teachers who hope to improve their
writing programs is complacency.

Do Teachers Need to Be Writers?

Brenda: Yes; Susan: No

SUSAN: I think we place a terrible burden on a teacher
           when we tell her she has to be a writer. Do I have
           to be an artist to encourage and foster my
           students artwork? Ditto for Physical Education or
           whatever. I do think teachers should write the
           same assignments they require of students—both
           because that will eliminate some tired old chest-
           nuts and because students enjoy reading what
           their teachers write. But I think teachers are
           human and they should be allowed to select their
           areas of strength—where they sort of give it their
           all. Recently, I volunteered in the classroom of a
           2nd-grade teacher, and I cringed every day at the
           way she taught writing. It was dreadful. But this
           woman loved art, and she helped her students
           produce truly awesome artwork. So they had a
           mediocre year in writing and an inspiring year in
           art. Somehow, I have faith in kids and in teachers
           that they'll get a good mix over time. I'd like to
           see us call a halt to demanding that teachers be
           Renaissance people. I say gnaw your own bone.

BRENDA: Imagine taking pottery lessons from someone
           who has never handled clay, or photography
           lessons from someone who's never touched a
           camera. It's not necessarily critical that teachers
           write well, but they do need to try to write well. I
           remember growing up and taking piano lessons
           from a kind, old Polish woman. Every lesson
           ended with her playing the piano for a few
           minutes. She really wasn't a great pianist—even

at age eight, I realized everything she played, from minuets to ragtime, sounded suspiciously like a polka. But the combination of her kindness, and her willingness to pound away at the end of each lesson, gave me faith that I could learn something from her.

I think we've done a lot of damage in emphasizing the teacher as writer by narrowly defining it—"teacher as writer" gets translated to "writing lots of personal narratives and reading them to your students." These narrow rules of what constitutes teacherly writing come from university types who have little knowledge of what it's like to try to write eloquently about planting your garden with your hand while your eyes scan the class looking for Timmy, who five minutes earlier, began to turn green and announced he was ready to throw up. Writing is intense, and teaching is intense, and they are intense in different ways. It's not easy to combine the two in the classroom, and maybe teachers shouldn't try. But they need to find a space for writing somewhere in their lives, and open up that space for students to examine.

To say it's okay for teachers to be weak writers, or for them to not even try to write well, leads us quickly back to the days when writing teachers were supremely confident about their ability to teach writing, because they could do one thing well—mark up spelling and grammatical errors on student work.

SUSAN: I wonder why we pick writing as the one curricular area that the teacher must do in her spare time. I think it was Paul Theroux who pointed out, "Writing is lousy on the nerves." I stand firm on belief that a teacher, a human being, is made better by having some overriding passion. I might draw the line at allowing "collecting beer cans" to apply, but I taught next door to a scary teacher, a real termagant, a skill sergeant. But the kids and I were entranced the one day during the year when she brought in her old bottle collection and talked about it as an introduction to some history unit or another.

I participate in an on-line chat group in mathematics. There are a lot of elementary teachers trying to become better math teachers. We aren't trying to become mathematicians, though, of course, we all think it's wonderful when we have a rare glimpse of the corner of some deep mathematical principle. But we do this not to become mathematicians but to enrich our teaching, to become more aware of mathematical teaching possibilities in our classrooms. Mostly we don't talk about math, but about teaching math.

The elementary teacher, of course, has a special problem because she teachers all subjects. But the issue is important to high school teaching, as well. I once participated in a huge National Endowment for the Humanities grant, wherein professors came up to Troy, New York once a week to retrain us in the humanities. They had constructed this wonderful model whereby each teacher would contribute to art theory according to his "discipline." So, in looking at a painting, the mathematics teacher would bring in the special perspective of mathematics, the writing teacher would bring in a rhetorical perspective, and so on. The project was a disaster. You know why? The good professors didn't realize we taught kids, not disciplines. Except in rather unique cases, a mathematics teacher is not a mathematician; she does not produce mathematics. Why do we pick on the writing teacher—and expect her to produce writing?

BRENDA: I think there's a difference between not having a passion for something, and outright fear and loathing. Too many teachers fear and loathe writing—and you get over those feelings by writing. If teachers don't acknowledge and confront those feelings consciously, they are in danger of transferring them to their students. Worse, they promote traditional school concepts of what constitutes "good" writing—in my experience, it's flowery prose filled with clichés. At the very least, when you try to write well yourself, you begin to get a sense of what constitutes good writing. It gives you a compass (however weak at the start) to guide you toward those students who have the talent and drive to make writing their grand passion.

SUSAN: You are absolutely right when you say that, when you work with things, you get less fearful and even better. At a deep level, I still fear math. But I enjoy finding interesting mathematical relationships in the real world. I keep a notebook of these. I suspect the equivalent for a writing teacher would be keeping a notebook of other peoples' felicitous phrases. If I were a college instructor of prospective language arts teachers, I'd have two requirements: Keep a notebook of good words they find in their reading—to make them aware of "possibilities"—and write at least three letters a week—and mail them. I think the world would be a better place if more people wrote letters.

We must realize that first and foremost we are teachers. That means that most of us are generalists, not specialists. Our professional expertise is in children, not in the real world practice of a discipline. Most writing teachers could not make a living writing. Not many writers make a living writing.

BRENDA: Of course I agree that teaching comes first. And just because you're a great writer, doesn't mean you can even be a so-so teacher. But the next leap, from noting and appreciating good writing, to trying to write something well yourself and get response from others, is still essential for me. As Ruth Nathan notes, "It is knowing how a writer feels when a piece is shared, the chemical twang, the wildly beating heart, the mental involvement, the 'I'm out there and feeling vulnerable' sensations that you must comprehend if you want to do a decent teaching job." I've visited too many classes where teachers ask students to do things with their writing, from on-the-spot readings to the whole class to oddball revisions, that just wouldn't happen if the teacher had even once experienced that chemical twang of putting her writing out for response, or of feeling like you've lost an arm when you have to whack off the first three pages of your writing to get to the good stuff. I don't think we're in danger of losing many teachers because they will be overwhelmed by the urge to "go professional" in their writing. If anything, I suspect the reverse would be true—they'd have much more respect for what hard work writing is, and how much we are asking of students with many writing tasks.

Should Students Keep Journals?

Susan: No; Brenda: Yes

SUSAN: A large part of my quarrel with journals is that they are developmentally inappropriate for young children. A journal is "internal," a record of one's reflections, thoughts, and dreams. In contrast, young children's writing should be social—reaching out to the world rather than looking inward.

I will admit that journals are an ideal and natural form for adolescent angst, but schools have no business meddling with the psyche. I like Jane Carlyle's observation in her diary, October 21, 1855: "Your journal, all about feelings, aggravates whatever is fractious and morbid in you." She also points to the hazards of journal keeping: "I remember Charles Butler saying of the Duchess Praslin's murder, 'What could a poor fellow do with a wife who kept a journal, but murder her?'"

I reject the term "dialogue journal." If we're going to write letters to kids, then call them letters. We should stop disguising what we do in the schoolroom by abstruse vocabulary that nobody understands.

BRENDA: But doesn't it make sense that some children may be able to best sort through their emotions through journal writing, and then be able to reach out socially in more useful ways?

I know some of my most important writings are screeds never meant to be seen by the person I'm writing to or about. Writing in this way is a great emotional release, and it's only for me. Just seeing the words on the page at times helps me get over that emotion, and deal with that person in more thoughtful, reflective ways.

Your response will probably be that my experience is more closely connected to the adolescent journal writing you're encouraging. But I've seen young children do similar writing "to get through" an experience, whether it's a fight with a brother or the sudden loss of a parent.

A true story: When I was a researcher in a fourth-grade inner-city classroom some years ago, a couple of the girls wrote graphically about being beaten by their parents. Sessions with social workers ensued, with much hand wringing about the best course of action. In the midst of it all, the girls admitted they had lied in their writing—their parents had never beaten them. They had written the stories to get attention. The social workers did a careful analysis of the situation, and determined there was no evidence of physical abuse.

I've written this as an "aha" story for you. I suspect your response will be, "See? This is what happens when you encourage kids to emote in journals." I admit that I get queasy too with all the "writing teacher as social worker" essays, and I fear too many teachers implicitly promote deeply personal writing about family secrets because they are more comfortable fixing personal problems than they are fixing the development of a metaphor in writing. I've read a couple psychosocial or emotional articles and books about writer's workshop where the students in the class who come from a family with two parents who love each other must feel woefully left out of the group community-building that comes from writing about abusive, transvestite stepparents, and the like, during workshop time.

But I still think writing is the stuff of our lives, and for many writers, sorting through that "stuff" to get to the writing that needs a social audience will involve personal writing. Keeping a daybook or a journal is a time-honored tradition. Just because writing doesn't serve that purpose for you, might it not still serve that purpose for many students? Teaching is about getting beyond what seems natural and right for us personally, and into what makes sense from research built upon the experiences of other learners.

SUSAN: Well, I wouldn't forbid journal writing. I've been known to encourage it for a kid or two. But I wouldn't require it either. By the way, I myself have kept a journal at several times in my life. And I now keep what might be called a reading log. I don't reflect on the reading—just write down the good lines, provocative events, or whatever.

One thing that very much bothers me about school journals is the responses teachers make in them. These marginal kinds of responses, "You must have been happy" or "You must have been sad," seem so "teacherly," about as inspiring and exciting as cold mashed potatoes. And if the journal is so special and so personal, then why do teachers have any business putting comments in the margins? Writing comments in the margins is an act of power and control. It has no place in the intimate baring of the soul. I mean, journals are either personal/ introspective or they aren't. Teachers can't have this both ways. If they start writing comments, then this is just another school activity.

Historically, in real life, I know of only one example of someone keeping a journal and someone else responding. Louisa May Alcott began a journal when she was 11. She told her mother she'd like to have her write in it and it became a medium for their notes to one another. That has a nice modern classroom sound, doesn't it? Now some people would call that an *interactive journal*, a term, along with *dialogue journal*, that I detest. It sickens me to see teacher and students writing back and forth about a novel nobody cares about. I don't warm to it even when they care about the novel. I say if it looks like a book report and quacks like a book report, then let's just call it a book report.

Whenever there's a hot item such as *journals* in education, then publishers aren't far behind. I have a whole collection of so-called professional books containing journal topics. Now there's a misnomer, right? Have a kid keep a journal and then assign the topics. Here are a few gems[1]:

Compare the national flag and your state flag.

Compare your haircut and one of your friend's haircuts.

Compare your front yard and your friend's front yard.

Plan a farm. What type of animals would you raise, what type of crops would you grow?

Explain the difference between a hobby and playing on a summer baseball team.

Would you rather be, an astronaut or a rattlesnake keeper?

Would you rather be a garbage collector or a teacher?

BRENDA: Well, Susan, by squirreling away those preposterous journal topics in a box in your attic, you show that educators often have the best of both worlds—we are teachers *and* garbage collectors. But how can you say journals are or aren't this or that for all students in a class, when writers through history have used them for such different purposes, and students really do have unique styles, needs, and processes as writers?

The difference between the journal a student keeps in school and the journal an adult writer keeps is that the adult writer isn't, . . . well, a student anymore. The adult isn't in the process of learning how journal writing can be used to help her develop both her writing abilities, emotional control, or world views—she knows how a journal does that for her, and that's why she keeps it.

Just because some teachers do lousy jobs responding to journals doesn't mean others don't do wonderful jobs. Even the teacher comments you cite as awful wouldn't necessarily be bad in all contexts. The teacher should always be the more experienced other, the guide to help students see the functions and uses of those daily jottings. I like writer Anne Lamott's quote, "Our purpose isn't to see through others, but to see each other through." I think it easily describes the difference for me between adult journal keeping and student journal keeping. Adults use their journals to see through the world and make sense of it. The students have teachers to help see them through the process of keeping a journal, and what it can or can't mean for their development as writers and people. Students aren't necessarily in a position to figure that out for themselves—but the teacher with comments that nudge in the right direction can assist.

SUSAN: I am sympathetic with right-wing fundamentalists who are scared of journals in the schools. I believe that children need to learn the difference between a public voice and a private voice. School is where you use your public voice. Letter writing is a good form because it is written for someone else and kids understand this is "public." Things get very murky with journals; kids don't readily see the distinctions.

Journal writing in the schools feeds into the current rash of personal memoirs and the TV schlock talk shows where people are anxious to "tell all." I urge teachers to cast off their therapist's couch and stop encouraging agony overload in schools.

Journals in the schools reflect the current societal vogue that all secrets are bad, that secrets that don't dress up and parade in public will fester. But in The Bellarosa Connection by Saul Bellow, the narrator remarks, "Deeply experienced people . . . keep things to themselves." This is an important point. Teachers are exploiting children's lack of experience when they announce that the school journal is the place to "tell all." Secrets are an integral part of our privacy, and we need to help children learn how to protect their private spaces. We do that by letting kids know some writing isn't appropriate in school.

BRENDA: Rashes, exploiting, festering, scared. Good thing you wouldn't stoop to using any kind of inflammatory language here, Susan!

The reason journals are called dialogue journals or learning logs or daybooks is because they are used for different purposes by different teachers. As Vygotsky points out, there is a world in a word. Teachers rename and rethink journals all the time, because of public/private issues and curricular purposes. I honestly don't recognize the purposes you cite in the teachers I work with daily. The last incident I remember from a "secret" shared in a journal came in Jane Doan's multi-age class last fall. A second grader wrote about running away from home in his daybook. Jane read the passage, wondered what to do, and finally called home at lunchtime. The dad said, "Oh yeah, he's been talking about running away. He's even got a bag packed. He's really been reading a lot of survivalist literature. Kids!" And then he thanked her for the call. So many of those "secrets shared" are the normal sorting out students go through in figuring out what's public, what's private, what makes sense to write down, what makes sense to talk about, what makes sense to ignore. I personally know of no teachers who actively seek private, prurient information in journals. We deal with that stuff all the time from students, without having to demand it in a journal.

Is Writing a Political Act?

Susan: Yes; Brenda: No

SUSAN: I shunned the very idea that writing is a political act until I was invited to speak at some NCTE session on writing as a political act, and Pat Shannon said, "Tell your toilet-paper story." I thought: Oh, is that all it means—telling a story about who you are and where you fit in the hierarchy?

Maybe that's a naive interpretation, but when the professors wrote their grand texts on writing as a political act, I had rejected it as anything touching my life because the schema was too grand, too universal. Me? I tell stories. And of course the stories we choose to tell (and the ones we reject) is the essence of politics. As Tip O'Neill said, "All politics is local."

The toilet-paper story? It is the story of my 4-year struggle to get toilet paper in the lavatory that would actually fit into the toilet paper dispensers. I went to the principal and to the union. The principal would come up with bizarre plans to solve the problem—such as putting toilet paper in shoeboxes on the floor in back of the toilet. And the union would inform me the problem had been solved. I ended up phoning the County Health Department, the County Environmental Protection Unit. I talked to a public health nurse, to a senior public health sanitation officer, who told me the maintenance of health in public school is the responsibility of the New York State Education Department. After three phone transfers at the State Education Department, I learned that they could not find any lavatory regulations. They referred me to the local Board of Education.

I phoned the Occupational Safety and Health Administration (OSHA) in Washington DC. They referred me to my local PTA.

I phoned the New York State Department of
Labor, Division of Safety and Health. I insisted
that they search the codes and they found that
"an adequate supply of toilet paper should be
provided." One official said I should write my
congressional representative about getting provi-
sions added to the Public Employee Health and
Safety Codes.

Our faculty became divided between those
who claimed there had never been a toilet paper
problem and those who marched in the hallways
carrying toilet paper rolls on broomsticks. I have
since divided the world into two groups: those
who see that the toilet-paper story reveals the
craziness of bureaucracy and the willingness of
teachers to be victims, and those who don't. After
a number of rejections, my article about the affair
was eventually published in Phi Delta Kappan
and awarded EdPress prize as best article about
education published that year. So, some people
did get the point.

BRENDA: I agree that all politics is local, and politics in its
most basic sense is nothing more than a power
exchange between two people. I love that toilet
paper story, but I don't notice that you set your
students off on a letter-writing campaign to
change the TP status quo, and I'm glad you
didn't. It was your issue, and in dealing with it,
you learned a lot about political systems. I guess
where the analogy breaks down for me is in
finding a clear link to teaching kids to read and
write. At this point, I fear I'll be bombarded with
stories of how kids wrote letters that changed the
cafeteria menu or did reading projects that
brought about social justice. But I worry whose
agenda this really pushes at times—the students',
or the teachers'? And in much of the material
written about teaching literacy as a political act, I
see the agendas of professors and scholars more

than the agenda of teachers. Again and again, when I and the teachers I work with read articles about how political our choices are in writing programs, we ask, "If this is supposed to empower me, how come it isn't written in language I can understand? How come it makes me feel stupid?"

I think Frank Smith was right when he wrote about literacy advocates overstating the claims for what literacy can do (and what literacy instruction can do). One of the reasons whole language is viewed so suspiciously by much of the general public is that advocates say, "This isn't about reading and writing as much as it is about teaching students to speak up and out, and to challenge the curriculum and the status quo." Parents justifiably want to make sure reading and writing programs are indeed about reading and writing first, and they worry that the "empowerment" of students through literacy is really just a cloak for pushing the teacher's political agenda (whether that be jabbing at the administration or hounding colleagues through students, to abandon their workbooks). Writing programs should fulfill students' needs more than teachers'.

In my darker moments, I think some teachers use their students as a tool for reinforcing their views or pushing their political agendas. Consider these words from a popular literacy study meant to be read by teachers:

Literacy itself can be understood only in its social and political context, and that context, once the mythology has been stripped away, can be seen as one of entrenched class structure in which those who have power have a vested interest in keeping it.

I think that's a lot of baggage for the poor first grader who really only wants to know which way the big "D" curves in the Disney World story she is writing, and instead must grapple with the hegemony of oppression the Disney empire creates in our classist culture. I say, kids are pretty vulnerable, but they are also smart enough to do some sorting on their own. Let 'em write, and don't push political agendas that community members may or may not share.

SUSAN: What bothers me is that teachers refuse to recognize even the tiniest local politics, which translates into being responsible for the choices they make. Being political doesn't mean you have to stand up on a soapbox and orate. It does mean you have to assume responsibility for the choices you make. Each teacher is responsible for the books she brings to children—and, for example, if those books exclude access to some children, if those books reinforce certain power structures, or whatever, then she has made a very political decision.

In my darkest moments, I think that some teachers like putting themselves—or letting themselves remain—in the role of victim. Victims don't have to accept responsibility—not for themselves, the children, or the curriculum.

Do Students Need to Publish Their Work?

Susan: No; Brenda: Yes

SUSAN: As a writer, I hate the fact that, once a book is written (I've been working on my latest one for nearly 20 years), it takes another year for it to come out. Early on, I learned that if you wait to see your bound work, you lose a lot of time. I've trained myself to give myself about one day of relief after finishing a project. Then it's back to scribble-scribble on something else. By the time I finally get the bound work, I'm a different person than the one who wrote it. And I don't much care about it any more. I don't think I've ever read one of my books after it was a book.

I try to bring an immediacy to my student's work. Seventh-grade students once wrote a murder mystery set in our middle school. We "published" each chapter as it was written by taping it on the media center walls. So the public could read the mystery as they walked by. But there was never a hard copy for the writers. And, as the public reacted to the work, the writers kept adding more. There was daily excitement among writers and public alike—everyone wanted to see what each new day would bring at the writing wall.

When I taught 3rd grade, my students were segregated as the worst readers of 3rd grade, kids who had failed 3rd grade already, kids mainstreamed in, kids in many ways identified by the school as "losers." They hated writing even more than they hated reading. And so, I began assigning topics. For example, on the first rainy day I read aloud many poems about mud and then we all wrote about mud experiences. I acted as their editor, bypassing all the writing-process steps. I explained all this to my students. I told them that's what editors do—"fix up" spelling, grammar, punctuation.

We wrote on a common topic at least three times a week. I typed up all the students' pieces, the average length of which was only four sentences. I also included what I had written and an excerpt by someone whose words students loved, say Jack Prelutsky. Then I gave every child a copy. Their homework was to read everybody's words to an adult, who was asked to sign the paper. I guess it's publishing in a way. It violates all the (good) principles and I'd defend it anyway. I had proof of the power of this technique: when a child was absent, parents would phone to see if it was a "good" homework day. They didn't mind missing spelling or whatever, but they didn't want to miss a broadside. And the custodian told me about the night Dads were reading one of the very funny and clever broadsides aloud at the local bar . . . but that's another story.

BRENDA: I don't disagree with any of the improvisations you cite about bringing work to a larger audience. Taping chapters to the wall, conversing with parents—that's all work that exposes students to writing for different audiences and purposes. But it's not the sacred cow of writer's workshop I'm advocating, which is a bound or stapled volume by each individual student in the class that has gone through an editing process.

When I argue for the importance of this, I'm reminded of an experience a few years ago when a friend gave birth to her first child after 26 hours of labor. I was chatting with her husband the following week, clucking about how hard that must have been for her. He demurred, saying, "Oh no, I was the coach, and it's not as hard as people think. I mean, the pains only come every five or ten minutes. You have long breaks—you can read a magazine, or almost catch a nap between each one."

As a university teacher arguing for teachers to find time to edit with children, type, and bind books, I run the risk of seeming as insensitive as that husband. I know how hard it is to teach, and how hard it is to find time to publish work. But I don't know it from the inside of an elementary classroom in the same way as a teacher does, and I'm the first to admit it's probably harder than I'll ever know to find time for something like publishing books. I can say I do publish my undergrads' work every semester, in a collective, bound, desktop published volume. Many semesters I'm finishing the work on it in the wee hours of the morning before the last class, wondering if it's worth the effort. But years later, when I see students, they remark that they still have their class book, and they still pull it off the shelf.

I don't know any other task that gives students such a sense of distant audiences, of how they have to take the long view in constructing meaningful plots and characters because they won't always be on-site to clarify their meanings for others. And my belief in publishing comes from visiting more and more classrooms where there is nothing in the writing program that resembles the editing, polishing, and binding in final form I write about. The feel of the writing program in many of those classrooms is flat, and the teacher's first question is often, "How can I get some creative spark here when students are choosing their own topics?" Publishing does a lot of work toward keeping workshops lively, because students have goals in sight beyond immediate response from teachers and peers.

SUSAN: I'm not sure that I as a teacher save any time—typing up student daily work and photocopying sets every day (we won't go into how much time it takes to get hold of that much paper). But students spend time each day writing new pieces, not rewriting and rewriting a single piece.

I worry that when so much time is spent on editing and revising—and making the cover—the kids don't write very much. They get a few finely honed pieces. I wonder at what cost these "products" are produced. If one assumes that, for young writers, fluency is the goal, shouldn't kids write a lot? Sort of full speed ahead—and damn the consequences as well as the commas.

With the 7th-grade and 3rd-grade kids euphemistically referred to as "reluctant readers," I made a daily letter exchange the heart of the writing program. At the end of the year, I took a look at how their letters at the beginning of the year compared with their letters at the end. There was a dramatic increase in length of letters; also in the length of sentence. I wonder if there is research evidence that supports the increase in fluency produced by kids making those beautiful books.

BRENDA: You're right—the Martha Stewart invasion has ruined many a fine teacher when it comes to publishing programs. I suspect that even as we sit here writing there is a mad teacher in New Jersey who is soaking pounds of flax seed at the bottom of the school pond, readying it for pounding and carding by the children later into the linen that will be used in their published book covers.

Too much time spent trying to make the books beautiful or, for that matter, forcing children to edit for days far beyond their competence can kill the love of writing and publishing in a child. What's hurt teachers further are edicts about how much should be published. I remember Mary Ellen Giacobbe published 400 first-grade student books the year Don Graves was in her classroom as a researcher, and that figure shows up as a model in his classic book *Writing: Teachers and children at work.* But Mary Ellen is the first to tell you that's a ridiculous number of books to publish in a year. That was a very hard teaching year for Mary Ellen, and publishing books was one thing she was doing well. Cranking them out helped her stay sane, and she wouldn't recommend that level of production to any teachers who are already feeling sane.

What I advocate is that teachers find a level of publishing that works for them, and then get parent or older-student support in the school to work at that level.

SUSAN: I have deep reservations about declaring kids "authors." My niece is a sophomore in high school and absolutely convinced she's going to be a writer. She knows she's going to be a writer because, after all, she has a collection of published books. She has been a published writer since first grade. She's been fed this line about being a real writer, a published writer, ever since she was in first grade. And she believes it. Last week she sent me about a million poems. The best ones have a Dracula theme. I can't bear to describe the worst ones. Does every kid who takes piano lessons hear from his teacher that he's going to be a concert pianist? Are kids in little league told they are going to be major leaguers?

I have made my living writing since 1984. Maybe it's because my bank balance is always precarious, but when people ask me what I do, until last year, I said, "I work in education." Sometimes I get brave and say, "I write." I have never announced, "I am a writer." Let's get a reality check. Anne Tyler is a writer. Gore Vidal is a writer. If we really believe in process, why are we announcing to first graders that they are authors? It's a terrible burden.

BRENDA: I would argue that the cautionary tale of your niece isn't about the dangers of publishing, as much as the dangers of easy praise from teachers. In one of my all-time favorite *Language Arts* articles, "Do Teachers Talk with Their Students as if They Were Dogs?" Lowell Madden argues that much of our talk in schools is hollow praise, intended only to provoke in students surface level behaviors that are appealing to us. In this scheme, a published book isn't much more valuable than a dog biscuit to a student—a quick reward that encourages her to keep writing.

For me, publishing is the end point of a process where students of any age really have to think through issues of audience and craft, at whatever developmental level they work. My model was Pat McLure, a first-grade teacher in Lee, New Hampshire. Her students didn't publish much, because each book was typed by Pat, with the child sitting next to her, and this was done after a few conferences about revision and form. Some children published a half dozen books in a year; others only a few. But it was hard work to think through, read, and make changes to the drafts.

I have graduate students who have been known to burst into tears at the most gentle of writing conferences when I suggest major revisions before they send something out for publication. I even had one recently tell me this shows I don't believe in the "writing process," whatever the heck she thinks that means. I don't relish those teary college conferences, and I wish teachers had used publishing conferences in earlier grades with the same intent I saw Pat use them—to teach craft and push students beyond the edge of their competence into better texts. Publishing programs that are thoughtful can be seen more as the solution to your niece's misconceptions than the source of them.

I suspect that if your niece didn't have that stack of published books, she'd still want to be a writer. But you're probably right—she's got concrete proof of her status as a writer, and that's only going to make her college professor's job that much harder.

SUSAN: Your point about easy praise getting mixed up with the publishing process is a really good one. I think the only other point I'd make is that I published my students' work in community broadsides (in 3rd grade there were about 3 a week), not in individual books. And this was because most of their public writing (as contrasted with our letter exchange) was on the same topic . . . and it allowed really weak students to participate. Oh god, I'm not sounding like a collaborationist, am I?

A teacher has to look at her students, at what they need, and then proceed accordingly. I worry about the "product" becoming too important. I taught in a school where second grade teachers taught the comma in apposition and third-grade teachers had big posters with the "Five Don'ts of Composition: Don't begin a sentence with 'and' . . ." That kind of stuff. I was just determined that kids were going to get some relief from this oppression, to have some fun. This is weird coming from me because I know that writing involves fierce discipline. But let's not confuse the profession of writing and what goes on in schools. Schools have gone kind of haywire insisting that every student must be a published writer. Every year.

I don't think any of my third graders left me confident that they were "authors." That is surely one of the most overused—and abused—terms in literacy education. It is a term I do not use in the classroom. My students did not leave my classroom with a collection of bound volumes. My students left knowing they liked playing with words, knowing that they needed an editor, knowing their writing had entertained a community of parents and other adults.

We hope our discussions have done more than provoke some new thinking about these issues. These conversations have made both of us think more about the power of being challenged on any long-held views. Good friends are often sympathetic to our viewpoints, and they will patiently listen when we tell our favorite stories for the fourteenth time. Perhaps the best professional friends are the ones who push us past the easy assumptions that come from well-worn tales and comfortable beliefs. E-mail is a wonderful vehicle for friendly, focused exchanges on crucial issues. We don't expect this essay to change beliefs—but we hope it encourages readers to find new ways to challenge their own most cherished assumptions about elementary writing instruction.

Note

1. Susan Ohanian found these journal topics at publishers' booths at the NCTE spring conference in Charlotte, NC.

2 Learning to Write: Honoring Both Process and Product

JoAnn Portalupi

> Writing teachers enter into an unspoken contract with students to help them become better writers by the end of a course.
>
> —Ken Macrorie

Since I remember so little about writing in elementary school, let me start with a strong memory from eleventh grade. I recall sitting side by side with my good friend Brad waiting for the teacher to return our writing. Inevitably Brad's work would come back with the teacher's affirmation—a neatly scripted red penciled A. My work chugged along behind with a B, perhaps an occasional B+. Brad had the edge on me: I knew this. What I didn't know was why. What was it that distinguished his paper from mine? What qualitative difference was there between this teacher's A and her B? The sparse marginal comments and staccato red dashes provided little information. I was never able to unravel that mystery well enough to pull off the A paper. But I survived eleventh grade English, passing with a respectable grade, and have since gone on to be a lifelong student of writing and teaching, particularly the teaching of writing.

Many of us teaching today have similar experiences of writing in school. Nothing about these experiences is characterized by the conversation, community, and attention to process that are so prevalent in classrooms

Reprinted from *Primary Voices K–6*, April 1999.

today. The approach my teachers used to teach writing centered on product to the exclusion of process and delegated the teacher as "expert reader," to the detriment of the student.

Today, elementary classrooms across the country bear the influence of writing process research that has shifted attention from product to process. In 1978 Graves provided research warning that the teaching of writing received little to no attention in most elementary schools. A few years later, his book *Writing: Teachers and Children at Work* was published, and thousands of teachers nationwide finally had a hand-book to guide them in how to teach writing.

Graves's early work and the onslaught of research that followed initiated a para-digm shift in instruction. Teachers no longer assigned and corrected writing. Instead they set aside regular time for students to write and be coached through the process.

It has been 20 years since that shift. The terms Murray (1968) first coined—rehearse, draft, revise, edit—have become commonplace in many classrooms and an integral component in current language arts textbooks. We now accept that teaching students to write requires attention to process. We understand that learning to write is no different from learning any complex task. You learn to play tennis by playing tennis; you learn to bake bread by baking bread. If you want to learn to write, you must write.

Many of us were initially drawn into the writing process movement by the fundamental respect and attention it paid to children. Writing process offered us the chance to listen to our students, to become careful observers of their learning, and to use those observations to guide us on how best to help them grow as writers. This focus on children required new teaching strategies that asked us to rethink everything from the way we organized time and space in the classroom to the roles we defined for our students and ourselves. This latter change was perhaps the most dramatic. As students took on a more central role in their learning, the role of the teacher shifted to one who guides students in the process of their own learning.

Murray (1982) characterized this shift as a move from "teaching as telling" to "teaching as revealing." If teachers were to instruct students successfully in the process of writing, they themselves needed a clear understanding of the cycle of craft. Teachers needed to write and they needed to make that writing public. They needed to demonstrate the messiness of the craft—the false starts, the ongoing dialogue a writer has with the emerging text (Calkins, 1984, p. 19), the way meaning is often found in the line that surprises (Murray, 1989, p. 5). This shift in turn precipitated a change in the tone of the classroom. Our classrooms became workshop communities in which teachers and students shared reading and writing together.

While there is no question we have come far since the assign-and-correct days of writing instruction, we are currently undergoing another shift. Process has come under recent scrutiny. A complaint I hear, often from administrators in the context of impending large-scale assessment, is that the focus on process results in a less than desirable product. "Sure children love to write," some say, "but what good is it if they can't write well?"

Effective writing teachers have known all along that attending to process and product is not an either-or endeavor. They take seriously the task Macrorie (1994) refers to when he says, "Writing teachers enter into an unspoken contract with students to help them become better writers by the end of a course" (p. 70). They understand that the care given to process serves the goal of developing writers who can create better products. And they know that this requires a knowledgeable and skillful teacher.

What must a teacher know in order to teach writing well? Effective teachers draw from two crucial wells: knowledge of how children learn to write and knowledge of writing itself. Teachers need to know what is involved in putting internal thoughts onto paper to reach a more distant audience. They need knowledge of the range of successful strategies writers use. They gain this knowledge by writing themselves, observing writers at work, and reading the many resources by professional writers about their writing processes.

But knowledge of a professional writer's process is not enough. Teachers need to view this process through a lens that takes into account the developmental capabilities of their students. This involves everything from understanding how students develop as spellers to how they come to think of narrative and the complex relationship between writer and reader.

In his work on teacher knowledge, Shulman (1986) makes a distinction between pedagogical knowledge and subject matter knowledge. Teachers draw on their pedagogical knowledge when they successfully manage writing conferences in a classroom with 30 students, create communities that encourage risk taking, inspire creativity, and successfully nudge the resistant student into writing. This knowledge also guides teachers in making the critical decisions of when to instruct in or allow for exploration and discovery.

Teachers need expert knowledge on the subject matter as well. If students are to become more skillful writers, they need teachers who know what constitutes good writing. This includes the standard conventions of our language as well as the range of literary elements that define artful writing. This knowledge of the discipline allows teachers to be responsive to students while guiding them to become more competent users of written language.

In my work with teachers across the country, it is this last area of expertise—knowledge of literary craft itself—that elementary teachers seem least sure of. Once our classroom workshops are underway—folders, materials, management systems in place—what next? How do we do extend the manageable workshop into an environment in which rigorous teaching about craft takes place?

What Is Craft?

Craft. It's difficult to define yet easily recognizable. In the literature written by teachers and writers, there is a range of definitions. Consider this variety:

> Good writing doesn't waste words. Its not sentimental. It dramatizes its crucial moments. If it's powerful writing, at the same time it rises above those moments and tells us what it's like to be alive on this earth. (Macrorie, 1994, p. 79)

> [Craft is knowing] . . . how to find the right word, how to rub two words together in a phrase that gives off more meaning than either word alone, the skill of allowing a sentence to find its own flowing course, the placing of emphasis within the paragraph. . . . (Murray, 1994, p. 59)

> I think of a writer as part-magician, part technician. A writer is the sort of wizard whose sorcery involves the use of words to create a particular effect: suspect, distortion of time, a character's inner life, etc. The writer's craft involves the use of words to deliberately create the effect you want. (Fletcher, 1997, unpublished journal writings)

What does this mean for the elementary teacher, particularly teachers working with the youngest writers? Is craft something to be reserved for older students once they have mastered the conventions of language? Certainly not. When Graves (1983) pronounced that first graders can write on the first day of school, he asked us to reconsider our definitions of writing. For many six-year-olds, writing involves the same goal that more experienced writers hold—putting thoughts onto paper. Researchers (Calkins, 1984; Clay, 1975; Graves, 1983; Harste, Woodward, & Burke, 1984) helped us understand that a child's representation of thought matched her developing knowledge of print. If the writer had little awareness of letters, the meaning was inscribed in drawing. If he had mastery over a handful of letters, those letters might be added to the picture to further represent the story. Regardless of their product, children were representing their thoughts and experiences of the world.

In the same fashion, we need to rethink our understanding of craft when working with young children. Consider this conversation I recently had with two eight-year-olds.

JP:	When you read a book you really like or write something you think is really good, what makes it good? What would you say is good writing?
DAVID:	I think when people talk back and forth that makes a good story. What's that called?
JP:	You mean conversation?
DAVID:	No, it begins with a D—.
ROBERT:	Dialogue.
DAVID:	Yeah, interesting dialogue—like yelling.
ROBERT:	I'd look for interesting parts and things.
JP:	What do you mean, interesting parts? Can you say more about that?
ROBERT:	The beginning. Leading?
DAVID:	A good lead like the first few words.
ROBERT:	Yeah, a good lead.
DAVID:	Mostly the end is interesting to me.
JP:	Is there anything else?
ROBERT:	The story. What it's about.
JP:	Hmm, let's see. If there's a book about a subject you don't like, is it possible that someone else might like it and think it's a good book?
DAVID:	Yeah. Not everybody's interested in the same thing.
JP:	Okay then. Let's say you don't like the book but others do—what might make it "good"?
DAVID:	Talking to each other. Conversation. Arguing is the most interesting part of the dialogue.

It's interesting to note the way in which Robert and David reach for specific language to describe their concepts of good writing. David seems to recognize that the label—dialogue—empowers him to communicate in a common arena with others. The language provides a kind of shorthand and facilitates discussion of craft.

It is not surprising that these boys' descriptions of good writing are different from those offered by older, experienced writers. What is surprising is the way in which definitions of good writing serve similar purposes for writers of all ages. Writing involves shifting from the role of writer to reader, back to writer again. Write a little. Stop. Read. Write some more. This rereading may happen when a draft is finished, but it also happens many times during the process of drafting. The writer pauses to reflect—on either what's been written or the feeling that accompanies the writing—and then moves onward. Much of this "rereading" is not visible to an outside observer. What happens in that reading mode has everything to do with the way the writer thinks about craft.

Claire is seven and doesn't want to leave out a single detail about her weekend camping trip. As she rereads, she considers: "Have I told it all?" Jamel is 11 and reads mysteries. He knows what it feels like to be held in suspense and wants to create that effect for his readers. He reads what he has written and wonders if he's told too much or given enough clues to spark the reader's curiosity. How Claire and Jamel answer these questions will ultimately determine their next writing moves.

But knowledge of craft applies to more than rereading a draft. Writers use knowledge of craft to generate texts as well as to conceive ideas. Recognizing that an incident has potential for a story requires knowledge of craft. David writes a scene with dialogue because that is what he likes to read. Craft is like a map that helps you as you move through writing and reading. It helps you understand the lay of the land and steer with more authority.

Do children do this naturally? Not without particular conditions in place. Mem Fox (1990) says, "Writers don't improve their craft unless they have a real purpose, a real audience, and a real investment in their writing" (p. 471). These three conditions set the stage for teachers to encourage students to read as writers and to write as readers.

The writing process movement has been buoyed by an extensive body of writing presented by teachers about the work they are doing in their classrooms. In these classroom portraits, we see firsthand the ways in which students and teachers together become students of craft. What these stories teach us is that learning to write well—with attention to craft—is not divorced from authentic engagement with reading and writing.

Reading as a Writer

We build our knowledge of craft each time we engage in discussion of literature. When we ask students to notice when a text confuses, surprises, or delights them and to reread the text to see what occurs on the page to evoke such a response, we help them study craft.

Calkins (1984) and her colleagues at the Teachers College Writing Project show how certain "touchstone books" become territory in which to study craft. Peterson and Eeds (1990) show how students and teachers study craft when they engage in "grand conversations" about books. When we read and reread in order to dwell in a text we develop a new and deeper relationship with that text. Read once to experience, understand, enjoy. If you decide the book is something to aspire to, return to it and study it with a writer's eye (Fletcher & Portalupi, 1998).

Teachers can talk about leads, strong verbs, fully developed characters, five-sense description, writing small, creating a scene, beginning-middle-end (the list seems endless). And students like David and Robert can use that language to construct and define for themselves a concept of good writing. But ultimately their understanding of "good" will bear their unique ways of viewing the world and expressing those views.

Our goal then as teachers is not to teach the list of what's good but to become students of craft who continually ask the question, What is good writing? We need to ask it often and rigorously. It needs to be in our minds when we listen to student work, when we talk about books, when we read the words we are writing ourselves. Our students need to be asking the question as well.

In effective workshop communities, students and teachers recognize that "good writing" is a horizon to aim for, knowing that the horizon has a limitless ability to change. This is what my eleventh-grade English teacher didn't understand. While she set a destination for her students, she didn't recognize the learning potential of the journey we might take to get us there.

References

Calkins, L. (1984). *The art of teaching writing*. Portsmouth, NH: Heinemann.

Clay, M. (1975). *What did I write?* Portsmouth, NH: Heinemann.

Fletcher, R., & Portalupi, J. (1998). *Craft lessons: Teaching writing K–8*. York, ME: Stenhouse.

Fletcher, R. (1997). Unpublished journal writings.

Fox, M. (1990). "There's a coffin in my office." *Language Arts, 67*: 468–472.

Graves, D. (1978). *Balance the basics: Let them write.* New York: Ford Foundation.

Graves, D. (1983). *Writing: Teachers and children at work.* Portsmouth, NH: Heinemann.

Harste, J., Woodward, V. A., & Burke, C. L. (1984). *Language stories and literacy lessons.* Portsmouth, NH: Heinemann.

Macrorie, K. (1994). Process, product, and quality. In L. Tobin & T. Newkirk (Eds.), *Taking stock* (pp. 69–82). Portsmouth, NH: Boynton/Cook.

Murray, D. (1968). A writer teaches writing. In *Learning by teaching.* Boston: Houghton Mifflin.

Murray, D. (1982). The teaching craft: Telling, listening, revealing. In *Learning by teaching: Selected articles on writing and teaching.* Portsmouth, NH: Boynton/Cook.

Murray, D. (1989). *Expecting the unexpected.* Portsmouth, NH: Boynton/Cook.

Murray, D. (1994). Knowing not knowing. In L. Tobin & T. Newkirk (Eds.), *Taking stock* (pp. 57–65). Portsmouth, NH: Boynton/Cook.

Peterson, R., & Eeds, M. (1990). *Grand conversations: Literature groups in action.* New York: Scholastic-TAB.

Shulman, L. (1986). Those who understand: Knowledge growth in teaching. *Educational Researcher, 15*(2), 4–14.

3 Putting Ourselves on the Line

Pat McLure and Linda Rief

This is a conversation that Pat and Linda tape-recorded in response to some questions Jane and Judith sent them. Pat teaches first and second graders, and Linda teaches seventh and eighth graders.

> Let's think back to your beginnings as teachers of writing. What do you wish someone had told you about teaching writing before you began? What advice would have been helpful for you?

P: I wish someone had told me about the important role that illustrations play for young children in their writing. Lots of times, in talking with teachers who are just starting to work on writing with their students, I find they almost devalue the illustrating part of it. Or they think of the illustrating as just a rehearsal for the writing. But really for young children, it's so integrated—their illustrations and their print are so integrated in terms of the way they're trying to tell their story on paper. Ruth Hubbard's [1989] research really helped me see the role that illustrations play. But I think that's really important. I guess I always liked the illustrations that children did, but I didn't realize the importance of them in the beginning. I think there is great value in having

Reprinted from Chapter 3 of *Teaching Language Arts*, edited by Judith Wells Lindfors and Jane S. Townsend.

children do the illustrations and giving them the time and materials and space to do that, as well as to put print down on paper.

L: It's interesting that you say that, Pat, because in seventh and eighth grade I think we devalue illustrations even more. It never occurs to teachers who work with older kids that those illustrations could be very important in telling the story. I'm thinking about Adam, who I had last year. Adam truly is a cartoonist. His journal is filled with cartoons and he hates to write, but he's got incredible stories in his comic strips that he draws. He really is a cartoonist . . . an artist. And I have to look at kids like Adam as artists when I look in their journals. It's not that they just use drawing to illustrate a story: Their art work is writing to those kids, so that it does play a major role.

You know, when I think about getting started as a writing teacher, I feel pretty lucky because of all the wonderful mentors that I had who helped me understand writing in a different way. When I was in school, I *never* had anybody talk to me about my writing. We were told to write an essay, [and] it got handed in, graded, and handed back.

P: And it might have some marks over it, and it might have a few comments in the margins (like a one- or two-word response), but that was it.

L: Right. But it wouldn't give you enough information to know how to make that writing an awful lot better. Actually, it never occurred to me that they *wanted* me to make the writing better.

P: No, it was a one-time assignment. I don't remember ever going back and working on a piece anymore after it was once handed in.

L: I guess I wish also that someone had told me how hard teaching writing is. Today even, I had two kids crying after I talked to them about their writing, because they handed it in as finished drafts, and I had never talked to them about it. They thought these were A pieces of writing and they liked the writing just fine the way it was, and for me—even gently—to say to those kids, "You know, I just think there are things that you could do to make this better writing," it just really hurt them. I think I have to tell myself *every single time* I talk to these children, one-on-one, or even when I talk to them on paper, that each child's whole being is so tied to that piece of writing that that conference is probably the most important thing. And when you get with older kids and the writing gets longer and longer, a lot of times I can't manage one-on-one conferences all the time in forty-five-minute periods. And so I end up writing things on the writing, I forget the child, and it doesn't work as well as it should.

P: That whole time factor—I guess that's one of the things, too, in the beginning: to understand that it's going to take a lot of time if you're going to try to get to everybody. And it takes a lot of time to bring pieces through a process. You can't rush it. You can't just speed it up. It's going to take time.

L: I also think something that I didn't really realize was how connected reading is to writing and how much kids need to use professional writers as mentors. That was pretty clear to me this year when my seventh graders were writing what they said were poems. I said to them, "How many poets have you read?" And they said, "*What?*" And I said, "Well, who's your favorite poet?" "Well, Shel Silverstein." Or a few kids knew Robert Frost. But to actually know poets, or to write fiction and to know fiction writers—I don't think they really make the connections until we make the connections more explicit for them.

P: Well, it is so intertwined, what they're reading and what they're writing. I've noticed that. You know, we've been doing interviews to get ready for these parent conferences that we're doing tonight. And so one of the questions I've been asking them is, "What will help you to become a better writer?" And several of them have said, "To read more."

L: Wow! See, that's great, for first and second grade, that they can say that.

P: Yes. They'll say, "The more I read, then the more I'm gonna be able to write, because I get ideas from lots of different writers to put in stories." It always impresses me. But I think that sometimes they lose some of this understanding as they move through the grades.

L: I think they do too, Pat. And I can't figure out when that happens. I know what *you* do with kids, and I know what other teachers do with the kids. And yet they will come to me in seventh grade and say, "No, I've never written anything before." They've written! I know they've written! And I know they've read too. I know they've got many authors at their fingertips. I don't know why this happens.

P: Is it just the age—the growing stages they go through? They get more self-conscious about it, and they don't want to admit to having written before?

L: I think that's part of it. They truly forget! There is something about seventh grade—many are not real committed to making something. I think it's hormones kicking in. What's most important to many of these kids is who they're sitting with at the table, who's looking at them, and who might have bumped them in the hallway. And truly, everything else seems to go right out of their heads.

P: Eighth graders do some wonderful things.

L: Well, I think there's a big difference between seventh grade and eighth grade. I think we work hard at getting the seventh graders to try to remember all the things they did in elementary school, because I really do know they did wonderful things.

But in a more positive light, I wish someone had told me what incredible fun it is and how it takes just one child's discovery in a piece of writing; that can keep me teaching for months and months.

P: It's so exciting! I mean, there really *is* excitement to it, and *they* feel so pleased. One of my children, Mary, shared with the class a book she'd written about the guinea pig. And one of the children, in responding to her, said that she thought Mary had done a very good job on it, and she wondered if she was thinking about publishing that. And Mary said that well, she didn't know. And so the other little girl said, "Well I really think you ought to. It's a very good book." And Mary just *beamed*. She just *beamed*. It was so pleasing to her to think that someone else in the class recognized her work as being good. I think that's something that we forget. And I forget that too. It's that one thing that you say that can keep a child writing.

L: And it's also the one thing you say that can *stop* them from writing. And it's that fine balance all the time—that in the *rush* . . . that's the hardest part for me. It's having twenty-seven kids for forty-five or fifty minutes and trying to conference with that many kids in each class in a week. And it's in the rush—it was in the rush that I probably made this little boy cry today. He thoroughly believed that he had done the best piece of writing he could do, and he felt an A was what he deserved; and when he ended up with a B on

it, the tears just flooded. And it was so honest that
I thought, "Wow, I really missed the boat." I think
of Tom Romano's [1987] comment about
evaluation. He says that evaluation should keep
the writer writing. So if what I'm saying is
stopping them . . . every time before I try to give
feedback to them, I have to ask myself, "Am I
going to stop them, or am I going to keep them
moving forward?" And that is so hard!

P: Oh, it's terribly hard! And with the little children
it's hard too. You have to *really* be careful
because they're just trying things for the very first
time. You need to keep giving some positive
feedback, but also keep talking to them so that
they will take a few more risks and try something
different and experiment a little with their
writing.

L: It's tricky at all stages. It seems like a balancing
act.

P: Even with adults. We're vulnerable when we're
talking about our writing. But in a classroom, we
tend to forget that. It may not look like the kids
are emotionally tied to the pieces they write, but
many of them are.

What about as your students proceed through school from the first
graders you teach, Pat, to the seventh and eighth graders you deal
with, Linda? What kinds of teachers would you want them to have
over the years to help them develop as writers?

P: I guess I would hope that it's teachers who can
appreciate the work they're doing and can
respond to them as individuals.

L: Yes. When I think about older kids, I hope it's
teachers who see they're teaching children, not a
subject. I mean, I certainly want the kids to get
the content of what makes a good piece of
writing, and I want them to know authors and do
a lot of various kinds of reading. But I think I've
learned over the years that those kids know if you

don't like them as human beings, and if you don't, you'll never teach them anything.

P: Yes, it really comes down to knowing each one as an individual, and I think one of the pluses of teaching writing is that through their writing, you get to know them in a way that you wouldn't normally get to know students if you weren't doing something like this. They share so much of themselves, and you're sitting down one-on-one and talking with them, and I think you have an opportunity to know each of them as individuals.

L: Absolutely. You know, when I'm working with teachers in other schools, I find that a lot of times they're afraid to do some things with kids because of the parents. I just worked with some teachers in another state, and they said, "How can you let kids keep journals? We've got parents who are afraid kids are going to say things in the journals that they don't want teachers to know."

P: Oh really?

L: And so they don't want their students keeping journals. And that was a really legitimate, serious question that I had to think about. You and I have a lot of autonomy here. We've been in the district a long time, and it's a very liberal district. We're trusted as teachers, and I think you and I can do a lot with kids that a first-year teacher may not be able to do. Things that I couldn't do when I first started teaching either. I knew in my gut what made sense to me, but I wasn't prepared to defend a book if it was controversial. I wasn't prepared to explain to a parent why it was OK for kids to be truthful in their journals or why I think it's important they're truthful now. But I feel more experienced at that now. I was pretty stunned when some beginning teachers I was working with said, "This list of books that you've given us—the books that your kids most highly recommend—more than half of them on here are incredibly controversial, and we would never be able to have them in our classrooms." And so I think sometimes, until you've got enough experience to understand how you're using something and why you're using it and why you feel perfectly comfortable doing something, you do kind of hesitate a little bit. I also think there are teachers who deal with things that we don't have to deal with here.

P: So maybe some of the advice to people starting out is to be cautious and to really think through everything that they're doing, being sure that they can justify or they can give reasons for what they're doing—really understanding what they're doing.

L: Right. I think it's *knowing why* you're doing *what you're doing.* I think what it boils down to is you know yourself. You know where you're coming from in your own experience, you know your children, and you know the district in which you teach. And if you know the district and you know your kids and you know your community, then you know what you can do. I just worry sometimes that beginning teachers are dealing with some really difficult issues, and we have no idea how hard it can be for some of them. It surprised me that those teachers I worked with said they were no longer allowed to have their kids keep journals. Although what I did say to them was that these were academic journals. I really make that a point with seventh and eighth graders—that they're not diaries. And I think that's something that we really need to clarify with teachers as well as with the kids. This is not a confessional, it's not a diary. And if you've got something really difficult going on in your life, certainly I would help you in any way I could if you needed to talk to somebody about it. But I

P: think we have to use the journals as academic journals. This journal is who you are as a reader and a writer. But if it's honest, it's who you are as a thinking, feeling human being.

P: And it's also a journal that they know is being read by someone else.

L: Absolutely.

P: It's not just for personal reflection, just for yourself, so that's known right up front—that there is an audience.

L: And that knowledge changes what's written in the journal. Definitely.

Could you talk a little bit about what you see as the easiest aspects of teaching writing?

P: Well you know, with the little ones—and I know this sounds funny—but we just put out blank books and paper and they write. I mean, it sounds too simple, but they do it. They really do. You know, from the first day of school, they start with—some start with pictures, some start with words, some—you know, it's back and forth. It's not always the same thing they do. It depends on what they're writing. But they just write.

L: OK. So what happens between first grade and seventh grade? They come into seventh grade, and they often don't want to write.

P: There is something, though, about a six-year-old or a seven-year-old: They're really quite uninhibited. And they're very giving and open about what they're going to do. And so they enjoy putting their ideas down on paper. They love to show their writing to other people—or most of them do. Not everyone. I mean there's always some child that's a little hesitant, somebody that waits before sharing with the class. But a lot of them are quite open about it and want to show their work and want to do their pictures and put words with them, and they really seem to move through it so easily. Now, I know there's effort on their part; it's not so easy, but at the same time, it's not a big struggle for them or for me. Of course there are some that you have to work with a little more, but a lot of them just—you have the paper, you have the markers, you have the pencils—and they come in and they write.

L: And actually, I have to say that most seventh and eighth graders—the majority—want to write. They have things to say. Some even come in with journals already. They know they're going to be reading and writing so they're prepared to do that. But I wonder what happens to those few kids who are hesitant. I wonder if what's happened for five or six years is that it's been so painful for them to get words down on paper, that they'd rather do nothing than have to go through what they've gone through. Maybe they expect negative comments. And maybe they really feel they're not as good a writer as somebody next to them. I don't know.

P: I do think it's true that some students judge themselves in ways that we would never judge them. I mean, there are some that just are overly harsh on themselves. And that's all tied in, I guess, with self-image and other things that are happening for them. But I think that probably gets in the way of their writing.

L: Oh yes. I think another thing that gets in the way, too, is that now these kids have five major teachers, and so they're trying to figure out what does this one want, and this one, and this one. And that's very hard! I can't imagine going from classroom to classroom to classroom and having to figure out what does *she* want, what does *he* want. Every forty-five minutes, going to another class. It's *very* hard.

P: And yet, that's the way middle schools are set up.

L: I don't know why! We keep talking about getting to block scheduling, but we can't quite seem to make it work—at least in *our* middle school—because there are so many places these kids have to be.

P: But that comes back to that time thing that we talked about before—how if you've got them all day, even though we have one segment of the day that we call Writing Time, still we are writing all through the day. They're writing about their reading, and they're writing about the guinea pig and they're keeping journals for that, and—during Free Choice Time—some are choosing to do writing then. Writing's not really a compartmentalized subject for them.

L: So they can see writing in all the different areas of the classroom because you're in a self-contained classroom. For me, it's a lot harder, and it takes a lot more encouragement for me to say to those kids, "Look, you told me that you feel very comfortable when you're writing a science lab report. That lab report that you love should be in your portfolio." And the kids'll go, "But I didn't write it in here." So it's very hard for me to convince them that that social studies current event piece that they absolutely loved, or the fabulous comparison–contrast piece they did (a wonderful persuasive piece)—that these belong in their portfolio too, even though they didn't write these pieces in my classroom.

P: Well, I'm sure there are probably other writing teachers that wouldn't recognize these pieces as valuable writing that should be in the students' portfolios.

L: That's true. They would separate those.

P: So I think it's not only the students that maybe
        separate those topics or those subjects. Some
        teachers would separate those subjects too.

L: Probably. But you can't separate subjects, despite
        the fact that you're in walled rooms and you're
        divided by forty-five-minute segments. You would
        hope that writing teachers would value the kinds
        of literacies that kids can bring from all the other
        disciplines that they're in, whether it's art, or
        social studies writing, or science writing, or
        pictures, or photography—all kinds of things.

P: So whether it's called an integrated program or
        not, in fact, writing *is* an integrated medium: It's
        something that you're using through every
        subject.

L: I'm lucky to be on a team of teachers that really
        understands that, because in every single one of
        the disciplines—whether it's math or social
        studies or science—the teachers on our team
        write really positive comments back to the kids
        and ask really good questions and give
        suggestions like, "This lab report could be a lot
        better if you did this or this," or "Would you
        consider giving an opposing side for this current
        event, and you're more than welcome to turn this
        back in as a second draft." I don't see that
        happening in an awful lot of classrooms.

P: True. But the teachers on your team really are
        responding to the writing as well as to the
        content of the piece.

L: Absolutely. Definitely. And so the kids begin to
        see that writing matters in all their classes. And I
        think that's helped them see that the writing they
        do in other subjects should be part of their
        portfolios also, to really show who they are and
        what they can do. You know, Carl (who doesn't
        have any writing in his portfolio) was telling me
        last week, "I only work well when somebody

tells me what I need to write." And I said, "Well, why don't you have your social studies or science in here?" And he said, "I didn't know I could put them in here." And I've *said* it again and again, but they don't *hear* it. So he felt an awful lot better when he knew his social studies and science writing could be part of what I'm looking at to see what he can do as a writer. So it does matter.

Well, I'm not sure I just answered what's the easiest part of teaching writing, but I know that the most engaging thing for me is to see kids draft a wonderful piece of writing and feel that they've really worked hard at it, and then kids burst into applause when they read it out loud. That is so exciting! I don't know if I could teach if language arts was not writing and reading.

You've talked a bit already about some of the challenges of teaching writing: the time pressures, the special emotional and social pressures of adolescence. Is there anything else you find particularly difficult or challenging as you work with student writers?

P: Certainly, the conferences. Conferences can be wonderful, but they can be hard too.

L: Absolutely.

P: Because there's no way to really prepare for them. The university interns in my classroom always have questions about how you do conferences, but you can't really set them up for it because it's such a responsive way of teaching. It's not until that student shares the writing with you that you can respond to it. You can't prepare that ahead of time; you can't know what you're going to say ahead of time. You just have to be there with the student.

L: And I don't know if you do it the same way I do, but I do ask the kids to read their writing to me so that I can really focus on the content. But by the

time kids get to eighth grade, there are some kids
who've written ten, fifteen, twenty pages. And so
I find that sometimes I have to say to the kids, "I'd
like you to read the part that you're having the
most difficulty with" so that I can at least hear the
voice and maybe focus on that one thing. Often
they have to give me the pieces of writing to read
for myself, but that's where I run into trouble. If I
don't hear the voice of the writer, I may make
faulty assumptions, and then when I hand that
back to kids, sometimes the tears just flow, and I
know I've missed something that I wouldn't have
missed in a one-on-one conference.

P: If he had read it to you and you had talked to
       him about it, you would have understood him
       better.

L: Absolutely. And so I realize every time I take a
       piece of writing home, and I don't have the writer
       read it to me, it's very different. And I think I need
       to try and make those conferences happen more.

P: There is an advantage to working with the
       younger children because their pieces are
       shorter. I notice by second grade, and certainly
       by the second half of second grade, some of
       them are starting to write longer and longer
       pieces, and then we will sometimes just choose a
       part of it that the child wants to focus on right
       now for this conference. But up until then, often
       they can just read the whole thing to you—six,
       seven, eight sentences. Each sentence is another
       page of the book, but they can read till they get
       through the whole piece of writing. So it's usually
       not until [they get] into second grade that we're
       choosing a part to focus on for a conference.

L: I think that's the hardest part for me. I've got
       twenty-five kids in a class (and now we've got
       twenty-seven, twenty-eight kids), I aim for one
       conference a week with each one. And it still

doesn't happen. I can't quite get it in. But I noticed something last year. I had a doctoral student in my classroom, and he was trying to pay attention to how I listen to kids, so he recorded many, many conferences I had. And what was so ironic was that sometimes the conference would go on for twenty minutes, but after I'd listen to the tape of it, I felt I could have done the same thing in twenty seconds because the kids can only take in so much information. And if I had just shut my mouth and stopped asking all of these questions, I think I could have targeted right in. It was very helpful for me to see that.

P: Well, that's probably another important thing to say about conferences, that conferences can be very short. In my room they can be. You know, sometimes one or two comments is all it takes, and you move on to somebody else. Conferences aren't always very detailed sorts of meetings. And not formal meetings, either.

L: By seventh and eighth grade, though, there's so much that you're focusing on. Sometimes, with the kids who really want to make their piece the best they can, I'm going through three and four conferences over the same piece of writing before we even get to editing. So it takes a couple of weeks for them to really construct a thorough piece of writing.

P: Oh, I would think so.

L: Then there's that time thing again too. You've got to have plenty of time to do it. Sometimes people think you need to get students to keep finishing pieces, and yes, it's important to bring pieces to conclusion. But you need time to keep working on a piece too.

P: Well, I want the children to bring their pieces to conclusion, but I also want them to begin to realize all the hard work that goes into making a piece of writing the best that it can be. And I just have to know the stopping point. I mean, kids look at me and go, "This is my final draft!" and I go, "OK. We've done enough for today!"

L: I know what you mean. Sometimes I just push it too hard, and I make them go back too often.

P: That reminds me of something Tom Romano [1987] wrote. He says if you know that the students are going to be doing several pieces of writing—it's not just a one-assignment kind of writing—then one piece might have really good dialogue in it, maybe the rest of the piece doesn't hold together real well, but that's OK because you know there's going to be another piece coming along, and you can work on something else with the next piece. You don't have to get everything just right in every piece of writing. There are going to be other opportunities.

L: Yes. And what I do now, too, is I just tell the kids I really want to see three to five rough draft pages a week so that they can't ever say to me, "I'm really done. What do I do now?" We're *never* done! (Which probably aggravates the heck out of them.) But I just want them to start to be able to evaluate for themselves: With all these pages of writing in front of me, it's pretty obvious that in this piece the dialogue's working really well, but this other piece holds together better because it's got some other characteristics that make it a better piece of writing. I just want them to do volumes of writing so that they can begin to identify what makes a better piece.

P: Yes, and unless you do a lot of writing, you just can't develop that.

L: Maybe we should talk a little more about how we set up conferences.

P: Well, I tend to roam for conferences. The students come in each morning, and they get

their writing folders, and they get started with
writing right away. As soon as the first people are
here, I start roaming and settle down beside
somebody and talk with them about their piece. I
keep lists for myself or use a name list so I know
who I've talked to already this week and who I
haven't, and so I know who else to get to. And
then, once we get into publishing pieces, I keep
a whole stack of notes on the table that say, "I
would like a conference for publishing." And the
children sign up for that and leave the note there
for me.

L: Oh, that's a good idea.

P: And so I pick up that note and know that that's
somebody I need to get to that day. And then we
continue to use the notes, so that if I sit down
and I'm having a conference with a child and we
decide on one thing she's going to do for that
piece of writing, I'll make a note about it on the
back of this little slip of paper and I give it back to
her. Then when she thinks she's done that, she
just puts the note back on my table and that's
kind of a signal to me that she wants another
conference to go over that. But mostly I'm just
roaming unless somebody has told me they want
a conference.

L: That's fairly similar to what I do. All of the kids
have conference sheets in their working folders.
They sign up for conferences, and I tell them my
goal is to have one good conference with each of
them during the week. But I keep a list too, and if
they don't sign up after a couple of weeks, then
either they have to give me the piece of writing
they're working on or they need to talk to me
about it. But that conference sheet that they have
is kind of a record of how I responded to their
piece, and it's in their working folder so that they
can see—and I can see—if it's blank; then I need
to talk to those kids I haven't talked to. Our class
periods are about fifty-two minutes now, and I

tend to do something at the beginning of the
class to get them started. Maybe it's a quote I'm
asking the kids to respond to, or I might put up a
piece of poetry and ask them to do a one-to-two-
minute quick-write about it, just to kind of get
some juices flowing. And then I say, "Whatever
you need to get, you know you've got so many
pages of writing due this week," or "Now we're
at the deadline, so you need two finished
pieces." And then they work on those things they
need to work on. I go to the kids who've signed
up first, or I might put kids' names up on the
board to go to them because they haven't seen
me for a week or two. It seems to work pretty
well.

P: I would think that if writing is coming, say, in the
middle of the day or they're coming from
something else to writing (like they do in middle
school), you would need a mini-lesson or
something to get started with, to kind of move
them into it. But I've found now, by being able to
do it just first thing in the morning, they often are
thinking about their writing on the way to school.
They come in with ideas; they know what they're
doing. And some need that time to kind of roam
the room a bit before they settle into it. But that's
OK. That's part of coming into school.

And where do your kids get their ideas for their writing?

P: Well, you certainly can't minimize the
importance of sharing writing. I notice that so
much. You have whole class sharing times for
them to share their writing with the group, and
you start to notice some ideas that spread from
one to another. This little boy's got a space story
going and in the space adventure story he's
taking other classmates, and so then you start to
notice somebody else doing that too. "Oh, I
could have my friend in my story." So they start to

include classmates in their stories, and you start to notice these conventions that sort of spread throughout the room. Or somebody realizes that someone else wrote about his cat. "Well, I need something to write about. I can write about my cat." I think having lots of opportunities to share their writing is really important, whether it's informally because there happen to be four people sitting at this table and they're gonna say, "Hey, look what I just wrote!" or whether we set up the time for the whole class, and a couple of people share their writing with everyone.

L: In my classes, it's with those four or five kids sitting at a table—that's where the most sharing happens. Very informally. And I see more teaching going on—those kids teaching each other in an informal situation—than when I try to set up response groups when they have a formal sharing. That does *not* work really well with my kids. And I do a *terrible* job (I admit it and I feel guilty about it), but with 50 minutes, I'll look up and there're three minutes left, and nobody has read what they've been working on. Plus the fact that with adolescents, trying to get them to share in whole class is like pulling teeth. No matter how safe it is, it takes *months*. I was just noticing today there were some kids who, for the first time, began talking to the kids at their table. And this is the end of October. It has taken eight weeks for those kids to feel comfortable enough to even share with three other kids. They're so self-conscious.

P: And see, that's the difference in ages too, I think. Although I've had some young children who took awhile. I can think of some through the years. With one little boy, I remember it was February before he would share with the whole class. But that's more the exception than the rule with younger kids.

L: Well, you know what I've also been thinking, Pat? For years I've said, "The sharing has to be done by the writer." But a year ago I started to wonder about this. I try to write when I'm asking kids to write. I don't mean that they're writing a particular thing, but I'm usually writing something too. When we were writing a musical last year, I was trying to write song lyrics. Now, I didn't get up on stage to sing what I had written, but the kids who sang that song that I contributed lines to—I was so excited! I felt like one of the kids! It was so exciting to hear somebody sing words that I wrote. "Oh! That's the line that I thought of!" And I thought, "This is really stupid. What on earth made me truly believe that other kids can't present a finished piece of writing someone else has done?" When you go public with a piece of writing, I think it *should* be almost a performance, if the writer chooses it to be, and maybe somebody else could read that poetry, say, far better than the writer could. Writers don't come with their books; poets don't come with their poetry. I think that writers don't have to be the only ones who present a finished writing.

P: Yes, I think most of us have that mind-set to it.

L: Well, I really have been thinking about that, and thinking we just really need to teach the other kids how to take another child's piece of writing and consider, "How would you present that to us? Would it be in a performance? Would it be in some different kind of reading? Would you have multiple voices presenting this?"

P: There really is a performance aspect with *any* kind of sharing with the group. It is an element of the sharing.

L: Oh, I believe it is. Yes.

P: In the last few years I've had some students that have gotten into writing poems for two voices.

They really like the books by [Paul] Fleischman [1988]. Well, that's performance to read those poems for two voices. But then they started writing their own and then performing their own. And it sort of made me step back and think about how much performance is part of any of the sharing that they do.

L: Definitely.

P: When they take that space in front of the group, that's a performance.

L: It's taken me twenty years to learn that before I read something out loud to those kids, I'd better know it really well. In a sense, I'm performing it too, because if I'm reading poetry to them, I really want to read it in a voice that I think the poet would be pleased with. So even when we're reading books out loud—if we're reading a novel together—I want the kids to know we need to practice ahead of time and really take the parts, so that we're listening to each other, and it's not just some deadly boring reading like I did when I was in high school. You know—don't look at the teacher because she'll call on you.

P: And then you'll have to read!

L: Yes, you'll have to read, so don't make eye contact! Oh, weren't we talking about where the kids find writing, and you were saying how the kids kind of find writing from each other?

P: Also from books that they're reading. And one of the children said to me the other day that he just looks around the room at the pictures, and he sees a picture, and then that gives him an idea for something to write about.

L: I have to almost point all those things out to my kids! I'll point out that I've got quotes hanging all around the room. And I do a lot of quick-writes with the kids—I might put a piece of poetry up on the overhead and just ask them to do a one-

to-two-minute write from it. I read a piece from
Cynthia Rylant, "My Grandmother's Hair" (I love
that piece!), and I asked them to respond to that
for one to two minutes. And they've got a lot of
writing in their journal that they know they can
go back to again and again. What else do I do? I
might read the lead of something to them. They
construct a positive–negative chart so that they
might aim towards the good and the bad things
that have happened in their lives. Then a couple
years ago kids said, "Could we just do dislikes
and likes?" And they did. They actually did a
great job on those. Just to be able to say to Jan,
"Tell me more about these things that you really
hate," or "Friends are at the top of your list. Tell
me more about friends," or "Tell me about the
beach. What do you love about the sound of the
ocean? What happens here?" So when they're
stuck for writing, they have another source to
draw on.

P: Well, you know, Linda, you mentioned the
        difference between first graders who are
        clamoring for their turn to share, and middle
        school students who are reluctant to share with
        the whole class. We do try to build in two times
        right at the end of writing time for children to
        share their writing, and then later in the day
        there's always a time for somebody to share some
        reading with the class. Then we end the day with
        another sharing time, and that can be either
        writing or reading or something from their
        portfolio or any kind of work that they want to
        share. So there's at least four students who are
        sharing with the whole class just about every day.

L: That's great. That's really great. But you've also
        got them in that self-contained classroom. I'm
        fighting that fifty minutes all the time. There are
        some other ways that I get the kids to think about
        finding ideas for writing. I do set up a whole

bunch of things at the beginning of the year where I'm doing a lot of quick-writes with them, I'm reading some professional writing to them—short pieces or pieces from previous years—and asking the kids to respond with whatever comes to mind. Or I ask them sometimes to borrow a line and write off that line for a minute or two. So they've got their journals *filled* with possibilities. I've got quotes hanging all over the room; there are pictures hanging all over. I also share a whole bunch of writing contests with them and say, "Here's a possibility, here's a possibility, here's a possibility." I suggest they write book reviews for *Voices from the Middle*, because we try to publish twelve book reviews in each issue. But I know how hard it is for teachers to get kids to send their writing out at middle school level, and so I'm always pushing our kids to do that. But most of them have ideas. It's the kids who don't feel good about their writing or have never felt good about it who have a hard time. It's trying to convince those kids that they have something to say so that they will write.

P: Part of it, too, is creating those opportunities for lots of different kinds of writing.

L: Definitely.

P: Or if there is a student who's really reluctant to share a personal narrative writing, she has the opportunity to try a book review. There's something else that she can write and still be part of the writing community.

L: I think that's tied to reading too, Pat. For a long time I just had novels in my classroom and I was having the kids read novels, yet I couldn't figure out why they were all writing fiction! Well, that's what they were reading. You have to start to kind of put two and two together and say, "I need to get a lot more nonfiction in this classroom. I need to show them that it's perfectly OK for them to be reading some skateboarding articles because that's what they want to be writing." So let them look at how somebody else constructs something like that. So it *is* important to surround them with a variety of kinds of reading. And with the middle schoolers, they're writing in every single genre or discipline: They're writing in science, they're writing in social studies, they're writing in geography. But our kids don't seem to see the connections unless I make them explicit, saying, " *Please* make your portfolio as full as it can be with these wonderful pieces of writing you're constructing in other classes. They matter to me too because they show me what you can do as a writer."

P: So for a middle school teacher, it's really important to invite that writing into the writing classroom.

L: Definitely. To see their language arts classroom as a laboratory for the language arts. And it may not all happen in that room during that fifty minutes, but you certainly hope that those kids show you what they are capable of doing as writers.

Some teachers say that revision can be a problem—that their kids just don't want to revise their writing. What's your experience with this?

P: Well, for young children revision tends to be just adding some information. Maybe we can work on sequence sometimes, but rarely is anything ever taken out of a piece of writing. That's very difficult for young children to deal with. More often than not, revision is just adding information—trying to make something clearer so that everybody can understand what the writer means. But that's the bulk of our revision, and most of our revision conferences are just about adding information.

L: I think for us, especially at eighth grade, it's quite a bit more sophisticated. Kids are actually looking at what makes a good lead: What should a good lead do (and let's practice a few)? How should that lead look different depending on the kind of writing that you're doing? What is it that makes this such a good piece of writing? How does the ending work?

P: Now that comes up sometimes with first graders too. That's an issue that all writers deal with: How do I bring this to an end? But for the little children, sometimes it's just 'cause they come to the last page in their book. And that's the end.

L: You know, Pat, when I think about it, I'm not sure there are so many real differences between your kids and mine. It may be a little more complicated at seventh and eighth grade levels, but truly the characteristics or elements of a good piece of writing that six-year-olds are looking at are very much the same. They're talking the same elements, but the older kids just have more information. But they're reluctant to take away, too, when they revise. But then, so am I. I'm reluctant to take away.

P: Oh yes! What writer isn't?!

L: I've spent hours writing this twenty-page article, and then somebody tells me it doesn't start till page eleven—well, it's pretty hard to take out the first ten pages.

        When I'm thinking about teachers that I've worked with who have never done much writing themselves, I realize it's awfully hard to have conferences with kids and help them revise their writing if *you* don't know how *you* have been affected by this experience as a writer.

P: I think what's really important is just writing *yourself*. Whether it's having a conference or sharing a piece of writing, if you haven't done it

yourself, you really don't understand it in the
same way.

L: No. No. And I believe that even if you're working
with 125–150 kids, every teacher at least has
time to keep a journal and can do a one-to-two-
minute quick-write, when you're asking kids to
do that. That you *can* get that seed of an idea, just
so you're getting the feel of what it's like to
capture a moment even in one wonderful
sentence. It *is* important—really vital—to
teachers of writing that they're doing some kind
of writing themselves.

P: Whether you're writing at the same moment the
students are, or whether you're putting yourself
in another writing group at some point in time,
it's just that you get that experience of being a
writer.

L: You know, there have been years when I haven't
done much writing or shared it. I'm always writing
in a journal, but there have been a couple of years
when I wasn't writing for myself (either a memoir
that I wanted to write or a fiction piece that I
wanted to try). But this year I'm working on a piece
of young adult fiction, and I'm also trying to write
the text for a children's picture book. Well, when I
shared this writing with the kids, their comments
were so helpful because they knew these weren't
fake pieces of writing that I was working on. I really
want to send these out: I really hoped that this
could be a picture book someday, and I really
hoped that this could be a young adult novel. I
used the kids' interaction with me as a model for
how I wanted them to be responding to each other.
I showed them how helpful their responses were to
me and how their comments helped me change
my writing. It made such a difference when I
responded to them in conference: They were much

more receptive to the kinds of comments I was making to them because they saw me as a writer more than a teacher. I don't know how we define ourselves. I hope they see me as both writer and teacher. But I hope they never see that one is off balance from the other. I hope they see that I can't separate teacher from writer and writer from teacher. I hope my writing is teaching them as much as what I'm *saying* to them is teaching them. And *they* are teaching *me.* They truly have helped me revise those pieces.

P: I think our students need to know that there are things that we can learn from each other and that it's not just a one-way street. We do value the help and the comments that they make to us.

L: Well, I'm thinking something else, too, Pat. When we put ourselves on the line—if I'm writing about my mother's death, say—then the kids know that that's a serious piece of writing to me. And they don't laugh at it, and they don't make fun of it. So the kids see that I put myself at risk in front of them, and then they're much more able to write honestly and take some risks themselves. It may not be an emotionally-charged piece that they're writing, but it may be something that they really care about, and they're able to risk the writing of that if they know that other kids have not made fun of me. Then they know the kids are probably not going to make fun of them.

P: I think the important point is that, even if you don't have the chance to write all the time, you still build in some ways for you to be a writer. Whether you're going to have your own drafts of a children's book this year, that doesn't matter. But the fact that you, the teacher, do have some ongoing experience of writing and sharing within the community of writers—that *does* matter.

References

Fleischman, P. (1988). *Joyful noise: Poems for two voices.* NY: Harper & Row.

Hubbard, R. (1989). *Authors of pictures, draughtsmen of words.* Portsmouth, NH: Heinemann.

Romano, T. (1987). *Clearing the way.* Portsmouth, NH: Heinemann.

Rylant, C. (1991). My grandmother's hair. In N. Larrick & W. Lamb (Eds.), *To ride a butterfly: New picture stories, folktales, fables, nonfiction, poems, and songs for young children.* (p. 85). New York: Bantam Doubleday Dell.

Bibliography

Pat McLure

Professional resources that have been especially important to me include:

Graves, D. (1994). *A fresh look at writing.* Portsmouth, NH: Heinemann.

Hansen, J. (1987). *When writers read.* Portsmouth, NH: Heinemann.

Hubbard, R. (1989). *Authors of pictures, draughtsmen of words.* Portsmouth, NH: Heinemann.

Murray, D. M. (1989). *Expecting the unexpected: Teaching myself—and others—to read and write.* Portsmouh, NH: Heinemann.

Power, B. M., & Hubbard, R. (eds.) (1991). *Literacy in process: The Heinemann reader.* Portsmouth, NH: Heinemann.

Romano, T. (1986). Something afoul. From the video series *The writing and reading process: A new approach to literacy* developed by J. Hansen and D. Graves. Portsmouth, NH: Heinemann.

Wells, G. (1986). *The meaning makers: Children learning language and using language to learn.* Portsmouth, NH: Heinemann.

Children's books that I especially enjoy using with children include:

Fleischman, P. (1988). *Joyful noise: Poems for two voices.* New York: Harper & Row.

James, S. (1991). *Dear Mr. Blueberry.* New York: McElderry.

Jarrell, R. (1964). *The bat-poet.* New York: Macmillan.

Krupinski, L. (1992). *Celia's island journal.* Boston, MA: Little, Brown and Company.

Munsch, R. (1985). *Thomas' snowsuit.* Toronto, Canada: Annick Press.

Yolen, J. (1987). *Owl moon.* New York, NY: Philomel.

Linda Rief

Professional resources that have been especially important to me include:

Atwell, N. (1987). *In the middle: Writing, reading, and learning with adolescents.* Upper Montclair, NJ: Boynton/Cook.

Carnegie Council on Adolescent Development. (1989). *Turning points: Preparing American youth for the 21st century.* Washington, DC: Carnegie Council on Adolescent Development.

Dillard, A. (1989). *The writing life.* New York: Harper & Row.

Fox, M. (1993). *Radical reflections.* Fort Worth, TX: Harcourt Brace.

Tobin, L. (1993). *Writing relationships: What really happens in the composition class.* Portsmouth, NH: Boynton/Cook Heinemann.

Wolf, D. (1988). *Reading reconsidered: Literature and literacy in high school.* New York: College Entrance Examination Board.

Children's books that I especially enjoy using with children include:

Cisneros, S. (1991). *House on Mango Street.* New York: Vintage Books.

Cisneros, S. (1996). Eleven. In *Woman hollering creek* (pp. 6–9). New York: Vintage Books.

Fox, M. (1984). *Wilfred Gordon McDonald Partridge.* Brooklyn, NY: Kane/Miller.

Hesse, K. (1997). *Out of the dust.* New York: Scholastic.

Hinton, S. E. (1967). *The outsiders.* New York: Viking Press.

Janeczko, P. (Ed.) (1983). *Poetspeak.* Scarsdale, NY: Bradbury Press.

Lowry, L. (1993). *The giver.* New York: Houghton Mifflin.

Paulsen, G. (1993). *Nightjohn.* New York: Delacorte.

Philbrick, R. (1993). *Freak the mighty.* New York: Blue Sky.

Rylant, C. (1989). *But I'll be back again: An album.* New York: Orchard Books.

Rylant, C. (1990). *A couple of kooks and other stories about love.* New York: Orchard Books.

Soto, G. (1990). *A fire in my hands.* New York: Scholastic.

4 Understanding and Transforming the Meaning of Our Lives through Poetry, Biographies, and Songs

Cecilia M. Espinosa and Karen J. Moore

Background

Our school is a work-in-progress—a project where we teachers have the freedom to put our theory into practice, and the expectation that we will continue to grow in our knowledge about teaching and learning. This professionally enriching state of affairs is largely due to the vision of our principal and the teachers she has hired. Parents who grew up in the neighborhood and attended the school as children often comment that they were afraid to send their children to our school because they remembered what a horrible institution the school was. These same parents now wholeheartedly support our school, the work we do, and the community.

Our school, located in Phoenix, Arizona, is in an inner-city neighborhood whose population has changed tremendously during the past decade. During that period, the Spanish-speaking minority became the majority. Currently, our newest students are people who have just arrived in this country. Our teachers and administrators have worked to help make the school not just an institution but a part of the community, and so our school has many connections with the local university and social and health agencies. These other institutions bring us a wealth of knowledge and expertise; they also use our campus as a laboratory and teaching ground.

The flexibility we enjoy allows us to have multiage classrooms. Therefore, we can come to know the children and their families and build trust over a longer period of time. Knowing the children well helps us develop a

Reprinted from Chapter 2 of *Making Justice Our Project*, edited by Carole Edelsky.

curriculum that has depth and relevance to our lives. The work we present below grew out of these opportunities.

The Farmworker Study

Our kindergarten through second-grade multiage classes had been studying about "the desert" for about six weeks. We had studied it from many different points of view. We had read the work of some authors who live in the desert and dedicate their lives to writing about it. We had filled the classroom with desert artifacts brought by teachers and children. The children had done research about animals and plants. We had taken a couple of field trips to different places where we could observe firsthand the desert habitat. Parents had volunteered in the classroom with their expertise about desert plants and their medicinal uses. Each week the children's talk about the desert had became more and more complex and knowledgeable. We thought our "desert study" was coming to an end. We were planning to integrate our knowledge into different projects in order to make an exhibit or presentation about the desert and invite other classes and parents to our "celebration."

Then we came across some work of Tish Hinojosa, a Mexican American singer and activist from San Antonio, Texas. One of her songs, "Bandera del Sol," had already become a symbol for our school that year. Many classrooms sang it and used it as a community ritual. Lately, singing had become a very important part of our school life. It seemed that when teachers and children joined in singing songs that described peace, hope, love, and injustice, then our spirits, our minds, and our actions joined together as one voice. These magical moments, when our hopes were connected to make what seems impossible become possible, confirmed what the Chilean poet Pablo Neruda had reported in his autobiography *(Confieso Que He Vivido)* about the Turkish poet Nazim Hikmet. Once, when Hikmet was being terribly tortured, accused of trying to incite the marines to revolt after reading his books, he began to sing, quietly at first, but later very loud with all his strength. He sang all the songs he knew, all the poems he knew, the songs of the people, songs of the struggle; he sang everything he knew. By singing he overcame his torture. Neruda's response to Hikmet was, "You sang for all of us, we have no doubt in what we need to do. We all know now when we need to start singing" (p. 274).

As we became more familiar with the work of Tish Hinojosa, we understood better about the "need to start singing." We discovered and learned the words to many of her bilingual songs that dealt with injustice and change. Soon Tish Hinojosa's songs inspired our young poets and writers to write their own songs. Samantha and Jessica dedicated hours to writing them. An excerpt from their lyrics for "Peace and Love," one of our favorites, deals with topics of great concern to the children—gangs, drugs, and guns:

> My promise is to care for the world
> no gangs of danger, but say now is peace
> I am going to sing all day long Peace for the World
> Not drugs, not gangs, not even bad guns
> Stand up and say no guns for the world
> guns are not for me and you.

It was during the time when our classes were studying the desert that we heard Hinojosa's song "Something in the Rain." In this song she talks about the struggles of the farmworkers over the use of pesticides in the grape fields in California, about children being poisoned by pesticides and crying at night from the pain, about parents watching helplessly as their children suffer. This song evokes issues of human rights, of respect for the land and its people, and of the insatiable need of some people to make a lot of money regardless of the consequences. Yet, at the same time, the song is full of hope and humanity. We took some time as a class to pay attention to each one of the words and ideas chosen for this poem/song. We reflected individually and collectively. Our discussions were full of feeling and evoked many scary thoughts. Through this song we experienced images of children dying or being born with impairments because someone wanted to make money. We could hear the pain of the parents, and their desperate need for these practices to stop.

> There must be something in the rain
> Well, what else could cause this pain. . . .
>
> —Tish Hinojosa, from *"Something in the Rain"*

As the children became interested in what was happening to the farmworkers in California, they raised many questions and issues. Some of the children were aware of farmworkers' labor conditions because they had relatives who were working or had worked in the grape fields in California. So we decided to change the direction we had anticipated for our desert study. We embarked on a journey of inquiry in which there was no "knowledgeable leader" (no "teacher"). We had never intended to take this path, but the children's questions and interest gave us no alternative.

We went to the public library, made phone calls, and talked to people in order to become better informed about farmworkers and desert agribusiness. We found out about different organizations, such as La Causa, that could help us gather materials and locate guest speakers. A law student who had taken a semester off to volunteer with the migrant workers in California came to talk to our classes. He represented La Causa—the workers' movement initiated by César Chávez. He was full of passion for his work as a volunteer and for the possibility of enacting change. The children sat around him for more than an hour, listening to him and asking him questions. His words were very serious and convincing as he talked to us about the poverty and abuse that still exist in spite of all the work of César Chávez. He asked us not to buy grapes and to wear the buttons he gave us that said "NO GRAPES." He reminded us to take the time to ask managers at supermarkets where the grapes came from, and to voice our opinion if they came from a place where pesticides were being used. He taught us that as consumers we had the power to make changes.

He told us about César Chávez's ideas, his love for his people, and his dreams and hopes. We learned from him how much César Chávez had read and studied different laws in order to be knowledgeable and to be able to help his people. He stressed that the struggles of farmworkers still continue due to poor working conditions, low salaries, and pesticide use that persist years after César Chávez death. Finally, he showed us some films with interviews and explanations about the effects of pesticides in the fields and the surrounding areas. The films showed many Hispanics united and taking a stand on the farmworkers' situation.

Soon we realized that we needed to learn and study in depth the life and work of César Chávez. He was going to give us strength to change and deepen our understanding. As a class we read his biography, and kept a close watch for any information the news had about his life, work, and ideas. We also went to see a play about his life and work. After the play one of the children said, "He was like Martin Luther King. He wanted people to be treated with respect."

Slowly, César Chávez and his work impacted our hearts and lives. He was a model to us for putting into practice one's ideas and beliefs. One day the school lunch included grapes. Many of the children refused to take them. The cafeteria manager was upset and asked, "How could they choose not to take the fruit?" However, the children were determined not to take them, and didn't mind explaining why. A few parents visited one day with concerns because their children would not let them buy grapes any more. They complained, "Don't you know that grapes make it easy for us to pack lunches and snacks?"

One day the school librarian had a "Breakfast with Books" for children and their parents, and she served grapes. One of the children told her, "Don't you know you are not supposed to buy grapes? They are putting pesticides in the fields, and the children are being born sick. You need to put them away. Haven't you heard about César Chávez?" The librarian had no choice but to remove the grapes. On another, occasion when we were making posters for a bake sale, the children wrote "NO GRAPES" in the middle of the advertisement for the items we were going to sell. The children had taken something they learned at school, applied it to their lives, and took action. They were also challenging us to do the same and to be more vigilant about the way we lead our lives, both personally and professionally.

This experience taught us that it *does* matter how we use our time at school and that it matters what kinds of studies we choose to do with the children. With the right kind of opportunities and experiences, children learn to care deeply about the world, to be eager to take action and to fight for justice.

Now as we reflect on these events, we think that as teachers we probably did not take this study far enough or deep enough. For instance, the children could have created their own play about César Chávez, his life, and his ideas. Our lives at school are fast and full of interruptions. There is really very little time to reflect, and to take the time to see all the possibilities of moments like the ones we described in the paragraphs above. We know that these young children would have been able to express so much of their knowledge about César Chávez through enacting his story in drama.

Biographies

After the study of César Chávez, we struggled to make more connections that were valid for the children. We were looking for our next step. Since we teach multiage classes, most of the children remain with us for three years. We wanted to provide them with related, but not repeated, experiences in the years to come. Therefore, we began the following year with a study of biographies about people who had fought for human rights, animals, the environment, and so on. Students signed up for groups that would each study one of these people. The groups were led by a teacher assistant, a student teacher, and a teacher. Our goal was to fill our classroom environment with the lives of people who had made a difference in the world: e.g., Helen Keller, Rachel Carson, Rosa Parks, Vilma Martínez, Jane Goodall, Martin Luther King Jr., and Benito Juárez. Starting that year to learn about the lives of people who stood up for their beliefs gave us a vision to follow and a center to be grounded in. It also helped us in making decisions about how to lead our own lives. How was it that Helen Keller learned to control her temper? And what inspired her to become an advocate for unsighted people? What made Rosa Parks finally say one day that she wasn't going to give up her seat anymore? How did Benito Juárez manage to become a lawyer when, as an indigenous person, he was not allowed to go to school? How did Vilma Martínez overcome the oppressive societal thinking that women did not have a place in college or that bilingualism was a problem rather than a resource? What inspired these people to take a stand? Who inspired them?

The biographies were intended to make these famous figures become part of our students' lives and also to inspire them. We wanted them to see that fighting for one's own and others' rights is a struggle everywhere; we have to think globally about it, but we must start with the vision of people's rights in our own homes and classrooms.

Not all the biographies we studied were "teacher-initiated"; many were chosen spontaneously or with very little teacher intervention. One day in Cecilia's class, Julisa, a second-grade fluent reader, did not seem engaged in her reading. She would pick a picture book, finish it, and move on to something else. After conferring with Cecilia, she decided to read the book about the life of Benito Juárez. She started reading the book that same morning. By the end of reading time, Julisa was still reading; she read all through the morning and asked to take the book home. As soon as she saw us the next morning, she told us she had stayed up very late, past her bedtime, because she could not stop reading, and she wanted to share the book with the rest of the class. So Julisa shared "everything" that she had learned about Benito Juárez the day before. Even when we wanted to move on to something else, she said, "Wait, I am not done yet, I have more to tell you." The children listened to her intently, asking questions and giving their opinions. Julisa said she wanted to write a book about Benito Juárez. For many days afterward, she kept reading about his life and taking notes. As she wrote about Benito Juárez not being allowed to attend school because of his race, Julisa said, "I understand now. He had to go to a special school for indigenous people; he couldn't attend the same schools other people attended."

What was amazing to us was not only that Julisa learned such "lessons," but also that she was able to elevate what "reading" meant for the whole class. In only "one day and one night," as she said, Julisa discovered the power of reading someone's life *into* her own. Benito Juárez will be a part of Julisa's life for many years to come. We were truly fascinated when we heard Julisa say, "Wow, yesterday I didn't know anything about Benito Juárez, and look at me now. I know so much about him."

These studies of those who fought for their rights and beliefs helped us to remember that the human spirit has amazing capabilities, even in the midst of very difficult circumstances. It is our responsibility as teachers to help maintain this vision of our students being enthusiastic, successful learners so that we can help them see the possibilities, and at the same time so that we can see the possibilities for ourselves.

Standing up for one's beliefs and one's rights is always difficult, but it is especially hard for our students, given the complex issues they confront. Many of their families are immigrants, many are undocumented, and many families have escaped poverty and political persecution in their native land and have come here only to continue their suffering. The language they speak isn't necessarily highly valued in our society. The news and the media continuously present them from a very negative point of view. Most do not have access to medical care, and they are constantly afraid that "la migra," the immigration service, might come and take them away. Many of the places they rent do not meet even the basic standards of safety and health. Their landlords are not always the most helpful, and so they learn to live quietly because often the consequences of speaking up are damaging to their already fragile sense of "security."

For instance, in our school neighborhood there is a very large apartment complex, notorious for its drug traffic and prostitution, where many of our children live. Originally, the apartment had both a front and back entrance. To cut down on the amount of traffic going through, the managers closed off the back exit with a large fence. The front entrance is on a very busy street, so the school district would not allow the bus to stop on that street to pick up the children. The children were forced to walk a long distance around the complex to meet the bus in the back, in front of the locked gate. Many children climbed the steel-pointed gate or squeezed through holes in the chain-link fence. After several children were injured, the managers greased the gate so that it could not be climbed. When parents complained to the managers about this unsafe and unfair condition, they were told that if they complained to anyone else, they would be evicted from their apartment and reported to "immigration." A parents' group that was formed to talk about children's rights and safety in the community began to focus on this issue. The attitude of the parents who talked about it was that nothing could be done. It was only because administrators from the school district, members of the media, and some state legislators became involved that the problem was able to be mediated. The bus driver now has a key to the gate.

Many people at our school have been fortunate enough to work closely with Patricia Carini, former director of Prospect School, and current director of Prospect School Archives. She has influenced our thinking and our teaching in terms of seeing children through their strengths and building on those strengths. She has written (Carini, 1986) that

> Given the attitudes currently dominant in our society, I believe that it is important—indeed, crucial—that those of us deeply concerned with children and childhood learn to be attentive to, and to draw upon, children's strengths (and our own) in order to modify and counteract these adverse influences. This requires vigilance in guarding the rights of all children to an environment conducive to growth and to an education. It also requires the ability to observe and build from children's strengths as thinkers, learners, and persons. Finally, it requires us to create classrooms and other environments that are responsivex to the broad and diverse range of children in terms of interests, potentials, and needs. It is, I think, only from a firmly grounded knowledge of children's strengths that we will be able to offer effective alternatives to current and proposed school practices that undermine children's long-term potential for growth. (pp. 3–4)

Our children bring to the classroom a beautiful language; strong family ties; minds, hearts, and bodies full of hope; an intense desire to learn and to share who they really are. They also bring aspirations, high expectations, dreams, wonder, freshness, and a world full of possibilities. These are just some of their strengths. It is up to us to make sure that we create the space for all their strengths to work for them.

News

The time we set aside for "news" is one of these spaces. We have struggled for years to balance between frivolous news conversations that hop from one topic to another without really affecting our thinking, and the kinds of conversations that really make us think. For example, one year we paid attention to the way the media portray Hispanics and followed the news stories over a period of time. In class, we discussed a series of questions about the point of view of the articles: Who is really telling this story? Are we Hispanics really the way this article describes us? Do we all have parties with loud music and barbecues, so that our neighbors can't have any peace of mind? Why would anyone want to make such a general statement like that about a group of people? Why are we portrayed as trying to take jobs away from citizens of the United States? If we were writing the newspaper article or reporting for the TV news, what kind of stories would we write about ourselves? What are our many positive characteristics? We believe that if we do this critical analysis when our children are still young, they will not grow up believing that those stories are truthful, but instead will learn to read the paper and watch the news with a questioning mind.

Carole Edelsky (1994) urges teachers to think about how systems of domination are part of all classroom interaction. In our news time, we are trying to foreground and question systems of domination. We do that questioning at other times too. One day in Cecilia's class, during "Buddy Reading," the students were doing a study of fairy tales from a historical, literary, and critical perspective. We had spent days studying the different roles of the characters. We had plans to study nontraditional fairy tales in which females play a different role and witches are considered "smart and educated women." We had decided that in order to really analyze and pay attention to all of this, we needed to study the more traditional ones first. While reading the fairy tale "Snow White the Fairest One of All," Reneé, the fourth- and fifth-grade teacher, asked the children if they knew what the word "fair" meant. A child said, "It means if your mom is going to give you something you get the same as your brother."

We decided to look up "fair" in our thesaurus. To our dismay, many of the meanings were connected to "whiteness." The range of related words included "blond, attractive, gorgeous, beautiful, bright, pleasant, serene, clear, unclouded, clean, equal, equitable, even, honest," all the way to "just, unbiased, impartial, unprejudiced, and open-minded." Seeing "justice" connected with "whiteness" reminded us of Herbert Kohl's (1991) discussion of having to "unlearn" racist habits of mind. Kohl's student Akim challenged Kohl's idea of reading Conrad's *Heart of Darkness* because of its explicit and offensive racism. Kohl says, "Before knowing him [Akim] I was not attuned to many of the nuances of racist implication because I was not the victim of racism. I did not suffer through every offensive phrase I encountered when reading, nor did I experience rage when racism was cloaked in the authority of tradition or the language of excellence" (p. 32). As when Akim confronted

Kohl, the day we looked up "fair" was a turning point for us. It helped us see how the words we use every day are closely tied to those who are in power. The word "fair" will no longer have the traditional meaning for us; there is so much more behind it. In *She Tries Her Tongue, Her Silence Softly Breaks*, Marlene Nourbese Philip (1989) writes, "Language creates a bridge; to speak another language is to enter someone else's consciousness. Speech, voice, language, and word—are all ways of being in the world" (p. 16). Together we are learning to be "awake" in the world, to become conscious of "the ways of being" embedded in the language we learn and use.

Poetry

Poetry has a very important place in our classes. After many months of daily exposure to poetry, the children's assignment was to find their favorite poem from among all the poetry books in the class. While some of the children took the assignment quite seriously, others did not. Some children chose poems without paying much attention to aesthetics or intellectual weight. We had many discussions, therefore, about why one would like a certain poem. On the one hand, we wanted to support the children's choices, yet we also wanted to raise the "level" of their choices. We wanted them to be able to find poems that really moved them, that spoke to them, and that awakened something unknown in them.

There was a group of Spanish-speaking children who were looking at some of Rafael Alberti's poetry. One of the children in this group was looking for the poem, "Se equivocó La Paloma" ("The Dove was Mistaken"), a poem that is the favorite among many children in our class, and one that the children had practically memorized. Robert said, "Look, you can study about the life of Rafael Alberti in this book. We could study about his life." An intern from Arizona State University, Aída, happened to be there, and the children began to talk with her about Rafael Alberti. She had studied in Granada, Spain, and was also fascinated by the work of Alberti, García Lorca, Machado, and other poets of that period. The next time she came, she brought with her many books about Rafael Alberti and his poet friends. Every time Aída came, she worked with the children, helping them to take notes and "translating" the words of these books for adults into words and stories that the children could make their own.

This was another time when the children were engaging in inquiry that was quite unexpected for the "teachers" and when the teachers' knowledge was also very limited. But we learned. Rafael Alberti is another one of those poets who has fought for the rights of others. He became a poet of the oppressed and the persecuted and was himself persecuted and then went into exile for thirty-nine years. He was active during the Spanish Civil War, and became personally devastated when his friend and fellow poet, Federico García Lorca, was killed because of his beliefs and ideas.

One of the most persistent questions the children had was whether Rafael Alberti was still alive. They said, "If he is alive he must be older than ninety years. How could we find out if he is still alive?" One day while Cecilia was working on the Internet, she decided to find out if there was any information about Rafael Alberti. To her surprise, there was an article from a newspaper in Madrid, announcing that Rafael Alberti had been hospitalized on New Year's Eve and was very ill. The next day, during announcements and sharing, Cecilia shared the news about Rafael Alberti with the children. The classroom filled with silence. Another great poet was dying. Although Alberti was miles away, he had become very close to us, and it was hard to imagine that we wouldn't have any more new poems written by him.

That same day, another group of children, having noticed all the talk about Rafael Alberti, began to show an interest in the work of Gabriela Mistral. They went to other classes and gathered books about her poetry and her life. Here was another wonderful poet—and a teacher for twenty years— who had dedicated her life to putting books in the hands of people, writing poems for children, and helping reform schools and create libraries. Her desire was to write poetry for the poor and the most needy. Many children in our class wrote poetry inspired by the work of Gabriela Mistral. The following poem by Viridiana is one of our favorites:

> Paz
> Paz para
> los niños
> paz para
> los jóvenes
> paz para
> los maestros
> paz para
> los animales
> paz
> para tener
> un mundo feliz
> y con amor

> —Por Viridiana, 8 años

Peace
Peace for
the children
peace
for the youth
peace for
the teachers
peace for
the animals
peace
so we can have
a world
with happiness
and love

—Viridiana (age 8)

Working with poetry in our classrooms and reading essays by Adrienne Rich (1993) and Alastair Reid (1996) have helped us to re-view poetry as: poetry of the people, poetry for the people, and poetry by the people. Adrienne Rich says that she had "long known how poetry can break open locked chambers of possibility, restore numbed zones to feeling, recharge desire" (p. xiv). A poem, she argues, "can't free us from the struggle for existence, but it can uncover desires and appetites buried under the accumulating emergencies of our lives" (p. 13).

Adrienne Rich reminds us that in most countries, poetry has been considered dangerous and indispensable. For example, when the junta took control in Chile, there was heightened political repression. The military regime ransacked and sealed poet Pablo Neruda's house. But people from all walks of life came to write messages to him on the boards of the fence. These messages were full of resistance—brief phrases and names that conveyed a world of meanings. Neruda died twelve days after the junta took over power in Chile, but the poet and his life became a symbol of resistance. Alastair Reid (1996) says of Pablo Neruda's poetry, "He did not write poems for literary circles; he wanted them out in the street, read by everyday inhabitants of the language. He achieved just that, in his own time, as has no other poet I can think of. He accomplished what Whitman only aspired to; he became what Whitman had hoped to be" (p. 61).

We want our students to be awakened by poetry in such a way that their thoughts and feelings are given body and shape by its power. We also want them to know about the lives and work of poets like Pablo Neruda, Rafael Alberti, Alfonsina Stormi, Gabriela Mistral, Rubén Dario, Sandra Cisneros, Nikki Giovanni, Gary Soto, and others. As teachers we know that the struggle starts with us, that children won't take poetry as something indispensable unless we do.

Building Community

As a country we talk about the issues of human rights in faraway places, yet violations of human rights are taking place all around us, in our own country, in our cities, towns, and neighborhoods. Every day, the children tell personal stories that touch on issues of human rights.

Ana was in Karen's class for three years. From the first day she was able to express in some way what she considered to be her rights. She was not a child who easily conformed to the schedule of others. She had her own time frame and agenda. When she invested herself in her work, she was unable to stop just because the teacher said it was time to do something else. She could work for hours on writing or art and produce incredible work. This was difficult for us, but we also saw that Ana supported other children in the classroom; she was a good friend, and she showed us through the thoroughness of her work in class projects that she had a commitment to the class. It took time to get to know Ana and an adjustment on our part to be able to let her have her space and her own time frame.

After second grade Ana's family moved out of our school area. One day, in a phone conversation with Karen, Ana said that she wasn't happy in her new school. Spanish-speaking Ana had been placed in an all-English classroom, one with a narrowly prescribed curriculum. "They don't understand me," she told Karen. "They don't listen to me. They don't let me do my art. They don't know me." The closed curriculum and the language restrictions placed on Ana made her feel stifled; she was sure that the teachers at the new school saw her as not very knowledgeable or creative— a far cry from the thorough, responsible, imaginative child we knew. In *Life in a Crowded Place*, Ralph Peterson (1992) says that students must feel they belong and be confident that they have something of worth to offer others, that everyone need not participate in the same way, that voices differ. Ana needed the time and the opportunity to be herself, to make her own unique contribution to our community.

Building a community often means being an advocate for children and their families. This year Karen had a new child in her class who had just come from Mexico. He lived with his mother, his stepfather, and two brothers. A couple of months after the school year started, the family moved in order to be closer to the stepfather's work. Two weeks passed and one day at lunch we were reminiscing about the child and his entertaining qualities. At that moment the child's mother walked in with her children. She told us that for two weeks she had been trying to enroll her children in the school in the new neighborhood. She said the school would not accept the children because she had no identification and could not produce a utility bill or legal document to verify her address. The office staff and, later, the vice principal told her that too many people try to sneak their children into school, and there isn't room for them all. In desperation, the mother had returned to our school to ask for our help. We asked our principal to intervene. After getting the same story from that school, our principal called the district office and challenged their policy. Eventually, a higher-ranking administrator agreed to help. The children were enrolled the same day. Why did it take a principal calling a district office to get children into school who had been denied an education for two weeks?

Throughout the school year, but especially at the beginning, to build a sense of community and to become aware of our own and others' rights, we play games, talk about our expectations, learn new songs together, read books that touch on issues of human rights, and share personal and family stories. Every day we have a time together that we call "Concerns and Compliments," when children learn to talk about and solve their problems. In a school with a transient population such as ours, it is a challenge to provide the children with the feeling of community, safety, and continuity that they need in order to thrive in an academic setting. Nonetheless, when expectations are set for children to exercise their rights and to respect the rights of others, amazing things can happen.

Enrique started the year with a lot of difficulties in getting along with other children. He had many problems on the playground; children complained to him and about him. As the year progressed in Karen's room, through much talk about individual rights and the rights of others, Enrique became more responsible in his actions and more responsive to the rights, needs, and feelings of others. He made progress both socially and academically. The children often complimented Enrique for the progress he was making. But two weeks before the end of the year, Enrique was caught throwing rocks at the house of an incapacitated man who lived near Enrique's bus stop. The man was frightened by the violence. The man had dogs which Enrique and some other boys teased. Another day soon after, Enrique and a friend thought they had broken a window, so instead of getting on the bus and coming to school, they ran and hid in the neighborhood. Other children who had witnessed what had happened reported it to teachers. The children were very upset. We were worried about Enrique and his friend because they were not at school, and nobody—not us, not their families—knew where they were. The police were called in to look for them. They found them setting fires in the alley of their apartment complex. The police handcuffed the seven- and eight-year-olds and brought them to school—dirty and very scared. We felt such a sense of despair; the progress we had made during the year as a class and with Enrique as an individual seemed to have disappeared. We had worked so hard on thinking independently and making good decisions. This felt like a major setback, and we were angry and disappointed. But then we saw that the other children in the class were also disappointed. Moreover, they were not only disappointed in Enrique; they were also concerned about the elderly man who was being harassed by Enrique and the other boys. Even more impressive, instead of voicing anger, our students commented that Enrique needed our help and support more than ever; rather than punishing Enrique, they said we should help and guide him through this difficult time. We came to realize that even though, as a community, we were not perfect, the struggle was a process and our job was to keep working at it.

Our work with justice changes every year. We keep some basic principles in mind, like working toward bringing the idea of human rights into our classroom and into our everyday lives, as well as keeping a watchful eye in order to see the possibilities the children and life bring to us. We think of this type of work as a craft, a dance, a poem—the form the artist encounters as she works with the rock or the marble, a piece of clay we give shape to as we work with it. We are never sure what will happen, what will come out of it, what next year's children will bring to our class. We discover as we work together. And we create stories like these, which help us understand our lives.

References

Carini, P. (1986). *Building from children's strengths*. North Bennington, VT: Prospect Archive and Center for Education and Research.

Edelsky, C. (1994). Education for democracy. *Language Arts, 71*(4), 252–257.

Kohl, H. (1991). *I won't learn from you: And other thoughts on creative maladjustment*. Minneapolis: Milkweed.

Neruda, P. (1973/1993). *Confieso que he vivido*. Barcelona, Spain: Editorial Seix Barral,S.A.

Peterson, R. (1992). *Life in a crowded place: Making a learning community.* Portsmouth, NH: Heinemann.

Philip, M. N. (1989). *She tries her tongue, her silence softly breaks.* Charlottetown, P.E.I.: Ragweed.

Reid, A. (1996, June 24/July 1). Neruda and Borges. *The New Yorker,* 56–67.

Rich, A. (1993). *What is found there.* New York: Norton.

II CRITICAL LITERACY

What is critical literacy? Some people unfamiliar with the concept have confused critical literacy with critical thinking. Educators have worked for years to engage the critical thinking of learners. But critical literacy ups the ante and moves far beyond the distinction between, say, literal and higher-level responses. Not only are learners drawn into a critical stance to reveal, unveil, and contextualize any given text, but they also work toward using the tools of critical literacy to dismantle those texts and re-create new ones. Three takes on critical literacy include the following:

1. Having a critical perspective on literacy or literacies per se, where literacy itself is the object of critique

2. Having a critical perspective on particular texts, where the critique of texts and their worldviews is the object

3. Having a critical perspective on, for example, being able to analyze and critique wider social practices which are mediated by, made possible, and partially sustained through reading, writing, viewing, and transmitting texts. Here, social practices, their histories, their normative work, and their associated literacy practices and artifacts are the target of analysis and critique. (Lankshear 1997)

The educators whose writing appears in this section understand "having a critical perspective" from the third vantage point and as essential to their practice; at the same time, they acknowledge the challenges this position presents.

The excerpt from Linda Christensen's article "Critical Literacy: Teaching Reading, Writing, and Outrage" serves to define critical literacy and to frame the subsequent articles. Outraged by how her teachers positioned her as a student from a working-class home and as a student who spoke a variation of the standard dialect, Christensen later rereads her experiences, using them as a starting point with her own urban, working-class, predominantly African American students. Early childhood educator Karen Gallas uses the same tools—perspective, observation, field notes, analysis of social processes—to take a critical look at a literacy event in her first- and second-grade classroom. The event served as a "point of confusion" or rupture in the ongoing flow of activity and was the impetus to interrogate her own values and attitudes about what seems a benign engagement—story time. She was only partially successful in bridging the gap between the literacy expectations of school and the worlds of "at risk" children. Her story is a reminder that educators' complacent attitudes are also "at risk."

The world of school administration, a gendered space steeped in power and control issues, engages the analysis of Susan Church. She experienced small successes in carrying out "projects of possibility" that included alternative responses to disruptive special education students and a more systematic application of shared decision making. Her tenure as an assistant superintendent spanned a brief and highly politicized two years. She cautions, as do authors Barbara Comber and Helen Nixon, that the work is not simple, that it yields no easy answers, and that it's necessary. The commitment, whether in the workplace, the classroom, or within the larger culture, stems from the recognition that our work is about "who people are and who people might be."

Work Cited

Lankshear, C. 1997. *Changing Literacies.* London: Open Literacy Press.

5 Critical Literacy: Teaching Reading, Writing, and Outrage

Linda M. Christensen

From history to literature to language, my teachers' choices informed me to lower my expectations. I knew that the people who changed history were great men—Columbus, Washington, Lincoln. Because no one like me or my family was included in the curriculum, I learned I wasn't important, my family wasn't important, and I shouldn't expect too much. The women who made a difference were ordained by God, like Joan of Arc, or sewed their way to fame, like Betsy Ross. I clung to those few women and claimed them as my guides. I never heard of Fannie Lou Hamer or Frida Kahlo until I started teaching.

I was from a working-class family. My mother, the eighth child out of twelve, was the first to finish high school. My father only finished grade school. I was the fourth child in my family and the first to attend college. We didn't talk right. We said "chimley" and "the-ater." We confused our verbs. In the ninth grade, Mrs. Delaney asked me to stand in front of my English class and pronounce words like "beige," or "baj," as we said. I was an example of how not to talk. I became ashamed of myself and my family.

It wasn't until I studied the history of the English language that I realized there might have been a reason, other than stupidity, laziness, or ignorance, for the way my family pronounced words and used verb tenses. And I was angry that I hadn't been taught that history, that I'd been allowed, in fact, *made*, to feel ashamed of my home language.

Today I am outraged by the experience. And I want my students to be outraged when they encounter texts, museums, commercials, classes, and

Excerpt reprinted from Chapter 10 of *Making Justice Our Project*, edited by Carole Edelsky.

rules that hide or disguise a social reality that glorifies one race, one culture, one social class, one gender, or one language, without acknowledging the historical context that gave it dominance. I want to teach a critical literacy that equips students to "read" power relationships at the same time that it imparts academic skills. . . .

Some might say that the role of language arts teachers is to teach reading, writing, and language and that we should not be worrying about issues like injustice or racism. But I would respond that the teaching of literacy is political. Any piece of literature my students pick up—from cartoons to children's books to the literature we read in class—legitimates what Chilean writer Ariel Dorfman (1983, p. 7) calls a "social blueprint" about what it means to be men, women, poor, people of color, gay, or straight. And that vision is political—whether it portrays the status quo or argues for a reorganization of society.

How and when I "correct" students' language and writing is also political. If I do not teach students that the standard language in this country, or any country, is not based on the "best" language but on the language that the powerful, the ruling class, developed, then every time I "correct" their home language I am condemning it as wrong, as incorrect, as "nonstandard." If I fail to make that social blueprint transparent, I endorse it.

No subject in school, including literature, composition, and the study of language, is "value-free," as Ira Shor points out in *A Pedagogy for Liberation* (Shor & Freire, 1987). Too often, "[t]hese falsely neutral curricula train students to observe things without judging, to see the world from the official consensus, to carry out orders without questioning, as if the given society is fixed and fine" (p. 12).

Teachers must draw students into what Brazilian educator Paulo Freire described as a "critical dialogue about a text or a moment of society . . . to reveal it, unveil it, see its reasons for being like it is, the political and historical context of the material" (Shor & Freire, 1987, p. 13). But beyond illumination, students must use the tools of critical literacy to dismantle the half-truths, inaccuracies, and lies that strangle their conceptions about themselves and others. They must use the tools of critical literacy to expose, to talk back to, to remedy any act of injustice or intolerance that they witness.

What Is Critical Literacy?

Several years ago, I attended a literature workshop at which we read a chapter from Olive Ann Burns's novel *Cold Sassy Tree* (1984). The workshop was wonderful, full of useful techniques to engage students in literature: a tea party, text rendering, writing from our own lives, using an innocent narrator as Burns does. Great methodology. And ones I use with almost every unit I teach. But the entire workshop ignored the issues of race, class, and gender that run like a sewer through the novel—from the "linthead" factory workers, to the African Americans who work as kitchen help, to the treatment of women. The workshop explored none of this.

For too many years of my teaching career, I also ignored the social text. I thought it meant talking about setting. I had not been taught anything different. Saying that the novel was set in the South during such and such a period was enough. But it is not enough. Not questioning why the lintheads and the African Americans in the novel were treated differently or not exploring the time Grandpa blamed Grandma for not bearing him a son— this allows readers to silently accept these practices as just. Young women internalize the idea that they must be beautiful and bear sons to be loved. Working-class students learn that it is their fault if they are poor like the lintheads in the novel. When I taught literature without examining the social and historical framework, I condoned the social text students absorbed.

Critical literacy does explore the social and historical framework. It moves beyond a description of society and into an interrogation of it. Why were the lintheads poor? Why weren't they accepted by the middle class? In a society that has so much, why do some starve while others get fat? Why do women have to be beautiful to be loved? Critical literacy questions the basic assumptions of our society.

In each unit of study I use the same basic format: (1) a question that provokes the examination of historical, literary, and social "texts"; (2) the study and involvement of students' lives; (3) the reading of a variety of texts, ranging from novels to historical documents, to first-person narratives, to movies, speakers, role-plays, and field trips; and (4) a final project that opens the possibility for students to *act* on their knowledge. Critical literacy is big and messy. It combines the reading and writing of poetry, fiction, essay, historical documents and statistics, lots of discussions, read-arounds, days of writing, responding, and revising of student work.

This kind of work takes time. We cannot race through a half-dozen novels. I am forced to make difficult choices about what I include and what I leave out. Often, one novel will provide the center, or core, and I will surround it with other texts, role-plays, videos, improvisations, museum visits, or speakers.

*   *   *

6 Story Time as a Magical Act Open Only to the Initiated: What Some Children Don't Know about Power and May Not Find Out

Karen Gallas

As a first- and second-grade teacher and the parent of two grown children, I know the importance of reading to preschool children to prepare them for formal reading instruction in school. In my classroom, story time has always been a habitual practice, a routine that is a central part of the literacy program. Over the years, however, I have had many students who were not read to at home. At first, they usually struggled with reading and, as a result, with other subjects. Often, the students were poor, their home life unstable, or both. I attributed their difficulties with school to some nebulous combination of circumstances resulting from poverty and believed that their socioeconomic legacies exerted a tremendous, perhaps insurmountable, obstacle to success in school. In my mind, their lack of exposure to storybooks loomed large as a seminal literacy gap, that is until I met Denzel, a 7-year-old African American boy. Until then, I had never examined the deep, symbolic meaning of storybook reading as a critical literacy event.

Denzel

Although I normally have students for first and second grades, Denzel came to my class as a second grader. He was nearly 7 and was one of the

Reprinted from Chapter 5 of *Teaching Language Arts*, edited by Judith Wells Lindfors and Jane S. Townsend.

healthiest students I have ever taught. He was not sick, hungry, tired, or hurt. He had no learning disabilities or handicapping conditions. He came to school well-dressed, well-fed, and well-rested, and was much loved by his working-class family. In fact, ten family members, including his mother, father, brothers, sisters, cousins, and nephews, lived in a four-bedroom apartment. Denzel knew more about the intricacies of his family tree than I knew about mine.

Denzel was also serious about school and worked hard to please his teachers. Therefore, I was surprised early in the school year when he would not listen to stories during our daily read-aloud time. It was a problem that began in September and lasted until June, and it perplexed me for three years. This article describes my year-long effort to help Denzel understand the purpose of storybook reading, and it also relates my efforts as a teacher-researcher to understand both his and my beliefs about reading. The article examines story time or the read-aloud experience, an implicit part of early education, for what it says about educational equity, for who has access to this equity, and for what our assumptions about the transparency of classroom rituals may deny some students. My interaction with Denzel and my ruminations about how better to serve him helped me to peel back the layers of story time, asking what it means to listen to a story being read aloud and to look at the pictures in the book, what are the intrinsic implications for reading and receiving other kinds of texts that are embedded in this activity, and what assumptions have we made about the "naturalness" of this activity for children.

Research Perspective

It is common for teachers' questions to be borne of the prosaics of everyday classroom observations. The contextual nature of such observations are often presented as anecdotes that are embodied with the observer's assumptions about the event. For example, I made the following observation in September:

> Denzel and I have a problem: He won't listen to story. Won't look at the pictures either. This just makes me crazy. He's a good little kid, and I can't for the life of me engage him in story time no matter what book we use or what devices I muster.

To someone unfamiliar with the context of the event in this anecdote, this entry in my field notes might suggest that something is wrong with the student or with my teaching. The anecdote isn't complete, but it does raise some questions.

Yet, before considering any questions, I must consider the origin of the observation. As Bakhtin pointed out, the unfolding of the ordinary events of daily life, of life's prosaics, has much to offer our understanding of a language, a culture, a social milieu (Morson & Emerson, 1990). Observations that describe points of rupture in the life of the classroom, points of confusion, missteps, or even chaos give access to the moments when teacher intention, as it is embodied in a method, encounters the prosaic world of the students' daily life. What Bakhtin called the "unfinalizability" of human discourse—the understanding that each new human encounter cannot rely on past scripts but rather must be freshly and mutually constructed in the moment—is captured in such moments.

My inquiry into storybook reading began with this perspective, but it is important to note that my efforts to understand why Denzel didn't like story time did not result in a clear solution or resolution. He never fully participated in story time as a whole-class activity. However, my lack of success in trying to get him to participate is instructive. It magnifies the value of classroom inquiry as it examines the meanings of habitual practices, and it helps us to consider pathways to equity for all students.

The Setting

I teach in an urban school that has a multiracial, multiethnic, and multilingual student population. There are approximately thirty-two different languages—and hence nationalities—represented in the K–8 population of about five hundred students. In my class of twenty-two students, four of them were non-English speakers. I had East Asian, African American, and Hispanic/Latino students. The Asian and Caucasian students were primarily from professional, middle, and upper middle-class families, while the African American and Latino students were from working-class families.

The classroom mix makes for a diverse site of inquiry. I have students who have had enriched home lives in terms of literacy preparation: They have been read two and three books daily since early childhood and have regular exposure to museums, the arts, and cultural events. I also have students who speak little or no English and have just emigrated from foreign countries. Some of these students are true immigrants, settling permanently in the United States, and others are here for only a few years while their parents pursue university degrees. I also have what I term less-privileged students whose families are on public assistance or live in homeless shelters or whose families struggle but remain on the edges of poverty. Some of these students have also been exposed to reading at an early age. However, others, like Denzel, have no preschool reading experience and may not have attended kindergarten.

Denzel in Second Grade

From the start, Denzel and I agreed that he needed to learn to read. He did not go to kindergarten, but he did learn some prereading skills in first grade, where he received Chapter I reading services as well as individualized instruction. Those interventions continued in second grade. When I met Denzel, he knew the letters of the alphabet, how to count, and some basic phonics skills. He set out with a vengeance to learn to read. All year, Denzel read and reread texts, constantly applying newly acquired phonetic and print understandings to the process.

Most teachers agree that reading is more than saying the words in a story. Reading includes understanding word meanings, and, as children get older, understanding the nuances of a story. Although he made it his goal to learn to read, there were times when not knowing the meaning of words frustrated Denzel's efforts. For example, he loved fairy tales such as *Little Red Riding Hood, The Three Bears, The Ugly Duckling, Thumbelina*, and *The Princess and the Pea*, but he was not familiar with them until I introduced them to him. There were many words of importance that he tried to read but could not—words such as *cupboard, shawl, porridge, swan*, for example—and, therefore, he stumbled over them. However, not knowing word meanings is a common problem for many new readers, especially those who do not have strong literacy backgrounds. I knew strategies that would help Denzel learn new words, and he willingly participated. In fact, he began to use his mastery of the books to acquire new vocabulary.

Denzel and Story Time

From the day Denzel walked into my classroom, he purposefully set out to learn to read. In contrast, however, he did not see a purpose for story time and listening during read-aloud. If he was not coaxed through a story in either a one-on-one or small group situation, with the context for all events in the text made apparent and the reading made a social event, Denzel would not participate. Variations in subject matter, narrative style, illustrations, main characters, or any other alterations we made in reading strategies and selections of texts had no affect on his participation. Denzel simply was not interested in hearing stories read aloud.

If the book read aloud was not familiar to Denzel or was one he had not heard before in a more intimate setting, he would not listen to the story or look at the pictures. He would sit doubled over with his head tucked between his knees or would gradually move beyond the group and direct attention elsewhere. Although he was not disrespectful or disruptive, he was clearly impatient with story time and often told us so before or after a reading. If we tried to engage him in conversation about the book to see if he had been listening, his remarks usually indicated that he was not paying attention.

Denzel's behavior is something that teachers might expect from a kindergartner or possibly a first grader. With a second grader who was already at a disadvantage academically, but who clearly worked hard, this behavior is a great concern. I knew Denzel took reading, books, and his teachers' efforts seriously, but he did not see the relationship between our whole-class practice of storybook reading and his own goals as a reader.

My earliest reactions to Denzel's behavior ranged from irritation to bewilderment. Because I couldn't characterize his resistance as a challenge to my authority, I examined his ability to listen and attend in other areas. He seemed to have no problems beyond his inability to listen during read-alouds. Thus, I began to question my own reaction to his inattention. I began to question the deeper implications of story reading and think about its purpose within the framework of school. I asked myself why it was important for Denzel to listen to stories and to look at pictures and what did I think was happening when students listened intently to a story.

My first strategy was to talk to Denzel to find out what he understood about books, asking him whether he was read to at home (he wasn't) and if he understood what books were for. The following excerpt is from our discussions of what books are for.

DENZEL: (Thinks a long time.) Books make you read more.

GALLAS: Books make you read more. But what do you do
            with them? Why do we even have them?

DENZEL: So you can learn how to read. You look at the
            books, and so that you know the words. And for
            little kids to look at the pages.

GALLAS: Do grown-ups ever use books? Do you ever see
            grown-ups using books?

DENZEL: To practice reading. In case they forget some
            words.

I realized during this conversation that he did not understand the purpose of
storybook reading beyond an instrumental word mastery function. The
stories, or the real, imaginative fictions, that he thought were worth listening
to *were* part of sharing time when he and other students told "fake" stories.
Denzel actively and skillfully participated in the sharing of personal stories.
Storybooks, however, were not associated with "reading" as he understood
it. Reading was where you would "look at the books, and so that you know
the words." During read-aloud time, he could only see the book's pictures;
he could not follow along with the words on the page, which seemed to be
necessary for reading to be worthwhile to him. Denzel's response to my
questions about books made complete sense within the context of his
experience with books, which he saw as utilitarian, or a means to an end. In
this sense, his not participating in read-alouds was understandable. Knowing
this, I asked: "How could I add to his understanding of storybook reading?"
and "What was missing from his interpretation of what storybook reading
means?"

Storybook Reading as Ritual

A few weeks after Denzel and I discussed what books are for, a colleague
who had been reading with him once a week on a regular basis said that
Denzel had told her that he thought every book in the classroom was
handmade. It occurred to me that for students like Denzel, who have not
been exposed to books and intimate readings with family, books and events
associated with them must seem mysterious. Indeed, the whole event of
hearing a story read aloud must seem magical. Imagine being in
kindergarten or first grade for the first time, and a woman whom you
probably only recently met makes everyone sit down on the floor in a group
or in a circle while she sits in a tall chair. Everyone looks up at her and is
quiet. She picks up this object, which you know is called a book but which
no one has ever explained what it is for or does, and she opens it, holds it up
in the air, and begins speaking. Some of the words you have never heard
before. As she speaks, she points to the pictures and turns the pages. Then
she closes the book and puts it back, and the next day, at the same time, she
does the same thing again, but probably with a different book.

If you're an uninitiated participant in this ritual, you may think it is magical. How does she know the words? Where do the words come from? Where do the pictures come from? In fact, where does the book come from? As the questions multiply, it is easy to realize how precarious the assumptions that I made about students' understandings of books and the event of story time were. I assumed that all students were like my children, were like me, were like my friends and their children, and that they understood everything about books and their purpose as cultural objects when they entered school.

"The Look"

Realizing that Denzel may have a different perspective on story time than my other students, I examined what the other students in my class—the already-initiated students—did to listen to stories. First, I noticed they became still, then their eyes glazed over, their mouths dropped open, and they took on what I call "the look." "The look" struck me as being slightly zombie-like or being mesmerized by the story and the pictures. As I read, the students examined pictures carefully. For example, if I turned the page too fast, they protested, often requesting a second look at the page. As I read, the students did not move for almost the entire story, unless there was an exciting or disturbing transition that took place in the plot. Then they gasped, moaned, or squealed. Their hands covered their eyes and mouths in fear or suspense.

All of these gestures were reactions to being inside of the story. Chapter books without pictures had the same effect, only students looked directly at me as I read, their faces reflecting "the look." If the books were nonfiction texts, "the look" was slightly different: brows furrowed in concentration, questions silently but sometimes audibly mouthed, but bodies still and mouths opened. I asked myself, "What does 'the look' mask?" and "What's happening in their heads?" I responded from my own experience as a reader and listener: The students were allowing themselves to be transported to another time and place; they were engaged in an imaginative exercise. In fact, the books were magical, producing an altered state of being.

I began to understand my motives for wanting Denzel to participate in story time. I also began to clarify what was not happening for him and tried to talk to him about some of those things, but we made little progress.

In late January, as she gathered the class for story, Denzel asked my intern, "Why do I have to listen to story? Couldn't I just read a book by myself?" She, as frustrated as I was by that time, asked the other students the same questions. Their comments implied that story time offered a window into this magical activity, into a different place and time. The following excerpt presents some of the students' responses to why we listen to stories. Although Denzel did not say anything during this discussion, he listened.

MIA: Because, so you can calm down a little after you've been running around, like at recess.

DONNA: It makes, like, your, some of the teachers want your imagination to, like, let go, because sometimes . . .

LATIA: To learn things.

KELLY: To read much better and listen.

NATE: To help you concentrate.

LATIA: If you listen, you'll know how to read the words better because stories have been told to people for centuries and centuries, and the people pass them on, and it calms them down.

CHARLES: It gets them still and interested in what you're reading. Well, I think that when you listen to a story you can learn new words, and like, you can learn a lot from stories, and people that don't understand things, they can learn words.

MIA: By reading stories you can also tell it to other people, and you can pass it on, and it becomes a big story.

MATT: One story has probably been passed on for centuries and centuries and they change them.

CHARLES: Can you explain that a little more?

MATT: Like, somebody thought of a story, and they passed it on to somebody and each person changed it a little.

YUAN: I think we read stories because we have to pass things on. It's not like we're immortals or anything, we have to pass it on. Just think about how bad the world would be without language, and then just flip it back to stories. 'Cause stories would just die out.

world of the storybook. Although that realization came too late for me and Denzel, it forced me to reconfigure my classroom approach to storybook reading, and it also set me on another path of investigation that will enable me to better serve students like Denzel, some of whom I have in first grade. I must now consider how to gain access to their imaginal worlds, how to help bridge the gap between their "now," or the prosaics of their lives, and the new worlds of the texts I want them to enter.

This year, I have Tommy, a Caucasian child from a working-class family who also has not been read to at home and does not listen during story time. I noticed this during the first day of school. He is eager, healthy, and respectful but has difficulty understanding the purpose or intention of a lesson in any new area. For example, in math, Tommy, like Denzel, does not easily master new strategies for computation in addition, such as counting up or using Cuisenaire rods. After thinking so long about Denzel and considering how I might have taught him better, I have changed several aspects of how I structure my classroom and my teaching to target Tommy's needs as I perceive them. For example, I offer many more opportunities for retelling of stories using drama, art, and storyboards. I have allotted more time to basic expressive opportunities like building with blocks, painting, clay work, and especially creative dramatics to help all the students develop personal narratives about new topics or texts that we are studying in all subjects.

I am using these structures in the hope that they will help Tommy and other "at-risk" students find different ways to understand new subject matter and to engage in experiences that seem disconnected from their lives. In essence, as a teacher-researcher, although I initially focused on a specific problem because of my inability to reach and understand one student, that focus has changed the way I teach all students.

References

Bakhtin, M. M. (1986). *Speech genres and other late essays.* Austin, TX: The University of Texas Press.

Cochran-Smith, M. (1984). *The making of a reader.* Norwood, NJ: Ablex.

Coleridge, S. T. (1907). *Biographia literaria.* London: Oxford University Press.

Heath, S. B. (1982). What no bedtime story means: Narrative skills at home and school. *Language in Society, 11,* 49–76.

Heath, S. B. (1983). *Ways with words: Language, life, and work in communities and classrooms.* New York: Cambridge University Press.

Heath, S. B. (1986). Separating "things of the imagination" from life: Learning to read and write. In W. H. Teale & E. Sulzby (eds.), *Emergent literacy: Writing and reading* (pp. 156–172). Norwood, NJ: Ablex.

Heath, S. B., & Thomas, C. (1984). The achievement of preschool literacy for mother and child. In H. Goelman, A. Oberg, & F. Smith (eds.), *Awakening to literacy* (pp. 51–72). Exeter, NH: Heinemann.

Morson, G. S., & Emerson, C. (1990). *Mikhail Bakhtin: Creation of a prosaics.* Stanford, CA: Stanford University Press.

Ninio, A., & Bruner, J. S. (1976). The achievement and antecedents of labeling. *Journal of Child Language, 5,* 1–15.

Rosenblatt, L. (1978). *The reader, the text, the poem: The transactional theory of literary work.* Carbondale, IL: Southern Illinois University Press.

Scollon, R., & Scollon, B. K. (1981). *Narrative, literacy and face in inter-ethnic communication.* Norwood, NJ: Ablex.

Taylor, D. (1983). *Family literacy: Young children learning to read and write.* Portsmouth, NH: Heinemann.

Teale, W. H. (1986). Home background and young children's literacy development. In W. H. Teale & E. Sulzby (eds.), *Emergent literacy: Writing and reading* (pp. 173–204). Norwood, NJ: Ablex.

Wolf, S. A., & Heath, S. B. (1992). *The braid of literature: Children's worlds of reading.* Cambridge, MA: Harvard University Press.

Bibliography

Karen Gallas

Professional resources that have been especially important to me include:

Ashton-Warner, S. (1963). *Teacher.* New York: Simon & Schuster.

Cazden, C. B. (1988). *Classroom discourse: The language of teaching and learning.* Portsmouth, NH: Heinemann.

Heath, S. B. (1983). *Ways with words: Language, life, and work in communities and classrooms.* New York: Cambridge University Press.

Children's books that I especially enjoy using with children include:

Wood, A. (1987). *Heckedy Peg.* San Diego, CA: Harcourt Brace Jovanovich.

7 Leadership as Critical Practice: A Work-in-Progress

Susan M. Church

Taking a Critical Stance

Becoming an assistant superintendent was never part of my long-range career goals. As a teacher, a supervisor of student services and curriculum, a professional development leader, and a part-time teacher educator, I chose to focus my energies primarily on teaching and learning rather than on the administrative side of leadership. Over the years, I became more and more active in district-level and province-wide curriculum-reform efforts, taking a lead role in promoting whole language philosophy during the 1980s. My experiences in attempting to effect change led me to ongoing inquiry into why so many of our well-intentioned efforts to improve teaching and learning have so little impact. I read the professional literature on school reform, took a critical look at my own practices as a reformer, and concluded that thinking I could just focus on teaching and learning was like a teacher yearning to shut her door and work with her class, avoiding the complexities of functioning within the broader context of school and community.

Drawing on the messages of research, I tried to work with teachers in the ways that I was espousing they should work with children, for example, creating professional development experiences in which they had opportunities to talk, read, write, draw, paint, act, and move within a

Reprinted from Chapter 14 of *Making Justice Our Project*, edited by Carole Edelsky.

supportive context. While there was nothing wrong with these forms of professional development—they were actually a major improvement over one-shot, talk-at sessions—and many teachers found them helpful, they took place within a larger organizational context that had a powerful influence over how teachers perceived and reacted to the district-level change initiatives. Even though many of us in leadership roles tried to invite teachers into the change process by supporting their learning, many of them interpreted our attempts as more top-down demands from supervisors who had power over them. I became very frustrated with what I perceived to be teachers' ill-founded resistance to changes that I believed were in the best interests of students. It was not until I shifted my gaze from the teachers to the social and political context within which they worked, that I could begin to understand their resistance. That shift came as I became familiar with the work of critical theorists (Giroux, 1987; Simon, 1987; Giroux & McLaren, 1986; McLaren, 1989) and of educators who were making the political agenda of whole language more explicit (Shannon, 1992; Edelsky, 1991, 1994).

It became obvious to me, in ways that it had not been before, that many of our systemic schooling practices perpetuate inequities—that these practices maintain the power of dominant groups and subvert our espoused democratic principles. I was persuaded by arguments that whole language needed to have a more critical edge—that we whole language educators, whether our learners are students or teachers, need to bring issues of social justice and equity to the fore in our teaching. I realized that if I hoped to have influence over teachers' beliefs and practices, I needed to understand how they are positioned within the highly bureaucratic, hierarchical school system. I came to see the teachers' resistance to the changes I espoused, not as individual acts of people who did not want to improve their teaching, but as a rather healthy reaction to what they perceived as top-down coercion.

I had not intended to be coercive, but I could not avoid my own positioning as a supervisor within a network of hierarchical power relationships. Many of the teachers saw me as an instrument of the system—another person from outside the classroom attempting to impose change on them. Historically, as layers of administration have been added to school systems and more and more regulations have been imposed, teachers have had less and less control over their work lives. Those above them in the hierarchy control their use of time, access to resources and to professional development, and, often, their curricular goals. It was no wonder that they saw the ambitious reform effort associated with whole language as a threat, rather than as an opportunity. There was nothing in the way in which we introduced the change to teachers that suggested that they had the right to question why the change was coming and how these new ideas about literacy fit with their current beliefs. They also had no opportunity to determine how and when they would explore these new ideas.

I came to the conclusion that it was not enough to have a powerful theory of teaching and learning; I needed to become more explicitly political. As Shannon (1992) helped me to see, "All teachers are political, whether they are conscious of it or not. Their acts contribute to or challenge the status quo in literacy education, in school, and in society" (p. 2). To effect the curricular changes I believed would benefit students, I would need to make the organization itself the focus of my reform efforts by challenging traditional power relationships and ways of working. While I still believed in many of the principles of whole language, I began to think and write about what it might mean to bring critique to the fore in the classroom, the school, and the institution as a whole (Church, 1996).

During the time I was grappling with these issues, the school district in which I worked was moving rapidly to restructure in response to a number of pressures: fiscal restraints, proposed governance changes at the provincial level that shifted power from district to site, and the district's own commitment to decentralization and more community involvement in schools. As well, a number of senior staff took advantage of an early retirement package. It seemed to me that the context was sufficiently fluid and open that there might be some opportunities to take action toward the kinds of changes I thought needed to be made. When the position of superintendent of education services opened, I decided to apply and, much to my delight, was the successful candidate. For the next two years, until our school district was amalgamated with two others in the summer of 1996, I explored what it might mean to lead critically—to be a leader who made issues of equity and social justice my business and who acted wherever I could to change systemic practices that disempowered groups because of race, culture, gender, class, ability, or position in the hierarchy.

Although the district's espoused agenda was to shift more decision making to the schools, the organization was still highly bureaucratic and hierarchical. The senior team, which included the chief education officer and five superintendents, had a great deal of influence over policy, the allocation of human and material resources, and many other decisions that affected schools. Therefore, being a member of senior administration endowed me with positional power. By behaving differently, I believed I could disrupt the status quo. I could bring about systemic change, especially in the important areas for which I was responsible: programs and student services. For example, I could share power more equitably across the levels of the system and make it possible for diverse perspectives to be heard. I could allocate resources within my control to support initiatives that advanced equity and social justice. I could challenge systemic practices, such as tracking, that research has shown disadvantage poor and minority students (Oakes, 1985). I could give my active support to the implementation of board policies in the area of human rights, specifically one for race relations that we had been attempting to implement for several years and a newly adopted one for sexual harassment.

Small Successes

As I discovered almost immediately, there are powerful forces that work against a leader who decides to take a critical stance. I learned a great deal during two years of grappling with the challenges of trying to lead in this way. I discovered how firmly many of our systemic practices are entrenched despite the rhetoric of restructuring and empowerment. Before I turn to a reflection on the lessons I learned and to some thoughts about where to go next, however, I want to focus on what it was possible to accomplish in collaboration with colleagues who shared a commitment to change. Those colleagues were the dozen program and student services supervisors and consultants I was fortunate enough to have in my department and the many principals and teachers who became part of our ongoing conversations, continually challenging us to act on our beliefs. Had the school district amalgamation not occurred, I believe the following small successes might have grown into real forces for positive change. I offer them as examples of what the critical theorists (Simon, 1987) call "projects of possibility."

Rethinking Disruptive Behavior

Over the course of ten years, the school district had made significant progress in eliminating tracking and ability grouping and developing an inclusive environment for children of all ability levels. Virtually all segregated special education classes had disappeared, and all students received support within the classroom or through pullout for focused intervention. For the most part, administrators, teachers, and the community had been supportive of this move toward full inclusion; however, many schools had concerns about their capacity to cope with children and adolescents with disruptive behavior. Community mental health services, like the education system, had been pared down through several years of fiscal restraint. This diminished community support had exacerbated the schools' difficulties in accommodating students whose behavior often had a negative impact on the learning of other children and sometimes threatened the safety of both children and adults. As a result of growing concerns about these young people, there had been ongoing discussions about the possibility of creating some segregated settings in which their needs could be better addressed.

While there were many who saw alternative classes as the solution, there were also voices, including mine, suggesting that we needed to recast the problem; specifically, to explore ways in which the "regular" system might change to become more supportive of these students. A number of us had taught segregated classes in the past and, while it is more than possible to create supportive learning environments in those settings, the programs seldom "fix" the students sufficiently to allow them to return to regular programs, and nothing happens to make the schools more hospitable. In the long term, removal from the regular stream cuts off many future avenues for these students. It seemed to some of us that we should put our energy into creating more flexibility and support within the students' home schools and communities rather than into expensive alternative programs that would actually further disenfranchise the students. As well, we felt it was important to look beyond the educational system to draw upon the expertise and resources of community agencies in a more coherent way.

We asked the proponents of segregated classes to consider the following sorts of critical questions. What is happening in these students' lives that makes them so angry? Are they reacting against social inequities that are based upon class, culture, race, or gender? How have the students and their families been affected by the ongoing decline in the economy? How many of the students are living in poverty? How do our schools perpetuate inequities? How many of the students have significant learning difficulties that contribute to their disruptive behavior? What might we do to change the system to become more flexible and responsive? A teacher who works in a junior high with a large African Canadian population once said to me, "They give these kids anger management workshops, but they don't look at all the reasons why they have every right to be angry. The kids know the system is failing them." Fine (1990) argues that we need to unpack the label "at risk" and "turn our critical concern onto the very ideological and material distinctions that privilege educationally those already privileged, and disadvantage those already disadvantaged" (p. 64).

During the 1995–96 school year our district became involved in a small pilot project designed to address the needs of this population of students. District staff developed the project, which focused initially on the junior high level, in collaboration with two other school districts and a number of community agencies. Although there were two or three segregated sites established as part of the initiative, we took this opportunity to explore options other than special classes. Two supervisors in our district worked with principals and teachers to design flexible programs for students within their home schools. The possibilities included part-time attendance combined with community-based experiences, academic programs designed around the students' strengths, outdoor education and other recreational activities, and even music and art lessons for students who expressed interest. Schools drew upon the expertise of a school psychologist, a family counselor, a youth counselor and a paraprofessional support worker to help them and the students design and carry out programs that would meet their needs. Although one or two of the schools were skeptical at first, over time they all acknowledged that this approach had real potential for making a difference. No miracles occurred, but all of the students were more successful. Moreover, different kinds of working relationships among professionals evolved, and the schools became much more open to and capable of responding to the diverse needs of students.

The results of this pilot program were promising. Unfortunately, the amalgamation brought it to an end. On the eve of the disappearance of our district as an independent entity, we allocated some additional funds to the project schools, and they continued on their own the following year. Recognizing the benefits of reaching younger students, we invited the elementary schools that fed into these junior highs to participate as well. The schools worked together to plan further interventions, contracting with some of the professional staff who had worked in the pilot project. I kept in touch with some of the principals, who told me that the groups of schools were gradually developing ways of working together and additional creative approaches for making the system more responsive. All agreed that focusing on elementary-age students was a positive move. As I write, it is unclear whether the new amalgamated district will continue to fund these small projects, and there is much discussion about the need for alternative classes. From my conversations with those who developed school-based alternatives, I am confident that projects like that will continue, despite the lack of district support. These teachers and principals seem convinced that engagement in long-term collaborative efforts to alter disenfranchising systemic practices is the only means of creating equitable learning opportunities for all their students.

Shared Decision Making

As the district set about to restructure in ways that would vest more control with schools and their communities, many tensions arose at the senior- and middle-management levels. District-level administrators struggled with how best to fulfill their roles; some supervisors actively resisted giving up their power over schools. While those of us in programs and services had many questions about how to shift more power to the schools and still sustain our involvement with and influence over teaching and learning, there was general agreement that we had to work differently. We spent time familiarizing ourselves with the research on school reform and explored what it might mean to apply its lessons. For example, we thought about how we could create a structure that provided the appropriate combination of bottom-up and top-down influence that Fullan (1993) and others have shown is most likely to have positive results for students. We recognized that there was little or no evidence that site-based management models in which schools are left to cope on their own—with no outside resources and supports—were any more effective in transforming student learning than traditional top-down approaches had been.

As a program/services team, we decided to work at systemic change—to renegotiate our relationships with schools so that they really could make decisions about issues that were important to them, including how they used available human and material resources. During the 1980s, when budgets had been richer, the district had developed quite a large cadre of district staff who took leadership for program implementation and for managing services for students. Although there were many fewer people working in district roles by 1994, there had not been much change in the expectations for how these individuals would operate. Both the district and many schools held them responsible in much the way they had in the past. Our goal was to shift the responsibility to the schools—to bring them to the center of the organizational chart and then build a flexible system of supports around them. We knew many schools would struggle with this, having become dependent on district staff. We also knew that schools would be skeptical about whether this proposed change really meant that they would have more control or if it merely meant that they would have all of the responsibilities and no right to make important decisions.

During the two years, we made some progress toward this goal. We put time and effort into helping schools develop school-based teams which would problem solve around the needs of individual students and draw upon expertise from outside the school as needed. The district set an expectation that principals would meet regularly in a self-governing family of school groupings (the senior high and its feeder school) to work collaboratively on issues of interest and importance to them, accessing district staff as needed. We assigned system staff, such as speech pathologists and psychologists, to these families of schools and asked the principals to decide how best to use these resources. The program and services supervisors took on leadership for projects that were generated by groups of schools, for example, facilitating connections with the arts community and working with secondary school principals in their school-restructuring efforts. As much as possible, we tried to configure system resources in response to needs identified by schools, but we also saw a role for the system in gathering and disseminating information about research, provincial program changes, and other issues of relevance to schools. We envisioned that the district could become a resource for schools as they determined for themselves how best to fulfill their obligations to implement provincial programs and as they worked on their school priorities.

There is no doubt that we experienced growing pains as we attempted to make these changes. There were pressures on the supervisors to shift back into their old roles—to take responsibility and control from the schools. Parents were not always satisfied to resolve conflicts at the school level; we still received a great many calls asking district staff to intervene when parents were not happy about a decision that had been made by a principal. Some district staff from other departments complained that supervisors in our department were not doing their jobs because they turned problems back to the school. Some supervisors clearly wanted to return to the predictability and stability of their old roles. Others found ways to re-exert the power they felt they were losing. Although some principals seemed reluctant to take on the responsibilities we devolved to them, most reacted positively and were willing to live with the uncertainties as new structures, processes, and relationships evolved. The self-governing family of schools groups gradually took shape and began seeking out district support for projects they wanted to undertake.

It is not possible to predict how the district structures would have evolved had the amalgamation not occurred. As I reflect on our two-year exploration, I can see that power relationships were changing. Principals and teachers were beginning to have more voice. District staff were moving—some reluctantly—away from command and control forms of leadership. We were, however, far from transforming the hierarchical nature of our bureaucracy. We had taken only small steps toward the creation of a different kind of organization and had only begun to envision what forms a system like that might take.

Advocacy

Having a position of relative power in the organization enabled me to be an effective advocate for equity and social justice through my proactive support of district policy implementation. In particular, I became the champion of a committee responsible for implementing the sexual harassment policy which the school board had approved just before I became superintendent. Of all my efforts to bring critical issues to the center of my work, the support of this committee was the least complicated and most rewarding. I became a mentor for the committee chair, ensured that the committee had resources and released time for professional development activities, and kept the policy implementation on the district agenda. We found funds to hire an outside resource person who helped district staff bring a gender analysis to issues of sexual harassment. My active involvement in the implementation process sent an important message to the system about the importance of the policy. Inquiries that began with the policy soon broadened to include thorny issues such as gender discrimination and homophobia that previously had been rarely, if ever, discussed openly.

Creating Critical Conversations

For me, becoming critically literate has meant tackling the political issues head on in my writing. As a superintendent, I tried to use writing to create critical conversations through raising questions about systemic practices that I saw as disempowering. For example, I wrote to my colleagues in senior management about the nature of the discourse in our meetings, pointing out how alienating and counterproductive I found the constant battles for control to be. Although I was unsuccessful in drawing any of my colleagues into sustained written conversations, this informal writing did help to generate some dialogue. As well, I contributed short pieces to the newsletters of several professional organizations, in which I critiqued top-down reform efforts, proposed changes in governance that had only the appearance of giving more power to schools and communities, and the dismal record of employment equity in the public education system in Nova Scotia.

Political Lessons

In my two short years as a senior administrator, I learned many lessons about leadership. I know that I was successful in leading differently and that I was able to effect change. Yet, I also became painfully aware of the politics of organizational change. Despite the rhetoric of restructuring—the fine-sounding words like collaboration, empowerment and shared decision making—most people who had occupied formal leadership roles in the hierarchy were loathe to give up the power associated with those positions. Furthermore, males had dominated for such a long time in district administration that their ways of leading and knowing had become the norm. When I, as the only female in the senior leadership group, questioned certain of their practices, they often could not see why I saw a problem with the way they had operated successfully for years. Having now moved on from that district leadership role, I can see how formidable are the institutional barriers to the kinds of changes my colleagues and I were advocating. We had many struggles in trying to enact our rather modest agenda, for example, giving schools more control over resources, inviting more voices into decision making, and taking a proactive stance in support of human rights' policies. In light of that, bringing about the systemic changes needed to make public education truly socially just and equitable seems quite daunting. While I recognize that these systemic changes can only occur through the actions of individuals like me, I also know the high personal cost of being proactive in an environment in which one feels like an alien much of the time.

That sense of alienation was particularly strong in my interactions with my male colleagues on the senior team. It is clear that more than one factor contributed to my marginalization. Gender was an issue, but so were professional orientation and philosophy. I had taken a nontraditional path to senior administration through teaching and curriculum leadership; my colleagues collectively had many years of experience as managers in educational and private-sector settings. When I offered my perspectives on leadership, one of my male colleagues would often deliver a lecture on the fine points of management. When I tried to talk about how we were doing our work, specifically, to point out the contradictions between what we said the system was about and what we were actually doing, the others soon brought the conversation back to the real business—the more urgent, practical matters of "running the system." As Australian researcher Jill Blackmore (1995a; 1995b) has documented in her ongoing studies of gender, educational administration, and restructuring, many senior female leaders in organizations experience being simultaneously insiders and outsiders.

Blackmore interviewed seven female senior bureaucrats in the Australian Ministry of Education, all of whom had a history of voluntary and paid community work and social action before coming into government to provide leadership for policy development. These so-called "femocrats" were "part of the mainstream of everyday bureaucratic life and yet marginalised because of their concern with equity as a primary motivation for being in administration." Like me, they entered administration with the idea that they could change the system: "to make it more equitable and empowering, and all saw it as an opportunity to influence policy-making at the centre. Their ambivalence about the bureaucracy derived from the tension between their past experiences which confirmed the view that bureaucracies were largely disabling structures, and their personal experience as leaders in many organisational contexts which led them to understand that administration was about people not things" (1995a, p. 300). One of the women quoted by Blackmore could have been me talking: "Bev recalls how her attempts to promote debate or reflection meant 'a lot of people see me as oppositional, others see me as a dinosaur left over from the seventies who hasn't realised the world has changed'" (1995a, p. 302).

When the women moved inside the bureaucracy, they discovered that their beliefs about how policy should be developed, through an ongoing, recursive consultative process, and about how the day-to-day work of the organization should be carried out were at odds with the dominant, masculinist, technical-rational modes of working. Moreover, they found that there was

> an often uncritical acceptance that bureaucratic rationality means fragmentation and specialisation of tasks, territoriality and hierarchy. It assumes that policy can be divided into discrete stages and that it is a neutral task. Julie commented that the dominant technical-rational approach meant that "what was a very masculinist, patriarchal environment was seen by most merely as bureaucratic practice." (1995a, 303)

In reading the excerpts from these interviews, I relived many of my own feelings of marginalization in senior administration and my frustrations at my inability to articulate my critique in such a way that the institutional practices that I found so alienating would be problematized for my male colleagues.

Like so many other women who have taken on leadership roles, I found that the atmosphere became chillier and chillier, the higher up the bureaucratic ladder I climbed. It is important to understand, however, that my concerns are not primarily about what happened to me personally but about the larger questions raised by my experiences. How can those of us who believe whole systems need to be transformed in order to create socially just public education have a greater impact on the organization? Is it possible to reform the system from within? I must say I am less optimistic about that than I was before I tried to do it. I am convinced that one person in a strategic position can make a difference, but it is very lonely work and I am skeptical about the possibilities of one individual having much impact on entrenched institutional practices.

Yet, everything I read about educational reform tells me that the institutional practices I found so disempowering on a personal level are the very ones that have proven to be barriers to successful, enduring change. As Hargreaves (1997) expresses it, "If our struggle is for the needs of all children and not just for the elite few, then markets and managerialism will help us little in our quest." What we need are "openness, informality, care, attentiveness, lateral working relationships, reciprocal collaboration, candid and vibrant dialogue, and a willingness to face uncertainty together," not only within the schools which have been the focus of so much of our reform efforts but within the bureaucracies that surround them:

> The struggle for positive educational change must now move beyond the school in order to enrich what goes on within it. It must fully engage our hearts as well as our minds. And it must extend emotionally beyond the internal management of schools themselves to the high-powered politics of educational reform and restructuring above them. City halls and school district offices should not be fortresses against feelings. (p. 22)

Leading from the Edge

Despite the difficulties I encountered, I would have stayed in senior administration and kept working at effecting change. In the spring of 1996,

however, the provincial government's decision to amalgamate twenty-one
school districts in Nova Scotia into seven regional organizations resulted in
our district being joined with two others in the area to create a school system
of nearly sixty thousand students. Unfortunately, the hiring process was
highly politicized, and many of us in leadership roles became caught up in
the turf wars across organizations as the three school districts being
amalgamated struggled for dominance in the new regional organization. Not
only I, but most of the colleagues who had been part of the community
working for change, found ourselves excluded from the positions for which
we were most qualified and in which we had the most interest. Like many
others who endured this process, I was exhausted and extremely angry by
the end of the school year. I chose not to move into another administrative
position at the district or school level and took a leave of absence to accept a
term appointment in the faculty of education at Mount Saint Vincent
University. A major focus of that assignment has been to explore ways in
which the university can partner with other members of the educational
community to enhance professional development and action-research
opportunities for teachers. Again I find myself at the center of an
organizational-change effort through which we are trying to share expertise
and resources and to create more flexibility within and across institutions.

I have a sense that working from slightly outside the school system, but
still connected, creates more space within which to experiment. Being
positioned at the center of the organization did nothing to decrease my
feelings of marginalization; if anything, they were exacerbated. Perhaps it is
from the edge that I will be able to foster the contexts within which the
critical questions about disempowering institutional practices can become
part of the discourse of organizational change. Leaving my administrative
position has given me the time to begin a doctoral program with a focus on
organizational change and leadership. My brief sojourn as an insider
generated enough research questions to keep me going for a long, long time.

I have had a number of conversations with principals, teachers, and other
educators both within and outside the district about what my colleagues and
I were trying to accomplish and about how those efforts were brought to an
abrupt halt by the amalgamation. It has been gratifying to learn that we were
making a difference and that many in the system are outraged that we are
not part of the leadership team in the new district. While I assumed that the
treatment we experienced in the hiring was just nasty interdistrict politics,
others have interpreted those experiences differently. It was widely circulated
that I, in particular, was passed over for leadership "because I was too

supportive of teachers." I also heard that I was considered a problem because of my politics. Many said, "If they can do this to you, imagine what might happen to us!"

Clearly, many believe that the treatment we received was punishment for trying to act on our beliefs and for speaking out. While there were certainly painful and difficult personal consequences for me and others as a result of the amalgamation hiring process, the more serious, long-term consequence may well be the silencing of those who fear that the costs of speaking out may just be too high for them. I recognize that the risks may be too great for individuals who have fewer options and resources than I have. Yet, as Michelle Fine commented at a conference several years ago, "silencing is the glue that holds the hierarchy together." Therefore, as I contemplate the bureaucracy from my position outside the system, I am more determined than ever not to be silenced and to prevent the silencing of others in whatever ways I can. I have no regrets about spending two years in senior administration and would return if the right opportunity presented itself. Now, however, I would have the advantage of a more informed critical analysis to guide me along the way. Meanwhile, there is no shortage of leadership opportunities, and there is an abundance of laughter, learning, and productive work out here on the edge.

References

Blackmore, J. (1995a). Policy as dialogue: Feminist administrators working for edu- cational change." *Gender and Education, 7*(3), 293–313.

Blackmore, J. (1995b). Where's the level playing field? A feminist perspective on educational restructuring. Paper presented at the Annual Conference of the Aus- tralian Association of Research in Education.

Church, S. M. (1996). *The future of whole language: Reconstruction or self- destruction?* Portsmouth, NH: Heinemann.

Church, S. M. (1991). *With literacy and justice for all: Rethinking the social in language and education.* New York: Falmer.

Edelsky, C. (1994). Education for democracy. *Language Arts, 71*(4), 252–257.

Fine, M. (1990). Making controversy: Who's "At Risk?" *Journal of Urban and Cul- tural Studies, 1*(1), 55–68.

Fullan, M. (1993). *Change forces: Probing the depths of educational reform.* New York: Falmer.

Giroux, H. A. (1987). Critical literacy and student experience: Donald Graves' approach to literacy. *Language Arts, 64*(2), 175–181.

Giroux, H.A., & McLaren, P. (1986). Teacher education and the politics of engagement: The case for democratic schooling. *Harvard Educational Review, 56*(3), 213–238.

Hargreaves, A. (1997). Rethinking educational change: Going deeper and wider in the quest for success. In A. Hargreaves (Ed.), *Rethinking educational change with heart and mind* (pp. 1–27). Alexandria, VA: Association for Supervision and Curriculum Development.

McLaren, P. (1989). *Life in schools: An introduction to critical pedagogy in the foundations of education.* New York: Longman.

Oakes, J. (1985). *Keeping track: How schools structure inequality.* New Haven, CT: Yale University Press.

Shannon, P. (Ed.) (1992). *Becoming political: Readings and writings in the politics of literacy education.* Portsmouth, NH: Heinemann.

Simon, R. (1987). Empowerment as a pedagogy of possibility. *Language Arts, 64*(4), 370–382.

8 Literacy Education as a Site for Social Justice: What Do Our Practices Do?

Barbara Comber and Helen Nixon

Each of us grew up in working-class families who saw education as the way to a better future. Like many women of our class and generation who "made it" with moderate success in school, we trained for a "helping profession" and became teachers. We saw ourselves as charged with a moral mission. We were ready to "give" other children the same chances that we had had, chances we thought were related to success in reading and writing. However as classroom teachers we found "no quick fix" for our students (Allington & Walmsley, 1995). Later, as teacher educators, we met hundreds of other literacy teachers who worked to make a difference in the life chances of their students. Yet, despite good intentions and successive innovations with regard to literacy pedagogies, statewide audits indicate that children disadvantaged by poverty remain statistically more likely to perform in the lower bands of the range on mainstream literacy assessments (Education Department of South Australia, 1992). As literacy educators in the university setting, we remain committed to social justice. But what kinds of interventions can we make? In this chapter we raise questions about the relationships between school literacies and social justice; we describe a project which foregrounds literacy, diversity, and socioeconomic disadvantage; and by referring to the work of three teachers, we illustrate the complexity and the possibilities in working for social justice.

Reprinted from Chapter 16 of *Making Justice Our Project*, edited by Carole Edelsky.

School Literacies and Social Justice?

> People know what they do; they frequently know why they do what they do; but what they don't know is what they do does. (Michel Foucault, quoted in Dreyfus & Rabinow, 1983, p. 187)

Language teachers often hold a social-justice agenda. We employ discourses of liberation and hope that our work has a positive impact on the immediate and postschool lives of students. In recent times, many of us have believed that the acquisition of literacy is best achieved through child-centred pedagogies. The removal of teacher direction would enable the child learner to grow naturally. Egalitarian communities of learners, including the teacher-learner, would behave in just and democratic ways. We have assumed that whole language classrooms were ideologically sound utopian sites, where students and teachers would automatically become better people through literacy. We have assumed that the power offered by school literacies would be the same for all students and equally divided among them; that school literacies would empower previously disadvantaged students. School graduates would be empowered, literate citizens committed to democratic ideals. This is the story we have told ourselves.

As whole language teachers we have, in Foucault's terms, known what we do and why we do it, but perhaps known less about what we do does! Our assumption that literacy offers power and justice arises from the realisation that language use always involves power relations. A whole language philosophy promises power for students, yet our theory tells us little about how power might be exercised in classrooms or in society, only that language and literacy are pivotal. We have invited children to join our "literacy clubs" now and promised them better futures, without thinking about whose clubs these are and what kinds of identities they require and who might be excluded. We have been reluctant to consider the unanticipated effects of school literacy practices, that certain formations of literacy, including whole language, may maintain disadvantage, may be normative rather than transformative, domesticating rather than liberating, alienating rather than connecting (Donald, 1993; Edelsky with Harman, 1991; Stuckey, 1991). Without an analysis of how language and literate practices work in social and political contexts for and against different groups, our philosophy is of limited use for a pedagogy for social justice.

Whole language educators have made many claims for literacy. Potentially, whole language repositions teachers as researchers and producers of local knowledge and students as active initiators of and participants in conversations and literate practices. These moves are important for a pedagogy driven by social justice agendas. However, we think it is time to further question the stories we have told ourselves about literacy and about the promises we have made for progressive pedagogies. Our questions include: What do whole language practices do? What kinds of students do they produce? What different effects might whole language practices have on different groups of students? Can we assume that removing the teacher from the centre produces democracy? Ironically, while theorists may make claims that whole language empowers disadvantaged children, the local enactment and effects of the pedagogy may be quite different. It is not so much that pedagogies do not "work," but that they "work" in ways we do not anticipate.

Studies of literacy practices and power relations in child-centred classrooms challenge claims that whole language produces justice or empowerment, either in the immediacy of the classroom or in students' life trajectories (Delpit, 1988; Luke, 1996). When classrooms are constituted as sites for individual children to find a "voice," *which* children produce *which* texts, and to *what ends*, must be the subject of ongoing scrutiny (Dyson, 1993; Gilbert, 1989; Lensmire, 1994). If literacy is socially constructed, how gender, race, class, religion, and geographic location make a difference in school literacy teaching and learning become urgent questions for language educators. Socially critical researchers emphasise that students learn to read and write particular kinds of texts that represent different kinds of worlds, different kinds of knowledge, and position readers in different ways (Baker & Freebody, 1989; Gilbert, 1990; Luke, 1993).

Recent research and theorising suggest that literacy practices are multiple, historically contingent, and culturally specific. Literate practices are not neutral or innocent; literate practices privilege and celebrate texts which maintain the disadvantage of minority groups (including women and girls, people of colour, rural people, religious groups, aged people, people with disabilities). In classrooms, teacher commentary and questioning around text interpretation and construction may reinforce dominant cultural ideologies. Choice of texts may maintain a literary canon and exclude other genres and formations of language use and literacy which are important in students' peer and family communities. Choice of pedagogical techniques, interaction patterns, and assessment tasks may maintain the advantage of students who are already practised with mainstream cultural norms. Choice of topics may limit children's inquiries to safe, apolitical studies. Whole language alone does not automatically counter such problems.

The everyday moment-by-moment choices teachers and students make, and how they talk about those choices, construct the literate practices of the classroom. Those choices and ways of talking may have little to do with democracy or social justice. Even where multiculturalism is the object of inquiry, for instance, our practices can trivialise and depoliticise the nature of study. In one elementary classroom, when children mentioned skin "colour" as one difference between them and a Hawaiian visitor, their teacher redirected them to investigate food preparation in traditional Hawaiian culture as a more appropriate topic. There is always the potential to explore topics in ways that either take children's questions seriously or that reconstruct them as neutral and safe. A review of what can be talked, read, and written about in the classroom, and what is excluded, may be a good place to begin in evaluating literacy curriculum in terms of social justice. If children are not allowed to talk about colour, how can an antiracism curriculum function? It may be that the sentiments teachers fear go underground. We do not wish to suggest that it is easy for teachers to talk with children about race, class, culture, wealth, poverty, injustice, gender, and religion, but failure to talk about such topics in schools which proclaim their democracy results in a romanticised and individualised view of difference.

To take another illustration of how whole language pedagogies and theories can unwittingly create difficulties for children, let us consider the importance which has recently been given to parents reading to children and hearing their children read—home reading. Family literacy practices have become central during the past two decades because children whose parents read to them and hear them read perform better on school reading. The aim of many projects is to ensure that parents read to children. In a national survey of early years teachers in schools serving socioeconomically disadvantaged communities in Australia, teachers reported the two most important strategies in their literacy programs were parents reading to children and parents hearing children read (Badger, Comber, & Weeks, 1993). Home reading events were considered more important than what the teacher or children did at school. It seems to us that there is a problem with such thinking; that as whole language educators who have advocated sharing books with children, we have created a problem rather than a solution. The reason why home reading events make so much difference to success in school is that school reading events are replicated upon them. So children who have more practice in such events do better; hence the rationale for getting families to do more at home of what teachers do in school. But surely there are other ways to consider the question of how children come to early literacy.

Other literacy practices go on in homes and communities which may be equally important to foster in schools and which may not disadvantage children without access to regular home reading practice (in English) with parents. Families read environmental print, the packaging on food and other commodities, the junk mail which arrives daily in mailboxes, the advertising and credits on television, the letters which arrive from relatives elsewhere. Any of the multitude of literate practices in the home and community could be models for what goes on in school. There is no developmental or biological reason why children must learn to read with storybooks, and many children who learn to read prior to schooling do so through their own writing, through access to computers, and so on.

Our point here is not to criticise literature-based reading programs, home reading, shared-book experience, or any of the wonderful activities generated from the insight about the importance of parents reading to children. We simply argue that parents reading storybooks to children is a cultural practice in some communities only. We need to ensure that it does not become a new form of "reading readiness," the absence of which is used to exclude and negatively evaluate children who come with experiences of other forms of literate practices. What is needed is an "opening out" of school literacies so that children are able to use the resources they do bring. Children may bring strong oral traditions; a knowledge of heroes and heroines of popular culture; songs, prayers, and poetry from religious and cultural communities; and the expertise of consumerism. They bring a multiplicity of language and literate practices, some of which are excluded from their school day and some of which are welcomed as "proper" and "appropriate."

When specific cultural practices such as home reading are seen as the norm, then children who have not participated in such practices can be seen as "deficient," "lacking," "without experiences," or "without proper models." Some teachers in the national survey referred to above argued that parents reading to children and hearing children read were so important that the absence of these events put children "at risk." But it is the privileging of such literate practices and their associated behaviours and knowledges at school which puts children "at risk." Clearly, this "deficit discourse" is the opposite of what whole language educators advocate when they stress the importance of family literacy practices. What this example shows, however, is that we need to check out how our recommendations are heard and taken up in local sites. Teachers' own life worlds and values mediate the uptake and enactment of pedagogical practices and curriculum theories.

It is not our intention to review the critiques of whole language in detail (see Comber, 1994; Willinsky, 1990). It is sufficient to say here that we no longer assume empowering effects for school literacy or for particular pedagogies, but we continue to explore what working for equity through literacy education might mean. What kinds of interventions towards social justice can educators make? As university educators with an up-front social justice agenda, how can we act against media onslaughts and economic cuts in order to work in positive ways with teachers in communities which experience material and educational disadvantage?

Documentaries about Literacy, Diversity, and Schooling: A Social Justice Strategy

During the past decade, cumulative research evidence and our own experience forced us to confront the possibility that our teaching, despite our career-long commitments to social justice, may contribute to silence about class, poverty, and race in the English/language arts classroom in both school and university settings. Teachers in disadvantaged schools[1] continued to tell us that mainstream approaches to literacy pedagogy did not work within their contexts, and recent graduates argued that the university did not prepare them to teach in disadvantaged schools. A recent national project found that issues of social justice were largely absent from university courses on language and literacy (Christie et al., 1991). In reviewing our teaching we recognised that our preservice and inservice courses about literacy and schooling failed to foreground educational disadvantage. How could we change our own practices so that equity issues were not ignored or treated in token ways?

We recognise that "social justice" is itself a discursive construction used to different ends by groups with different political agendas (Harvey, 1993). For us, social justice means an ongoing commitment to exploring the effects of our own institutional and discursive practices. In the interests of teachers and students in communities disadvantaged by poverty, this means resisting and changing deficit discourses which attribute blame to people who live in poverty (Kress, 1994; Polakow, 1993). A social justice commitment means disrupting images of disadvantaged students which perpetuate myths about "these kids" as literacy failures and consequently of their schools as the nurseries of potential delinquents. How could we put these principles into our university practice and at the same time produce something that might be useful for our colleagues in schools?

Rather than undertake a traditional research project, we decided to make educational documentaries about teaching literacy in disadvantaged schools.[2] Our aim was to produce polyvocal videos involving student teachers, academics, staff, parents and students from disadvantaged schools, policymakers, consultants from charitable organisations, bureaucrats, and educational researchers. We saw the production of educational documentaries as a positive intervention. By creating an easy-to-use video text about literacy and disadvantage, we might increase the possibility that social justice would be talked about in university literacy and language education classes, beginning with our own work site. In this way we could begin to work against the maintenance of "deficit" discourses. We intended to do this by making problematic the myths that surround constructs such as poverty, literacy, diversity, and disadvantage. We designed the videos to generate conversations and debates and at the same time to document some of the innovative practices of teachers in disadvantaged schools who were explicitly committed to working for social justice.

One of our first tasks was to identify schools where teachers built language and literacy curriculum around critique and social justice, where teachers and students questioned "systems of domination." Because we wanted the documentaries to work for change, we wanted to produce visions for possible action, not only critique. At the same time we did not want to make grandiose claims for the programs we documented. Finding educators in schools who shared our commitments and were prepared to make their work public, and therefore subject to potential criticism, was crucial to the project. Without school-based visionary educators working on socially critical curriculum action there would be no videos. Some of the most innovative teaching of literacy occurs in disadvantaged schools, yet some of the greatest stress and intensification of teachers' work is also present at these sites. We were conscious that we were asking a lot of these school communities. We were fortunate. A number of educators, parents, and students agreed to work with us. This meant student teachers, researchers, camera crews and producers in classrooms, staff rooms, and offices. It meant permission slips to parents and so on. It meant more work. But it also meant an opportunity to document the productive, positive work going on in disadvantaged schools. For us as producers of the documentaries, it also meant facing up to selections—which administrators, teachers, parents, student-teachers, and students in which schools would we show, involved in what kinds of language and literate practices?[3]

The documentaries are concerned with how teachers work for social justice through literacy-related projects in disadvantaged schools. There are six videos entitled: *Literacy, Poverty and Schooling*; *Becoming a Literacy Teacher in a Diverse Community*; *Teaching Literacy in Disadvantaged Schools*; *Communities, Literacy, and Schools*; *Teaching and Learning at Paralowie R-12 School*; and *Literacy Assessment in Disadvantaged Schools*.

Each video attempts to inform (e.g., we describe how material poverty is defined; numbers of people who are homeless; which groups are considered to be "disadvantaged"); to explain theories (e.g., we explain deficit, difference, and structural inequality theories of educational disadvantage; whole language, genre, and critical literacy); to problematise (e.g., we provide differing views on poverty and on the importance of literacy); to generate conversations (e.g., the voice-over and the images together pose challenging questions); and to work against deficit views of disadvantaged communities. We attempt to take viewers into disadvantaged school communities, to disrupt easy assumptions about what might or should be, and to offer some ways forward.

In the remainder of this chapter we try to reproduce in prose some "vivid portrayals of classroom scenes" from the documentaries to illustrate the struggles and possibilities facing teachers who make social justice central in their curriculum. We focus on the work of our colleagues in the project, teachers and school administrators who were aware that schooling sometimes reproduces educational disadvantage, and who made questions of equity central in their day-to-day work with parents and children. We begin with Barbara Fox's Aboriginal studies class, where students were writing an essay about Aboriginal deaths in police custody; we move next to Nigel Howard's community studies class, where students were producing a brochure about cooperative learning; and finally we focus on Jennifer O'Brien's classroom, where students were analysing gender representation in a picture book.

Barbara Fox: Foregrounding Issues of Race

Barbara Fox, a young Aboriginal woman with majors in Aboriginal studies and Australian history in her undergraduate degree, began her working life with the state's Catholic education system as a project officer for Aboriginal studies. In this position, she worked with others writing, implementing, and trialing the Aboriginal studies syllabus developed for the elementary and junior high school years by the state education department. In the year that our video project began, Barbara was undertaking a one-year postgraduate teacher education course to become a secondary teacher of Aboriginal studies and social science. This was her first step towards achieving her personal and professional goal—to work as a teacher for social justice and equity, with and for Aboriginal people.

For her first practicum as a student teacher, Barbara chose to work at Paralowie R-12 School. This school is located in a low socioeconomic area to the north of Adelaide, the capital city of the state of South Australia, and has more than one thousand students ages 5 years to 18 years. More than half of the school community lives on or beneath the poverty line, and more than half of the students' families receive government assistance for their children's schooling. Twenty-five percent of the students are from non-English-speaking backgrounds (Italian, Greek, Vietnamese, Cambodian, Polish, Spanish) and, important for Barbara, there were more than forty enrolled Aboriginal students (a high proportion for our city). The school had a reputation as a leader in Aboriginal education. In the practicum, Barbara taught Aboriginal studies as a senior school academic subject and worked as a volunteer in the after-school Nunga Homework Centre set up by Aboriginal parents to support Aboriginal students with their studies. The centre is staffed by Aboriginal parent tutors and teacher volunteers. Barbara agreed to being filmed during her practicum and again the following year when she was no longer a student teacher but an employee of the education department as a teacher at Paralowie R-12 School. This allowed us a unique opportunity to record and discuss with Barbara aspects of her development as a teacher working for equity, which we believed would be useful in teacher education classes about literacy teaching and disadvantage.

For this practicum, Barbara's Aboriginal studies lessons were planned with the (white, male, Anglo) classroom teacher, within the framework of a state-accredited tertiary-entrance syllabus. She could be flexible with the topic and pedagogy, but the syllabus required Barbara to help the students research and produce a formal essay which would count for their final assessment. Although young and inexperienced, her commitment to social justice meant that she went straight for a topic that "mattered"—Aboriginal deaths in police custody, thus foregrounding an overtly political and contentious issue within Australian society in general, and an issue of deep personal and political meaning for Aboriginal people in particular. She tackled this topic with a diverse class. Her students included a mix of sixteen- and seventeen-year-old white, Anglo and Aboriginal students who had come through the school in a traditional way, and several mature-aged Aboriginal students who were returning to schooling after many years' absence. These older Aboriginal students were also parents of students at the school, and the class included a father, mother, and daughter from one large family in the community, as well as one of her own middle-aged male relatives who had been closely involved with the school as a parent and tutor for more than six years.

Barbara's curriculum had critique at its centre and made use of typical whole language practices (e.g., drawing on the students' experience, interest, and knowledge; providing students with choices; positioning herself as a facilitator and resource to be consulted rather than an expert or transmitter of information). Barbara provided her students with a range of literacy experiences to draw upon in producing their essays, including viewing and discussing a documentary video on Aboriginal deaths in police custody, and reading and analysing a range of texts: newspaper clippings, transcripts from inquests, investigations into police brutality, and other public documents (e.g., government statistics about the proportions of various sectors of the Australian population arrested and convicted of crimes).

Barbara's situation illustrates what can happen when certain kinds of critique are made the centre of a curriculum and whole language pedagogies are used in a diverse school community. As teacher educators we cannot simply argue from a theoretical position that teachers should "take risks" in the interests of working for a socially just community. We also need to explore the possible real-world consequences of taking certain kinds of risks and using certain pedagogies. In the video project we use instances of what did happen to pose questions and to encourage different ways of understanding what such practices might do. Let's take the example of Barbara's Aboriginal studies class. First, we could ask how Barbara was positioned as a teacher in this class. Ideally, we could say, she was a role model for Aboriginal students; a successful Aboriginal woman training for a profession. But this is not the whole picture. We must also consider that Barbara's race, age, and gender put her in a complex personal and professional situation within this context—and that the personal and the professional are not easily separated. As a teacher in this class, Barbara was in a position of authority. Yet she was also a young, Aboriginal woman teaching male relatives and elders with whom, in other contexts, a very different set of social and power relations existed. It is possible that such a situation generates uncertainty and tension for all participants and affects student learning.

Second, we could ask how Barbara was using the content to work for equity in this class. Ideally, we could say Barbara was working in the interests of democracy by choosing a topic about structural inequality and injustice—Aboriginal deaths in police custody. But once again, this answer may be incomplete. The diversity of the class meant that Barbara could assume no consensus among her students, either before or after the topic was "taught." On the contrary, the topic of black deaths in police custody may have many meanings for that range of students. For some students it could be just another social science topic. Others may be angered by being placed in a situation in which a young, Aboriginal woman teaches them, as white Anglo Australians, about subject matter that includes strong indictments of the dominant culture to which they belong. For still other students, some of whom have direct knowledge of the experiences of imprisoned friends and relatives, the topic may be highly charged, emotionally and politically. We cannot pretend that classrooms like this will always be comfortable. There may be real and perhaps unimagined consequences—for instance, students in conflict with each other and the teacher, or students in distress. Dealing with unpredictable outcomes may not be easy. What Barbara attempted was ambitious. She was not playing it safe. She was putting on her classroom agenda a subject which many experienced teachers might baulk at, and which many students might resist. We do not necessarily know what real-world consequences ensue for teachers' teaching and students' learning when particular pedagogies are used in diverse classrooms.

In her first year as a registered teacher at the Paralowie R-12 School, Barbara continued to put critique at the centre of her curriculum. The outcomes were not entirely what she had predicted. She found, for example, that putting racism on the agenda in social science classes did not necessarily make the students more tolerant or rational about the issues. This was true even when she put her own and her students' experiences at the centre of classroom learning. Barbara describes incidents from her classroom:

> When they are actually working with each other, it doesn't matter what cultural background they've got, or where they are from. They seem to have these blinkers about who the "other" people are, until somebody actually mentions an issue like "immigration" or "the Aborigine problem." . . . Yeah, it's really strange, even dealing with the immigration issue. The kids are saying, "No, no. We really can't have 'them' coming in and taking over," and all this sort of stuff. And yet their best friend, if they are an Anglo-Saxon type person, is a Vietnamese person. "Oh, it's all right for *them*. He's my *friend*. He can stay."

Despite repeated placements of antiracist work at the centre of her curriculum, Barbara found that her students did not easily see a contradiction between their positive personal experiences of "the other" and their unquestioning alliance with institutionalised racist values about, say, immigration or Aboriginal land rights. This is not to say that no gains were made, but it illustrates that the outcomes of what we do, even in a curriculum we think is working for social justice, cannot be taken for granted.

Barbara was continually reminded that her own experiences as an Aboriginal person and teacher did not necessarily explain, or prepare her for, the ways in which her students and her classroom "worked." She had come into the school as a confident young woman, experienced in teaching to and about Aboriginal people and their culture. She knew the complexities of her Aboriginal students' lives. What was going on "behind the scenes" was not a mystery to her. She hoped that their shared culture would enable her to help Aboriginal students succeed in the school curriculum. But this is not how it happened. Long after the students had left school for the year, she kept hearing things about her students' lives and wondering whether, if she had known them earlier, she could have done something differently, done something else to make a difference for these students. For a teacher committed to equity, such doubts are deeply felt, both personally and professionally.

Like many beginning teachers in her first year of teaching, Barbara was concerned to establish her "identity" in the school. Yet what exactly constitutes the identity of a young, black, female teacher in a school? How do the various facets of that identity conflict or work together? For the video, Barbara explains that in her day-to-day work in the school, she found herself being positioned in certain ways because of her racial identity. She felt that colleagues and students held certain expectations of her as an Aboriginal person and teacher, expecting that her racial identity "explained" her actions:

> You know, they think, "Oh, she's Aboriginal, she's got some things that she's got to deal with, and that's why she's involved in it." . . . And that wasn't the initial idea at all. Like I was saying before, I was hoping to develop myself as a teacher, not go on this Aboriginal search.

Barbara is not accusing her colleagues of racism. She knows they work very hard for equity in their school, often at great personal and professional cost. What Barbara was beginning to articulate was that her racialised identity was both integral to, and yet somehow separate from, the struggle she was experiencing in her project to become a "good teacher." When used as a label, *Aboriginality* was not always as informative as first appeared, sometimes masking other facets of identity that need to be foregrounded.

Barbara's experiences illustrate that constantly placing equity issues at the centre of the curriculum can have unanticipated effects. In the video Barbara speculates that at her school a kind of antidote effect built up around the discussion of Aboriginal issues in the curriculum: i.e., students' "knew the problem"; it had been discussed before; it had been dealt with. Students' attitudes seemed to be that once it had been "covered," they should get on with learning about "mainstream" Australian history, politics, and culture. Barbara describes an incident from one of her classes:

> I think at Paralowie the Aboriginal community is starting to be an "it's them again"–type thing, which is sad in a way, because my year-11s, they said to me "Why don't we get some *real* Australian history?" And I asked them what they meant by that . . . and they said, "Enough of this Aborigines stuff. Give us some *real* Australian history." And I thought, "Oh, *this* is very interesting." So I gave them some *real* Australian history, as they put it, and I talked about the Foundation Act of South Australia and then, lo and behold, there we are negotiating with the Aborigines and I said, "Oh, I'm sorry I mentioned them, but they're *there*" [laughs].

What Barbara Fox's experiences show is that it is possible to build a curriculum around a critique of racism and to do this in ways which avoid teacher-centredness. It is possible to question systemic sources of inequity that disadvantage indigenous and minority racial groups. But it is not always comfortable, not always safe, and does not inevitably lead to more equitable, democratic classrooms. Our video project attempts to describe and problematise equity projects such as Barbara's by posing sometimes difficult questions about equity interventions and assumed "liberatory" pedagogies. Barbara did not anticipate what she or her students experienced and came to know as a result of tackling the difficult topic Aboriginal deaths in police custody. For example, whole language pedagogy suggests that a teacher should encourage the use of personal knowledge and experience in classroom work. But who and what might be jeopardised by doing this when working with "substance that matters" such as black deaths in custody? How might the answer to this question be different for an all-black class or a mixed-race class; with a white or a black teacher? Do teachers know what emotional distress might arise from using such content and such pedagogy? In what ways is such a classroom "safe," as we would want critical whole language classrooms to be? Who is safe, and from what, when personal discourses about such topics are present? Are absent? These are difficult questions, but questions which we must address if we are to explore what it is that our classroom practices do.

Nigel Howard: Teaching for Social Action

Nigel Howard is a male colleague of Barbara Fox's at Paralowie R-12 School. A secondary teacher of some fifteen years' experience, Nigel's professional commitment has been to work with students whose lives have often been lived "at the margins" of traditional schools: children with physical and intellectual disabilities, children with behaviour difficulties, and adolescents who do not readily engage with what has been offered them by traditional schooling practices. Nigel has also been a curriculum developer in the state education department. His work there has been to broaden the curriculum offerings for senior secondary students so as to make senior schooling more relevant to them, thereby increasing the retention rate of students at risk of failing and leaving school early, and increasing the chances that the full range of students can achieve personal and publicly accredited success.

Attendance and retention of students are key social justice and equity issues because research has shown that the longer students stay at school, the better chance they have of gaining employment. For this reason, Paralowie R-12 School, located in an area where there is more than 70 percent youth unemployment, counts among its greatest successes the fact that its retention rate of students beyond the age of fifteen years, the age of compulsion, has risen during the past five years from 36 to 90 percent. Nigel believes that this success has been due to two essential factors. First, at a schoolwide, structural level, there is an ongoing commitment to provide resources and programs with flexible pathways for completing senior school education and with a variety of choices for training for a range of possible futures. Second, at the classroom level, the students' lives are central to the curriculum, and the pedagogy is student-centred. Teachers know the community and their students, and the curriculum and pedagogies reflect this knowledge. Nigel argues that:

> There's a real effort to make this stuff fit the kids. At this school the kids are saying, "We would rather be here than out on the street or at other schools," and that's related to what's happening in the class-room.

Nigel maintains that the students are voting with their feet. Whereas in the past, many postcompulsory students at Paralowie R-12 School left school for the streets, significant numbers now attend school. Nigel attributes this difference to more attractive programs being offered by the school. By being connected to students' worlds, the curriculum and pedagogy work for equity, providing the possibility of better futures for a range of students who were previously alienated and marginalised by systemic practices.

Teachers at Paralowie R-12 School know how their students and local poor community are structurally positioned within society in ways that maintain disadvantage. They take an active role in lobbying state and federal governments for better resources for their school. They work through the state credentialing agency to have their curricula accredited for university entrance and other forms of further education and training. This is the work Nigel does at Paralowie R-12 School as the coordinator of work-related pathways. For our video project, we filmed Nigel working with a group of year-11 students who had a history of failure to attend and failure to achieve at school. These were students designated in their earlier years at school as students "at risk"—at risk of leaving school early, of not achieving a high school certificate, of not gaining employment. The introduction of a community studies curriculum at the school meant that at the ages of fifteen and sixteen years, these "at-risk" students were offered the opportunity to stay on at school in a state certificate-accredited course and spend a significant proportion of their time working with Nigel in a range of nontraditional ways. The community studies curriculum attempts to connect school and community, school knowledge and real-world knowledge, skills valued at school and skills valued in workplaces. On video Nigel explains the rationale behind his curriculum:

> We had a large number of kids who in the best of all possible worlds would be out there testing out their knowledge in very real ways, and so we wanted to produce that back in the school . . . the question was, "How can we get them to use those skills in real ways?"

How can a school curriculum replicate real-world situations? What are the possibilities and the constraints? How can a school pedagogy help students learn in ways that are potentially useful for gaining employment or for taking social action in the community? What risks do teachers take in attempting such work? These are questions we explored with Nigel in our videos. Nigel explains how one community studies project to produce a brochure came about and what it involved:

> In this project we had a group of students who were asked by the National Schools Network in the area to publicise some of the collaborative learning activities that were going on in the primary schools. One of the aims I had for these students was to get them to look at their own learning by talking to teachers about what they were doing in the classroom about collaborative learning, interviewing students, photographing groups, and putting together a picture of what people are trying to do in primary schools. An important outcome of this project is that it has a real product . . . that's the brochure and the poster that's got to be done now . . . to actually publicise what happened.

A key feature of Nigel's curriculum is that it is grounded in real-world activities and learning experiences. For example, Nigel's students acted as researchers and publishers to carry out a commissioned, funded project. They were commissioned to research and produce brochures to be used in the public domain to advertise the nature of the learning programs in neighbouring elementary schools. They had to plan and rehearse their research and interview questions; learn and adopt procedures for making contact and visiting local school principals and teachers; assume responsibility for booking, borrowing, and returning expensive audio and camera equipment; and visit schools and interview young students and their teachers. Once back at their own school, with Nigel's assistance and support, the students drew on their photographs and interview audiotapes to plan, write copy for, and illustrate a brochure and poster for the schools that had engaged them to do the project.

In carrying out this project as part of the curriculum, Nigel's students learned competencies valued in the world of work, such as the negotiation of roles in group work and collaborative action. These are also the skills necessary for successful social action both inside and outside school. While helping students gain access to paid work is central to the senior school curriculum at Paralowie, an important additional objective of Nigel's curriculum is to develop in students the desire and ability to be active participants in their communities. For Nigel, one indicator that this objective is being achieved is students taking action for change. Nigel describes one instance of this happening:

> Today we had a group come up to us and say, "This is the problem; this is what we intend to do about it; what do we have to do to get someone to listen to us?"

Although Nigel was not at liberty to discuss the nature of the "problem," he explained that a group of students saw a real-world issue of concern to them that needed to be addressed and wanted something to be done about it. More than that, they decided what they thought needed to be done and took responsibility for initiating that action themselves. They knew that they had to make someone with the power to effect that change listen to them. The students approached Nigel and the school's administration as equals, requesting guidance about how best to establish communication with the appropriate people. Nigel quotes this example because it demonstrates students achieving his objective for a curriculum based on social justice. Here were students taking action to effect change about a "matter of substance" to them in their lives. Teachers who work for democracy in this way are teaching more than language arts. For them, putting critique at the centre of what they do is not merely including topics often left out of the curriculum. It is not merely planning particular kinds of "language activities." It is teaching in a way that results in action for change in the real world.

Nigel is very clear about how his curriculum is based on social justice principles. On video he explains:

> The program addresses disadvantage because it works on what the students are doing now. It's not a program that is beginning to say "Learn these things so that in the future you can get a job, and learn these things so that in the future you can have some power." . . . It addresses disadvantage in that it's about working in socially just ways for now, with the understanding that, if we can keep that going, it's saying you will be part of the future and you will be an actor in your own future.

Nigel's project is a radical one. His approach requires teachers to step back from direct control. It requires shifting real power, and the responsibility that goes with it, from the teacher to the students. And for Nigel, if it is to be real power, it has to be effective in the present, not in the future. His project is not about teaching students skills in the abstract so that they might later apply them; e.g., so they might later approach local businesses or politicians when they want something done. For Nigel, teaching for social justice is about constructing a curriculum which provides opportunity, incentive, and support for students to do such real-world things right away, while they are still enrolled in school. He argues that if they do it "now," they experience power "now," and so they know that they can exercise this power for the rest of their lives. They can be "actors in their own future," active participants in their living communities, both now and in the future.

In working for social justice, Nigel begins from what the students know and can do. He helps students plan to use language and action to make a difference in their community. This may require thinking differently about literacy. Students may do more talking or audio- and videotape recording than writing. Teaching and learning objectives might be achieved using a variety of forms of English, or languages other than English. To implement programs like community studies requires innovative approaches to resourcing and timetabling. For example, the subject has to be timetabled in large blocks of time, challenging the way senior schools are traditionally structured. Students need the freedom and responsibility, often withheld by the school, to leave the school grounds to do community research. The tension between the "safety" of the school and the "unknown" elements outside presents difficulties for both the teacher planner and the student learner. Teachers may have to work hard to change school structures and procedures so that they have the time required to set up possibilities for student-community access. They may also find it hard to take the necessary risks in sending students away from the school.

Implementing a student-centred pedagogy in a context like this can be very hard for teachers. Standing back and allowing students to make their own mistakes and "learn by doing" can go against teachers' deepest impulses to lead and show, to take over and "rescue." The student learner may also find this kind of program difficult to accommodate. For example, students who have little history of success and little social confidence may suffer anxiety at being apparently cut off from traditional types of teacher direction and close teacher supervision. Nigel describes how student expectations might require courage and resistance from teachers:

> But also sometimes you're battling against students' expectations of what school is; that rather than saying "If you fail this essay, I'll give you a bad mark, and isn't that terrible," there's a lot more at risk. "If this project doesn't succeed, then you haven't done what you set out to do . . . and you can actually see that there are going to be pay-offs and consequences." And so, one of the difficulties is resisting students actually pulling the project back into schoolwork.

For Nigel's students, becoming an active participant in the community does not always feel safe. Students who have a history of being excluded and marginalised by dominant practices do not easily become independent "actors in their future." Nigel's community studies program encourages and gives credit to students for meeting challenges and overcoming obstacles, for taking risks and moving away from known, comfortable school practices. For Nigel, this is what makes the program powerful for students in transition to postschool lives.

Nigel's goal is to teach in ways that produce students who challenge the commonsense view that they somehow have to "accept their lot" as failures. Nigel aims to help students "at the extreme end of disadvantage and poverty" to change the relationships they have with the school and the community. But Nigel knows that this is not easy, and there is no formula for achieving that goal. The answer does not lie in exemplary programs or curriculum models. Schools and individual teachers must own the inequalities that exist, and must find their own ways to address them in local contexts. This requires commitment by individuals as well as whole-school support. In Nigel's view, teachers working for equity goals make complex ethical and pedagogical decisions, lesson by lesson, day by day, as they "proceed tentatively toward social justice" (Howard, 1995).

Jennifer O'Brien: Critical Readers from the Start

Jennifer O'Brien is an experienced teacher who has worked for a number of years as a teacher/librarian and also in a professional development role in literacy education in her school district. In these roles Jennifer worked with students and teachers to research student-centred literacy pedagogies, while continuing to take seriously teachers' responsibilities for making explicit how all students could be successful. In Jennifer's view it was important to examine how teachers helped students select, read, and use different kinds of texts. In her graduate studies Jennifer pursued feminist and poststructuralist theories about textual practices which suggested that texts are constructed, not vehicles of unquestionable "truths"; texts are not neutral and have specific and differential effects; texts represent people in ways which are gendered, raced, and classed; and texts can be deconstructed and critically interrogated.

Jennifer decided to explore with children in their first years of schooling the poststructuralist contention that texts are constructed objects which could have been constructed differently. Her starting point was investigating the representation of gender in texts. Her explicit standpoint was to disrupt the oftentimes-limited gendered identities produced in texts for children, where, as Jennifer puts it, girls are constructed as "pretty and compliant" and boys as "cheeky and naughty." What Jennifer tried to do was to give her students access to critical and feminist discourses so that other positions were made available for them in the classroom (O'Brien, 1994).[4] Together with her students, she began to research ways of changing what could be said in her classroom about boys and girls, men and women, mothers and fathers and as we will see below, "aunts."

While critical literacy has sometimes been seen as the province of high school, college, and adult education, Jennifer took on the challenge made by socially critical researchers that "children at the earliest stages . . . contest, debate, and argue with texts" (see Luke in Jongsma, 1991). She explains what she intended:

> My response to these challenges has been to alter fundamentally the interactions between my students, their classroom texts, and me. . . . I use critically framed conversations, questions, and tasks to put into practice two key decisions: first, to challenge the taken-for-granted nature of the construction of children's texts; and second, to ask students to think about the constructions of reality authorised by the text and to consider different possibilities for constructing reality. (Comber & O'Brien, 1993, p. 3)

These are important insights for young readers to grasp, and they are not necessarily obvious in classroom discussions, which sometimes give the impression that the characters in books are "real" or represent "people like that" in the real world. In Jennifer's classroom, the author and illustrator were referred to as people who make decisions to portray things, people, and events in certain ways. During the period of her research, she asked children to consider questions including the following: What do writers say about boys, girls, mothers, and fathers in the books you read? What do mothers/fathers/girls/boys do in this story? Who had the power in this story? What do adults think that children like to read about? If you only knew about mothers from reading this book, what would you know about what mothers do? What doesn't the writer tell you about this person? What does the writer tell me that I already know? What do I know that the writer doesn't tell me?

Jennifer's research project involved her consciously changing the ways in which she spoke about texts and changing the invitations she made to children to speak about texts. The preceding questions are examples of those which she found provoked different kinds of discussions. She did not begin with a set of new or politically correct critical questions; rather, with the children's help, she explored ways of generating new kinds of conversations which would allow them to argue with texts, to interrogate the apparently "natural" gendered identities that appeared daily in their storybooks, factual texts, and the media and everyday texts in the community. It was common to hear Jenny interrupt herself with comments like, "No that's not a good question," and then rephrase what she wanted to say. Hence, she continually demonstrated to children a critical reflexivity about her own discursive practices.

These are very different kinds of questions than were being discussed in other classrooms we had observed, where children were asked about their favourite characters, their favourite pages, and why the characters acted in the ways they did. Classroom conversations about shared texts frequently treat the characters as real, the plots as natural, as the ways things are. The rationalities and visions of the authors and illustrators are often seen as natural and as beyond question. The role of the children in these classrooms is to notice what the teacher notices and to match the teacher's interpretation of the book (Baker, 1991). In Jennifer's classroom there was the potential for children to engage in critical text analysis from the beginning of schooling. Our aim in the video was to capture Jennifer and the children in conversation around texts, in order that we could show students and teachers other possibilities for talk around texts in the early literacy classroom which deliberately foregrounded social justice issues. As an introduction, we asked Jennifer to explain what critical literacy meant in her classroom:

> Critical literacy, to me, is an important part of showing children a way of looking at the world so that they don't simply accept things as they are presented to them. For example, they don't just take for granted the presentation in their storybooks of themselves as being perhaps cute, perhaps dependent, if they are boys being cheeky and naughty, or if they are girls, as pretty and compliant; that in their writing, for example they will start to think first; instead of just taking on board the usual ways of thinking about women or of thinking about girls or of thinking about children and writing those things down, they'll think first, "Can I change it? Can I take a different position on these things? Can I look at the world differently?"

Jennifer's position was that simply by following children's interests and inquiries, no redistribution of power or social justice outcomes are guaranteed. Children's interests and inquiries are no more "disinterested" or "natural" or "innocent" than those of the communities in which they are constructed. In Jennifer's view, teacher direction can be proactive. Critical literacies don't necessarily emerge unless teachers work with children to construct spaces where such conversations can be safely had.

In the video we show several brief classroom episodes of Jennifer's teaching, selected because they demonstrate how she frames tasks and conversations in order to have children work on the ways that texts are constructed, the ways in which authors and illustrators choose to represent particular kinds of characters. The focus of this work denaturalises the text and encourages children to ask questions about the way texts are constructed. Below, we outline one classroom episode in which Jennifer leads the children in posing critical questions. One of the children in Jennifer's class had commented that writers often represent aunts as "mean" in stories. This observation is interesting in itself. In Jennifer's classroom, the decisions writers made—such as how to represent aunts—were the object of study, and the child readers were positioned to notice what writers often do across texts.

Shortly after the student's comment about "aunts being mean in stories," Jennifer spotted *Beware of the Aunts* (Thompson, 1991), on the new book shelf in the library. She realised that here was a chance to test out the student's hypothesis. Jennifer begins by having the children study the cover and think about other books which include aunts, and then focuses on the blurb where we are told that the writer and the illustrator "gently poke fun at the foibles of aunts," but that "there is one time of the year when you cannot do without them." Jennifer asks the children to predict a time when the writer will say children cannot do without their aunts:

> JENNIFER: What will Pat Thompson, who wrote this book,
>   decide to put in the book? Have a think. Do you
>   need to talk to someone near you about it?
>
> STUDENT: Or close my eyes and think about it?
>
> JENNIFER: Or close your eyes . . .

Here Jennifer breaks up the usual pattern of question-answer sequences which often go on around texts by encouraging children to share ideas with each other or to just think. The children quickly tap into the logic of the book and begin to offer suggestions: "On your birthday," "At Christmas," "At Easter." The children realise that the author's joke is that however odd aunts may be, they are still good for present giving. Jennifer scribes the children's suggestions as a list. Next, she asks them to work in pairs to draw and label pictures of the kinds of aunts the writer and illustrator might portray in this book. When they have done this, Jennifer begins reading the story, inviting children to interrupt her when they come across an aunt they had predicted would be in the book. Jennifer does not get far before groups of children start to call out, "Fat aunt," "I drew a fat aunt," "You saw I drew a fat aunt." The children's predictions were accurate. Here was another text which positioned aunts as people to be made fun of; the first character being an aunt who cannot stop eating.

Prediction is not new to whole language teachers. What is different about the way it is done in Jennifer's classroom is that she does not have the children predict narrative as though this is the way things are. Predictions in this classroom are about the ways authors commonly represent different kinds of people; in this case, Jennifer directs children's attention to the construction of gendered identities.

Later, Jennifer explained that there were a number of things she wanted students to learn from this lesson:

> [W]riters very, very frequently draw on ideas about the world, about women, about children, about men, that are already there; as if the ideas are ready-made and they just pick them up and slot them in and use them. So these ideas about aunts being figures of fun, being mean, all these sorts of things that we come across, I wanted to show the children that there was a distinct possibility that, that sort of view of the world would come through, but I also wanted to put the question to them: "Does the writer of this book, whose name is Pat Thompson, does she alter things in any way? Does she decide to treat aunts differently?"

Because Jennifer makes her agenda explicit by openly exploring how limited gender identities are portrayed in many children's books, it should not be assumed that the children neatly fall in line and reproduce her point of view. To the contrary, Jennifer's transcripts are full of instances of contestation, debate, and resistance. A few days after the lesson described above Jennifer returns to the discussion of *Beware of the Aunts*:

JENNIFER: OK, and what did Pat Thompson seem to be saying about the one who loved sewing? Alison?

ALLISON: She likes making her own clothes.

JENNIFER: OK, and is this a successful thing she does? Or is Pat Thompson making that out to be a good thing or a bad thing?

STUDENTS: A good thing.

JENNIFER: In what way?

ZOE: It's a good thing that she's recycling things like the bedspread.

JENNIFER: Is that what Pat Thompson's saying or what you're
            saying?

ZOE: It's what I'm saying. She once made something
            out of a bedspread, and she must have had a
            hole right in the middle of it which was big
            enough for her head so she must have made a
            dress out of it.

JENNIFER: OK, fine. You're saying it's a good thing. Do you
            think Pat Thompson is saying it's a good thing or a
            bad thing?

STUDENTS: Good.

ZOE: It's good that she's recycling.

JENNIFER: OK, what about this other comment here
            [reading the text], "I'm afraid she sometimes
            makes us things." Is that a good thing or a bad
            thing about an aunt?

STUDENTS: Good!

JENNIFER: Have a good look at the picture.

ALISON: Bad!

JENNIFER: What makes you say that, Allison?

ALLISON: Because the sleeves are too long and they don't
            look right on them.

In the preceding transcript, we can see that Zoe takes up a strong position as
reader, drawing on her knowledge of recycling, in order to read the aunt's
sewing as positive, in spite of the text and the illustrations. Other children are
convinced by Zoe and also see the aunt's sewing as positive. What follows
then is a close analysis of the text and pictures, with Jennifer drawing
children's attention to what is in the text itself, including the print and the
pictures. Jennifer listens and continually redirects their attention to what the
author and illustrator have produced. Each of the children's contributions is
taken seriously, which means not simply accepting each comment, but
asking children to expand on their opinions and justify them by making
reference to the text itself.

Some whole language teachers may find this interaction teacher-directed.
Jennifer does indeed direct children—for example, to look closely at what is
going on in the text. She deliberately challenges texts which maintain limited

and negative views of who women are and who they can or should be. She does not do this by closing down what children can say or by subtly imposing her interpretations. She *teaches* children ways of reading which allow them to see texts differently. How much respect for the child reader would have been demonstrated if Jennifer had simply accepted Zoe's reading and moved on to the next question? In this instance, Jennifer's questioning indicates that children's responses to texts are indeed important, too important to simply accept as one more idea. It is in closely examining children's responses to texts and analysing how texts work that literacy educators can lead children to question dominant inequitable representations in the worlds of print.

This does not mean that children stop having fun, or that they are simply trained in politically correct responses. On the contrary, it means producing students who argue and debate, who at five and six can sustain arguments not just across a lesson, but across days and weeks, who develop understandings about intertextuality so that they detect patterns in their reading, who read and reread from different positions. We can reconceptualise teacher direction as an ethical practice where the teacher inserts her voice to ensure the space for difference, contest, and justice. In Jennifer's classroom the children, along with their teacher, were engaged in new forms of inquiry about texts and their effects.

Jennifer's critical literacy curriculum was not restricted to analysing children's storybooks. As she explains in the video, she considers any text "fair game" and uses newspaper clippings, junk mail, encyclopedias, nonfiction books, books tied to movie promotions—texts that children might encounter in and out of school. More recently, Jennifer has documented her analysis with young children of the representation of women in catalogues advertising gifts for Mother's Day (Luke, O'Brien, & Comber, 1994). In this work, Jennifer and her students explored gender, race, and class and involved parents and caregivers in their inquiries. Jennifer and other teachers in South Australian schools have begun to analyse everyday texts: cereal boxes; corn-chip packets; tea-bag boxes; the texts on toy catalogues and on the associated television advertising (Comber & Simpson, 1995). These everyday texts and texts of popular culture may form important ways of establishing what Anne Dyson calls a "permeable curriculum" (Dyson, 1993), in which children might bring to the official school world text and story resources they use and play with in their peer and home worlds.

Jennifer's work has been an important catalyst for change amongst early literacy educators in the local and national educational community. Jennifer

demonstrated what might be done with very young children and made
public her work with and on theory. She generously offered her work to
other teachers, not as an exemplary model, but as work-in-progress and as
evidence of what children can do given the space and tools. The effects of
Jennifer's work are impossible to anticipate; however, we do know that other
teachers are following her lead in exploring other ways of talking about texts
while making gender, race, and class subjects that can be talked about from
the earliest days of schooling. What is needed are forums where teachers can
safely discuss issues about difference and social justice (See Dyson, 1995).
We hope that our educational documentaries about teaching literacy in
disadvantaged schools provide material to generate and support such
discussions.

Confronting the Silence
and Seeing Things Differently

As literacy educators, we can no longer take for granted that access to
reading and writing automatically works for social justice. Brave teachers,
such as Barbara, Nigel, and Jennifer, who are prepared to put themselves on
the line on video in the public arena so that others may learn, are crucial in
the educational community. Their practices generate possibilities for other
ways of doing school, for other kinds of school literacies. Each of these
teachers begins not with a set of "good literacy practices," but with a
theorised analysis of how power works in society and the ways in which
textual practices and schooling are implicated in the maintenance of
inequalities. In making decisions about what to do in their classrooms, they
are informed by their commitment to working against injustice, now, by
giving students the space to question the way things are and to take action
within the spaces of schooling and community.

   We take the view that as language and literacy teachers in a world
increasingly mediated by texts, we have a responsibility to foreground
relations of power and social inequities. In the production of our educational
documentaries, made in collaboration with Barbara, Nigel, Jennifer, and
others, we attempt to produce open-ended texts. We attempt to create for our
teacher-preparation students a range of ways of seeing literacy, poverty,
education, and disadvantage. One view we explicitly present is the framing of
the "poverty problem" as systemic, and state-constructed and legitimated
through a politics of unequal distribution of entitlements (Polakow, 1993). We
attempt to counter the silence that has surrounded this view in educational

sites. We acknowledge that teacher-training institutions as well as schools can play a part in the formation or the contestation of deficit images of children, their race, class, family, and culture. As Polakow (1993) argues:

> Teachers do not live above their culture; they too are participants in the pervasive poverty discourse that conceals economic and educational inequalities, state-induced destitution. (p. 146)

We hope we are collaborators with classroom-based literacy teachers in

> [c]onfronting the silence, naming the classroom world with different forms of talk, shifting our ways of seeing, opening up spaces for possibility that can shift the tenuous ground on which young children of poverty stand. (Polakow 1993, p. 147)

We conclude with a story about one teacher enacting this kind of "shifting the ground" to create new ways of seeing. Anne Haas Dyson (1993, pp. 41–43) describes a lesson she observed in an elementary, multiracial classroom where the teacher, Louise, had invited in parents to talk about their jobs. On this occasion, a father, who was white, spoke about his work as a scientist. Afterwards the teacher asked the children who would like to be scientists. Four children raised their hands. The teacher asked these children to go to the middle of the room. Then the teacher pointed out a problem: four white boys in the middle of the room. The teacher went on to ask a series of questions about who was there and who wasn't and how the group of future scientists could be changed. Gradually, other children went to the middle of the room—girls, boys of colour, girls of colour—with the teacher helping the children analyse how the group in the middle was changing and why that was important. Eventually the teacher asked the children again to go to the middle of the room if they might like to be scientists and all but the scientist's daughter went to the centre of the room. She wanted to be a vet!

This story is important as it shows the way in which a teacher who has a social analysis and who is committed to equity can use situations as they arise in the school day. This language activity is about who people are and who they might be; the teacher sees the possibility for a wider lesson about identity and futures and demonstrated to children a way of analysing life situations: Who is in the centre and who isn't? We do not see choices in regard to pedagogy as limited to the binary oppositions of teacher-centred and child-centred. Relatedly, we don't see power as owned by the teacher or students, but as constantly negotiated and exercised in different ways in different contexts. We do not see that the absence of teacher-direction necessarily results in democratic power redistribution amongst children, nor that teacher direction excludes the possibilities of democratic classrooms. Making justice our project involves teachers exercising power in positive ways to challenge untested and inequitable hegemonic assumptions at work in classroom cultures.

As teacher educators we believe it is important that the work done by teachers like Louise, Barbara, Nigel, and Jennifer is made central to discussions of teaching for social justice. They make literacy lessons the sites for social justice. They challenge accepted notions of what literacy might be and what it can do for students. The video documentaries involved an alliance between university and school-based educators and their communities. From this collaborative strength we were able to begin to explore the dilemmas which confront teachers as they work for social justice. We were also able to portray school communities actively working for change. But none of this is simple. We document no easy answers. Our strongest hope for our project is that it prevents a complacent silence and generates conversations among educators who see schools as potential sites of transformation, as places where democracy is learnt and practised.

Notes

1. Australian schools are designated as "disadvantaged" if they satisfy the criteria for federal government equity funding under the Disadvantaged Schools Program (DSP).

2. In 1993 and 1994, we were members of a team awarded national grants to improve the quality of university teaching in teacher education about teaching literacy in disadvantaged schools. With Susan Hill, Lynne Badger and Lyn Wilkinson, we have produced two sets of three videos under the titles *Literacy, Diversity and Schooling* (Comber et al., 1994) and *Literacy Learning and Social Justice* (Hill et al., 1996).

3. For an exploration of the ethical and practical dilemmas in implementing the project, see Nixon and Comber (1995).

4. The authors were involved in this project as co-supervisors.

References

Allington, R. L., & Walmsley, S. A. (Eds.). (1995). *No quick fix: Rethinking literacy programs in America's elementary schools.* New York: Teachers College Press.

Badger, L., Comber, B., & Weeks, B. (1993). *Literacy and language practices in the early years in disadvantaged schools: A report on the National Survey.* Canberra, ACT, Australia: Department of Employment, Education, and Training.

Baker, C. (1991). Literacy practices and social relations in classroom reading events." In C. D. Baker & A. Luke (Eds.), *Towards a critical sociology of reading pedagogy: Papers of the XII World Congress on Reading.* Amsterdam: John Benjamin's.

Baker, C. D., & Freebody, P. (1989). *Children's first schoolbooks: Introductions to the culture of literacy.* Oxford, UK: Blackwell.

Christie, F., Devlin, B., Freebody, P., Luke, A., Martin, J. R., Threadgold, T., & Walton, C. (1991). *Teaching English literacy: A project of national significance on the preservice preparation of teachers for teaching English literacy.* Canberra, ACT, Australia: Department of Employment, Education, and Training.

Comber, B. (1994). Critical literacy: An introduction to Australian debates and perspectives. *Journal of Curriculum Studies, 26*(6), 655–668.

Comber, B., & O'Brien, J. (1993). Critical literacy: Classroom explorations. *Critical Pedagogy Networker, 6*(1/2), 1–11.

Comber, B., & Simpson, A. (1995). Reading cereal boxes: Analysing everyday texts. In *Texts: The heart of the English curriculum.* Broadsheet ser. 1, no. 1, Adelaide, South Australia: Department of Education and Children's Services.

Comber, B., Nixon, H., Hill, S., & Badger, L. (1994). *Literacy, diversity and Schooling.* Three videos and user's guide. Melbourne, Victoria, SE Australia: Eleanor Curtain.

Delpit, L. (1988). The silenced dialogue: Power and pedagogy in educating other people's children." *Harvard Educational Review, 58*(3), 280–298.

Donald, J. (1993). Literacy and the limits of democracy." In B. Green (Ed.), *The insistence of the letter: Literacy studies and curriculum theorizing* (pp. 120–136). London: Falmer.

Dreyfus, H., & Rabinow, P. (1983). *Michel Foucault: Beyond structuralism and hermeneutics.* 2nd ed. Chicago: University of Chicago Press.

Dyson, A. H. (1993). *Social worlds of children learning to write in an urban primary school.* New York: Teachers College Press.

Dyson, A. H. (1995). (Ed.). What difference does difference make? Teacher perspectives on diversity, literacy, and the urban primary school. *English Education, 27*(2), 77–139.

Edelsky, C., with Harman, S. (1991). Risks and possibilities of whole language literacy: Alienation and connection. In C. Edelsky, *With literacy and justice for all: Rethinking the social in language and education* (pp. 127–140). New York: Falmer.

Education Department of South Australia. (1992). *Writing-reading assessment program (WRAP): Final report.* Adelaide, South Australia: Education Department of South Australia.

Gilbert, P. (1989). Student text as pedagogical text. In S. DeCastell, A. Luke, & C. Luke (Eds.), *Language, authority, and criticism: Readings on the school textbook* (pp. 195–202). London: Falmer.

Gilbert, P. (1990). Authorizing disadvantage: Authorship and creativity in the language classroom. In F. Christie (Ed.), *Literacy for a changing world* (pp. 54–78). Victoria, SE Australia: Australian Council of Educational Research.

Harvey, D. (1993). Class relations, social justice and the politics of difference. In M. Keith, & S. Pile (Eds.), *Place and the politics of identity* (pp. 41–66). London: Routledge.

Hill, S., Nixon, H., Comber, B., Badger, L., & Wilkinson, L. (1996). *Literacy learning and social justice.* Three videos and user's guide. Melbourne, Victoria, SE Australia: Eleanor Curtain. Howard, N. (1995). What does it mean to teach in an unjust society? Paper presented at the Centre for Studies in Educational Leadership, Underdale, University of South Australia.

Jongsma, K.S. (1991). Critical literacy (questions and answers). *The Reading Teacher, 44*(7), 518–519.

Kress, G. (1994). Text and grammar as explanation. In U. H. Meinhof, & K. Richardson (Eds.), *Text, discourse, and context: Representations of poverty in Britain* (pp. 24–46). London: Longman.

Lensmire, T. (1994, December). Writing for critical democracy: Student voice and teacher practice in the writing workshop. Paper presented at the National Reading Conference, San Diego, CA.

Luke, A. (1993). Stories of social regulation: The micropolitics of classroom narrative. In B. Green (Ed.), *The insistence of the letter: Literacy studies and curriculum theorizing* (pp. 137–153). London: Falmer.

Luke, A. (1996). When literacy might not make a difference: Textual practice and cultural capital. In C. D. Baker, J. Cook-Gumperz, & A. Luke (Eds.), *Literacy and Power.* Oxford: Blackwell.

Luke, A., O'Brien, J., & Comber, B. (1994). Making community texts objects of study. *The Australian Journal of Language and Literacy, 17*(2), 139–149.

Nixon, H., & Comber, B. (1995). Making documentaries and teaching about disadvantage: Ethical issues and practical dilemmas. *Australian Educational Researcher, 22*(2), 63–84.

O'Brien, J. (1994, July). It's written in our head: The possibilities and contradictions of a feminist poststructuralist discourse in a junior primary classroom. Unpubl. master's thesis, University of South Australia.

Polakow, V. (1993). *Lives on the edge: Single mothers and their children in the other America.* Chicago: University of Chicago Press.

Stuckey, J.E. (1991). *The violence of literacy.* Portsmouth, NH: Boynton/Cook.

Thompson, P. (1991). *Beware of the aunts.* London: Macmillan.

Willinsky, J. (1990). *The new literacy: Redefining reading and writing in the schools.* New York: Routledge.

III TAKING NEW ACTION

The last section of this book offers educators a range of possibilities for operating in the world—for us and for our students. "Columbine's Challenge: A Call to Pay Attention to Our Students" by Robin Stern is a rallying call for those who understand that increased security and the commitment of limited education dollars for metal detectors will not address the impetus toward violent acts in schools. The following articles concentrate on relatively small projects that have made a difference. Individually and together, they work to answer the challenge and represent an ongoing thread of critical education in this century.

In "Becoming Proactive: The Quiet Revolution," three educators open the doors of their classrooms into the community to share three categories of strategies that served to establish working partnerships with students' families: strategies for community building, strategies for informing parents, and strategies for involving parents. Over time, these strategies transformed these educators' learning communities. Next, Elizabeth Saavedra describes her own transformation from an educator who diligently used teacher-proof materials to the organizer of a teacher study group that, through self-conscious and informed critique, worked to expand teachers' control over their teaching lives. Like Linda Christensen, Saavedra confronted and transformed the ways in which she and her fellow colleagues had been defined.

In an extended example of integrated curriculum, again in a bilingual setting, southern California educators Barbara Yeager, Irene Pattenaude, María Fránquiz, and Louise Jennings provide guidance for primary-level teachers who are eager to create inquiry-based curricula that promote critical consciousness. The fifth-grade students in this classroom began by defining responsibility and then working through particular inquiry processes in a study of the Holocaust that challenged them to give life to their definitions. "Exploring Critical Literacy: You Can Hear a Pin Drop" invites teachers to begin new conversations in any educational context. The authors provide twelve extended annotations for both picture books and short novels that are guaranteed to promote discussion. Stories run the geographical gamut, from war-torn Europe to Vietnam, and the subject gamut, from biracial parentage to students "on the loose" when a teacher doesn't show up for class. Each book is provocative, ambiguous, and ripe with opportunity to provoke rich dialogue in the classroom and other educational contexts. Educators might use these suggested titles in the classroom, with teaching staff, or with a book club in an effort to engage new conversations.

The final article in this volume vividly illustrates the possibilities of a critical-literacy curriculum by taking us through a project on South Africa and apartheid that helped students develop feelings of empowerment and commitment to social justice.

9 Columbine's Challenge: A Call to Pay Attention to Our Students

Robin Stern

A teenage boy wakes up in the morning. Time to get dressed for school. The parents are fighting and his mother is depressed. Money is tight and she is angry. He forgot to finish his homework and is already in a bad mood and slow to breakfast. His father is yelling at his older brother about not filling the car up with gas the night before. The young boy comes down to the table. His mother musters up a perfunctory greeting. The boy throws a PTA notice on the table and she takes a quick look, saying she is too busy to go. The boy asks his father about going to his ball game with him this weekend, and the father responds with an off handed "we'll see." The boy goes to school. He didn't eat much of his breakfast.

A teenage girl leaves her house to go to school. She is waiting for the school bus. It is a few minutes late, and she is already nervous about a science quiz. She did study but it was hard to concentrate after a fight she had with her best friend. The bus is hot and none of her good friends are there today to sit with. She is distracted and sits alone. She gets to school and sees her best friend in a group of others talking and laughing, glancing her way and laughing again. She goes to her locker, fighting back tears and grabs her books for her first class.

Enter the teachers. Some of them had mornings just as difficult and need some time to simply get themselves together before they can deal effectively with the students. The teachers are exhausted anyway because of all the new

Reprinted from *Voices from the Middle*, September 1999.

standards in education. There was a bomb scare in the school the day before. More inservice training, fewer resources. More subject material to cover, more interruptions, less time to meet with students. More trouble, less assistance.

And what about the administrators? Maybe they were criticized publicly at the school board meeting last night. Parents want to know what they are doing to prevent a school massacre like the one in Colorado while at the same time demanding that standards be raised so that their children can get into colleges of their choice next year. The janitors are creating havoc because their contract is up. There isn't enough time to stay current with promising programs that could help the students in their school. The principal closes the office door and drinks his third cup of coffee before meeting with the teachers. Just another day!

So, what about the fantasy in which effective teaching and learning are going to go on in this school this morning. Forget it! Will they get by? Probably. Will anybody be any the wiser? Probably not. That is precisely the problem: no one will notice. Students can get by without touching base, without dealing with their feelings. Some of our students are falling through the cracks. We need to pay attention.

So what can we do to create an atmosphere that promotes learning for the whole child; that is concerned for the cognitive, affective, and physical needs of children; that insists on recognizing that emotional literacy is as critical as mastering reading and writing; that allows for partnership between home and school; that remembers that teenagers are children struggling with difficult, intensely personal emotions at a time where, for some odd reason, parents have decided to back off and stop parenting. Studies of adolescents indicate they spend on average a quarter of their waking hours alone, and there is a fear that the unsupervised computer time may be increasing this isolation. Parents, if there are two parents, are often too busy pursuing dual careers and chasing after the "good" life. Television has become more than babysitter; it is now teacher as well. Our teens' role models come more from the media than from the home. Games we buy our teens teach violence and killing. And then we yell at them when they spend too much time with the games and become aggressive!

It is up to all adults to provide the leadership that puts vision into action, a vision where schools strike a balance between the physical and emotional dimensions of a child and the cognitive one. A vision where systemic programs that promote emotional literacy are infused from pre-K on. A vision where we create safe, caring environments to learn to foster empathy and self-understanding, and to promote emotional management, problem solving, and conflict resolution.

Imagine this. You are a teacher in a school where emotional literacy is a standard, where kindness is the credo, where gossip is not tolerated at all, where teachers and students alike have groups they attend every day to focus on emotional management, problem solving, and conflict resolution, where these skills are infused in the curriculum and modeled for everyone in the day-to-day teacher-to-student, teacher-to-teacher, and administrator-to-teacher behavior. Class discussions are held wherein children critically evaluate the appropriateness of media, toys, and net access, where consequences of inappropriate access and violent games are discussed as social and educational problems, where the parents become partners with the school and community in the education of their children, where the school and PTA provide parenting discussion groups for teenagers, and where an intranet—with relevant content and extensions of discussions—is developed to encourage communication and distance learning among parents, teachers, administrators, students, and community members.

Imagine that your school environment invites challenging discussions—many run by the students—and encourages the expression of negative feelings as well as positive. In this school, trained professionals are available as part of a team to help deal with kids in trouble. The children are rewarded for emotional mentoring and mediating, everyone has a "buddy" or a "mentor." Imagine that classrooms are well equipped, spacious, and stimulating. Work tables replace desks lined up in a row. Children are engaged daily in physical activity that serves to empower, strengthen, and provide an outlet for some of the intense feelings that we all have. Sometimes you just have to scream or run. Better on a track or in a game than in the classroom.

For all the adults who impact the lives of our students, this is a call to action. It is true we're all pressed for time. That doesn't matter. Talking the talk is not enough. We must make the time if we truly value the lives of our students. It is not up to us, as writers, to decide your vision for the perfect school. Our goal is to challenge you to think about your vision and to move you closer to implementing it. Together, let us pay attention to our students, encourage their strengths, promote their learning, model considerate and pro-social behavior. Notice them. Acknowledge their achievements. Praise their gifts. Be aware of when things change, when they seem to be off track, when they are more isolated and angry, when they stop talking to you. Be watchful when they let go of friendships, stop handing in homework, stop combing their hair, drop off the team. Notice them collectively and individually. Talk to them.

When was the last time you let your students, for five days in a row, know that you are interested in what they are feeling inside—really feeling? That you are interested in what happened with their friends today—or in their other classes? That you are interested in what they are thinking about? When was the last time you let them know that it is important that they pay attention to their own feelings? When was the last time you modeled self-reflection in your classroom?

Let us not be guilty ourselves of one of the classic hallmarks of the teen years, not paying attention to consequences. If we can't make the time to spend with our students, there will be consequences. These consequences may not show up in dramatic expressions like drug abuse, anorexia, or violence, but they will show up—in who our students are and who they will become, in how far they are able to go, and in how alive and healthy their spirit will be. Make time for them, pay attention to them. It makes a difference.

10 Becoming Proactive: The Quiet Revolution

Cathy Fleischer, Kathleen Hayes-Parvin, and Julie A. King

The problem is, by now, a familiar one. The public conversation about educational issues—and in particular about curricular issues in Language Arts instruction—has become more of a monologue in which legislators, reporters, school boards, and ordinary citizens make claims about classroom pedagogy that only sometimes reflect the reality of schools and children. Frustrated teachers are at a loss about what to do. Already busy, they have little time to devote to educating others about what classrooms are really like or to take on the political forces that seem to define the parameters of the conversation. And so an unfortunate cycle develops: Most citizens get their information about school issues from the articles they read in the paper ("How Whole Language Became a Hot Potato In and Out of Academia: Reading Method Ditched Phonics, Won Adherents but Test Scores Tanked"), many of which call up memories of their own schooling ("We always had spelling bees when I was in school" or "I learned poetry by memorizing rhyme schemes and rhythm. I can spot iambic pentameter a mile away"). When these folks then talk to others about what's happening in schools, their understandings are based on these memories and supported by the negative press they read about new methods, methods those of us in Language Arts know are grounded in sound theory, sound research, and sound teacher practice. Based on these misunderstandings, and fueled by public opinion, school boards in turn

Reprinted from *Voices from the Middle,* March 1999.

make decisions about curriculum and methods that directly impact the classroom.

A perfect case in point was the recent furor over Ebonics, a furor fueled by a wire service story reporting that teachers in Oakland, California, were going to initiate a program to "train teachers to conduct classes in the nonstandard English speech familiar to many African-Americans" (Chiles, A15). Immediately, citizens across the country reacted with strong, sometimes vitriolic stances. And despite the fact that the story was later acknowledged to be "inaccurate," the report had done its damage, leading "the rest of the country initially to believe the Oakland school system was going to 'teach' ebonics"—rather than to train teachers to recognize patterns of speech common to some African Americans and use that understanding as a way to nudge these students into standard English. This inaccurate version became the version of truth believed by both ordinary and prominent citizens around the country, encouraging strong opinions, but opinions based on misinformation.

What can teachers do to change this cycle, to help get the right information into the public eye and ear? The three of us—one university English educator and two middle school teachers—have been part of a group of elementary and secondary instructors talking and working together for the past few years to think about how to do just that, to have our voices, the voices of *teachers* informed about issues of language arts curriculum and best practices, heard in the public conversation. And what we have come to believe is that the place to begin is with parents: As we educate parents about what *really* goes on in a classroom that incorporates writing workshop or authentic assessment or choice in reading, we have a way to break the cycle . . . or at least to introduce some alternative stories into it. Parents who are educated about why we teach in certain ways, who are invited into our classrooms to see how we go about certain practices, become informed. And the next time they read an article in the newspaper or hear another parent on the soccer field bemoan the lack of sentence diagraming in the schools, they have access to another story that might factor into their response, a story that counteracts the messages that bombard us every day.

It sounds easy, of course. Teachers educate parents; parents educate others; the conversation about education changes tenor as it becomes much more inclusive. But for teachers, this step of becoming advocates for our own teaching practices is not always an easy adjustment. For many of us, that kind of job description conjures up images of Norma Rae or Ralph Nader on a soapbox chastising people to think in a certain way, a role that most teachers are not particularly comfortable with and that may not be the most appropriate or effective for us. First and foremost, our priority is to teach children, a job that takes an inordinate amount of time. It is vital, then, that any attempt to work with parent education and outreach becomes integrated with the job we already do, so that instead of being perceived as an "add-on" to an already hectic schedule, it's seen as a "part of." Equally important, we know that the relationship we forge with parents is always a precarious one, as we balance their vast knowledge about their own children's needs, strengths, desires, and interests with our own knowledge about best practices. While we have a lot of information to share with parents, we must always remember that this can't be a one-way agenda, carved in stone and unresponsive to individual needs. We can't become preachy, informing those "uninformed" parents how to think about our pedagogy.

What we're talking about is more of a quiet revolution, a revolution that depends on talking and listening, on teachable moments, on stolen time. It becomes a balancing act that factors in the needs of parents and students, as well as the knowledge of all parties, in a time frame that can be carved out of busy lives. It is a quiet revolution that needs to be waged *proactively* rather than *reactively*: reaching out to parents on a day-to-day basis, helping to inform them about certain pedagogical practices and why those practices are part of our classrooms, understanding that the most effective approach to changing people's minds is to address a problem before it arises, before defensive postures take the place of ordinary conversation. We've found that this proactive approach allows teachers to help educate parents in positive and collaborative ways, so that when a news story leads a small group to raise objections and to protest certain practices, these parents are able to approach other parents, administrators, and even a State Board of Education to argue for what they now understand. These parents become articulate defenders of best practices because a teacher has taken the time to explain to them *why* process writing, *why* choice in reading, *why* grammar in context.

What kinds of strategies do the teachers in our group use? We've found the techniques vary, depending on the context of the community, but certain categories of outreach are common: *strategies for community building*, which help bring parents and teachers together so that a team approach to problem solving is possible (Figure 1); *strategies for informing parents*, which help teachers educate parents about curricular issues in the classroom (Figure 2); and *strategies for involving parents* in classroom learning experiences, which help parents understand the curriculum by their participation in it (Figure 3).

Strategies for community building

- introductory picnic or party
- early conferences with parents to learn about their children's strengths, needs, activities
- handout for parents with ways for them to become involved—for all parents, with all kinds of schedules
- notes sent home with positive feedback about students
- public displays of student work (book signings, poetry readings, family writing nights)

Figure 1.

Strategies for informing parents

- introductory letter describing curricula
- student-written newsletter about classroom
- casual conversations before and after school or on field trips
- parent inservice nights on topics of their choice
- parent lending library of professional books
- parent-teacher reading and study group
- parent-teacher writing group
- teacher-written booklets about curriculum, with multiple student examples
- teaching letters connected to student published work

Figure 2.

Strategies for involving parents

- parent comment sheets attached to student published anthologies
- student-led conferencing
- parent responses to student portfolios
- occasions for parents to write along with students (joint published projects)
- student interviews of family members
- walking journals in which parents and students write about class, pass on to another parent and child
- parent involvement in reader response journals

Figure 3.

In the pages that follow, Kathleen and Julie will each share from their mix of strategies, approaches that are specific to the very different contexts in which they teach: Kathleen's sixth-grade classroom is in a school with a heterogeneous population, in terms of socioeconomics, race, and background experience. Julie's context is an eighth-grade classroom in a very homogeneous, middle- to upper middle-class community.

Kathleen Hayes-Parvin

After 18 years of teaching, I still feel proud every day to say, "I'm a teacher." I've taught in parochial and public settings, in both inner city and urban environments, in special education, regular education, and in inclusion formats, yet one constant remains: parental support is essential to an effective practice, a teaching practice where students, parents, and teachers all feel connected to a community of learners, where all members of the team feel the same pride.

It is because of this belief that I begin each year by building community—inviting, welcoming, and nurturing this coalition of parents, students, and teachers. Invitations may take a variety of forms, but most years, my first communication is a letter asking parents to attend a beginning-of-the-year conference. My colleagues and I compose this letter that we believe honors the parents' voices and allows a format for them to contribute to a conversation about their child, letting us know their child's strengths, challenges, passions, and in particular what methods or techniques have been successful in the past. This is an important first step to let parents know that we really do want their input, while it serves to establish a positive connection before the year even gets going.

This initial contact letter is written in English, but is also translated into Chaldean, as many of our students and their parents are of Iraqi ancestry. We do not want them to be left out due to a language barrier. This added effort, supported by our ESL department, often results in parents from other countries coming to school for the first time. Over the years, we've also become more sensitive to time constraints, understanding that many of our households are supported by single working parents. Thus, we've broadened our invitation to allow for a conference via phone or letter, both kinds of contact still providing us with the parents' insights and giving us that positive first contact.

A few weeks later, I extend an invitation to attend our school's open house. Oftentimes I spend a half hour or so personally calling to reinvite parents who, for some reason, were not able to respond to that first conference, knowing that they may benefit most from a positive school contact, and may be resisting for reasons I can't possibly know. These calls take a bit of extra time, but are usually effective and prove to be time well spent; I want parents to know from the beginning that each of them is welcomed into our learning community.

Open house gives me a chance to talk about my curriculum face-to-face with parents in a warm and welcoming environment. They get a chance to see the kinds of literacy I value, simply by being in the classroom. Books are everywhere, both a large collection of young adult novels and my own collection of professional literature that informs the stances I take. I place a number of these books in a parent lending library, and each year invite parents to check them out. No one has ever borrowed a book from it, but it sends the message that I'm confident about what I'm doing, have theory behind it, and am willing to share.

Contacts and conferences of this sort continue throughout the year as I extend multiple invitations to parents in hopes of both building the community and introducing them to various aspects of their children's literacy education. Sometimes I use student-led conferences in late May, where students lead their parents through their writing portfolios, graphic representations of both what they've learned and what they know about what they've learned. Most recently, I've introduced an end-of-the-year conference in June, providing a time for us to sit together, talk, reflect on our journey, and contemplate where to go from here.

By establishing these contacts, I try to help the parents feel invited into the community of learners of our classroom, paving the way for some more explicit collaborative projects. Our curricular collaboration begins with the students' first project: a genre study that culminates in a student-written poetry anthology. I place their poems in a three-ring binder, placing a teaching letter in the front. In that letter, I carefully explain what the students have been working on and the strategies for writing poetry that students have incorporated. ("We began the year with poetry so we could focus in on the structure of language. You might notice some of the writer's tricks we've incorporated into our poems.") I then ask the parents to respond in writing to what they have read, making a few suggestions about what they might look for in the student's writing ("Look for detail, alliteration, line breaks, the use of threes, and using old words in new ways. . . . Watch for the use of the five senses. . . . And just as published authors do, we're writing about things that really matter to us."). I start by sending the binder home to a parent whom I know will respond in a creative and positive way, hoping that subsequent parents who receive the binder will get some good ideas for how to respond. Again, parents are urged to write in the language they are most comfortable with. The kids and I translate and transcribe later. Parent responses usually indicate both a celebration of the work the students have accomplished plus an understanding of the techniques we have stressed in class.

The next invitation to write, read, publish, and celebrate our literary journey has become an integral part of our sixth-grade language arts program. It involves parents and students copublishing for our class book. Again, the initial invitation is put into a letter urging parents to compose a piece along with their child's for our next class anthology, usually devised around a theme or genre (for example, "heroes" or "memoir"). A number of parents write, but we've also broadened our scope to include grandparents, siblings, and step-parents. Joyfully, many have accepted over the years, composing stories about their children, their own childhoods, family stories, and a number of other subjects.

We do send home reminder letters or nudge with phone calls occasionally. But we try to make this a low stress, positive experience for the parents. We know writing for publication can be intimidating, so we reassure the writers that we'll edit their pieces for them. Parents occasionally drop by the classroom when they've gotten stuck in their writing and need some help revising, and students regularly report on the peer conferences they've held with their parents at home. Parents who have the chance to experience the joys and frustrations of writing and revising a piece begin to get a clearer picture of what their kids are doing in class—and start to see the differences between how they were taught to write and how their children are being taught.

We ask our guest writers to come in to read their pieces whenever they can, thus modeling quality literacy for our students. Once a mom, step-dad, grandma, or big brother has entered our literary sanctuary, a special bond is forged: the kids never forget, and neither do our guests.

Through conferencing, copublishing, and becoming intimately involved in the workings of our classroom, parents begin to understand in some detail the kind of literacy environment in which their children are taught. The terminology and the processes we use take on new and important meaning. Included from the beginning in a proactive way, parents become my best allies and advocates—an invaluable resource.

Julie King

Let's face it; none of us has the kind of time we'd like to spend communicating with and involving parents in our classrooms, but I've come to believe that we need to make the little time we have count a lot. As I try both to inform parents about my teaching and to involve them in the curriculum, I hope it becomes time well spent.

My first year, I radically changed my practice from a traditional approach to one incorporating workshop, choice in reading, and authentic assessment. I spent a great deal of time working to inform parents about what students were learning in the classroom—through both an initial letter home (which described what their child would be doing in school and what they might look for at home) and a student-generated newsletter (which described, in the students' own words, things like peer conferences, workshop, reading response journals, and author's chair) so the parents might begin to picture our classroom. While I continue to use these strategies, this year I added a new outreach idea to my repertoire: a booklet I wrote for parents, entitled "Seeking Common Ground: A Parent's Guide to Process Writing and Assessment." In this booklet, I describe terminology related to my teaching, such as stages of writing, portfolios, and authentic assessment. I believe parents need to understand the language of best practices, as well as the whys of our teaching. The booklet contains definitions, classroom portraits of students (including samples of their writing), as well as tips for how to help their children with writing at home. Handed out to parents at conference time, this book helps to explain my philosophy of teaching in friendly language with concrete examples.

While providing parents with this kind of information does help, I began to realize that even though I was *telling* them how our classroom and homework activities would increase student literacy, many of them never had the opportunity to see these activities in action. For many parents, the only feedback they received was a letter grade at the end of every ten weeks. Because of this, I've added yet another layer of outreach—involving parents in the actual classroom work.

The first outreach I tried was with our reader response journals. Students in my class were responsible for reading 30 minutes a day and writing three pages a week in response to the books and articles they were reading. Once a week, students wrote a letter to someone else (to me or to another student) about their reading, asking that person to write back. After the students became accustomed to this format, I began requiring a rotation of letters to parents or other adults at home, once every three weeks. While a few parents' letters responded merely to the mechanics of the writing, most responded with excitement, recommending reading the students might like, or offering models and stories about their own literacies.

An immediate advantage to this process was the way in which students explained to their parents the classroom practices and expectations for their reading. Marshall writes:

> Ms. King is making us write to you for our reader's response letter. Usually we talk about the book we are reading. I'm reading *Call Waiting* by R. L. Stine. You wouldn't probably like these books that much because they aren't as long as the books you read and they are mysteries.

His mom responds:

> I am thrilled that you are reading books and enjoying them. Reading has been one of my all-time favorite things to do. I like all types of books, including mysteries. Keep up the good work. I love you.

Later in the year, Marshall begins to describe his learning:

> I have been reading a lot more books lately and I think I've improved in my reading skills. Such skills include better understanding of vocabulary and faster reading. And I know that you like that, right? Well, I think after this year, I'll be a much better reader and I'll like reading a lot more, but that isn't for a while.

His mom responds:

> I am so happy that you are reading more (even if Ms. King is making you). The more you read, I'm sure you will come to love it as much as I do.

In addition to informing parents about our classroom learning, the letters gave my students extended models of literacy beyond the classroom and facilitated conversations about reading and home. Jenny's mother writes to her:

> You asked about what book I'm reading in my spare time?? What spare time?? . . . I'm reading all my nursing books and the dosage books for my classes now. You would probably find these books boring and very difficult, but I enjoy them somewhat.

She continues throughout the year to write about her reading for classes and to recommend some books that Jennie might like to read:

> "I really enjoyed *Face on the Milk Carton.* Hopefully someday you'll read that one."

These conversations gave students exposure to a variety of adult literacies. Many parents recommended books for their children to read. And frequently students took those recommendations seriously. In Dawn's case, her parents recommended the classic, *To Kill a Mockingbird.* While this book was a challenge to her, the letter exchange with her parents helped her to move from a literal level to a level of deeper questioning. Her mother writes:

> Your book sounds very interesting. I've enjoyed the parts when you read them out loud to me. Do you think the Radley house sounds like a creepy place?

Dawn begins to ask her parents questions about the reading:

> I don't know why the book is called *To Kill a Mockingbird,* because it has nothing to do with a mockingbird. Jem and Scout got air rifles for Christmas and their dad, Atticus said that it was a sin to kill a mockingbird, but that's the only time they ever said, "To kill a mockingbird."

Her father responds:

> Try and take some more time to think about the book and see if there isn't a hidden meaning to the title.

By reading and responding to the letters, parents were exposed to the ways my students were learning about reading. They saw the different texts students were exposed to, as well as their developing understanding and analysis of those texts. They could see in those letters their children's developing literacy. I didn't have to singly educate parents about what we were doing; the students themselves did the teaching and parents could see the value in our learning experiences.

A second outreach practice I incorporated this year was involving parents in the portfolio process. Every marking period, each of my students puts together a portfolio that includes a reflective letter articulating a personal evaluation of his or her learning over the year. In the past, some parents have had difficulty understanding how this works, mainly because they do not have the opportunity to see the writing their children have done.

This year, I began requiring my students to take the portfolio home to share with parents before my evaluation. The emphasis was on the students "showing off" their work, and taking their parents on a tour of their improvements over the year. Parents, in turn, filled out a Parent Response sheet, which asked them to respond to several questions designed to give both the children and me feedback about the work in the portfolio. I also designed a teaching letter for the parents, inviting their participation and asking them to be constructive in their responses: "It is a place where you can give positive feedback, ask your child questions about his or her writing, as well as give suggestions."

As with the reader response letters, the parent responses to portfolios provided an ideal way for students to share with their parents the kinds of classroom practices I use. Rather than merely telling them about the kind of literacy experiences students had in my class, the portfolios gave parents evidence to see how students were improving in their writing skills.

Students received helpful responses from their parents, particularly in terms of their improvement: "Better vocabulary," one parent wrote. "Expressing himself more clearly." According to another, "I have seen a definite improvement in Jennie's writing style. Her scenarios are enjoyable to read (not boring) and the spelling and punctuation is really improving. Her writing is at a more mature level."

When parents ask questions on the response form, it gives me the opportunity to contact them individually to address their concerns. Sometimes questions are addressed to the student regarding his or her writing, and other times parents use this as a time to address their specific concerns to me. Through the portfolio responses, I have been able to continue conversations with parents about how specific instruction works, or even how they can provide greater help at home.

My goal with parent outreach is to increase parent involvement in student learning. In a state where standardized tests drive real estate markets, it is increasingly difficult to continue to balance what I believe my students need in the classroom with mounting pressure from the school community "to raise scores." While I am passionate about continuing best practice instruction based on current research, I cannot ignore the expectations and needs of my parent community. Quite often, we fall short in education by not extending what we know about how our students learn and what they need into the community. As I develop as a teacher each year, my goal is to increase the blend of classroom learning with community involvement, beginning with the parents. If we are to gain support for what we do, we must begin there.

Seizing the Moment(s)

As teachers in the '90s, we are well aware that our ability to continue to teach in the ways we believe depends heavily on the understanding and good will of the communities surrounding us. Horror stories abound of places where teachers are no longer allowed to teach in certain ways, as mandated curricula turn into mandated practices, all too often based on outdated and rigid approaches to teaching. We've chosen to use that reality to push us to do something we know we should be doing anyway: educating the parents in our communities before the attacks start, helping them see what we are doing as sound educational practice based on research and experience. We aren't naive about this; we know that our proactive approach may not work in every situation, given the political nature of schooling and the strongly organized forces that are opposed to many of the practices we see as vital. But our own attempts to work with parents show us this: a proactive approach can make a big difference in helping parents recognize a different story about schooling, based on the positive experiences of their own children. And parents do talk about these experiences and their new understandings—at the soccer game or in the grocery line, often inadvertently spreading the word to other parents and other community members. Parents who understand what we are doing can become our strongest advocates in the community—and as teachers, we need to take advantage of the opportunity this affords us to have our stories heard in circles larger than our immediate classrooms.

Teachers *can* make a dent in the repetitive monologue about what's wrong with schools; by becoming proactive, we can help write the next chapter in the story of educational practices in our country. In our minds, it's no longer a choice; it's a matter of survival.

References

Chiles, N. (1998, June 7). ABCeething: Ebonics just might work out. *Ann Arbor News*, p. A15.

Cooney, C. B. (1991). *Face on the milk carton.* New York: Dell.

Duff, C. (1996, October 30). ABCeething: How whole language became a hot potato in and out of academia. *Wall Street Journal*, p. A1.

Lee, H. (1988). *To kill a mockingbird.* New York: Warner.

Stine, R. L. (1994). *Call waiting.* New York: Scholastic.

11 Transformative Learning through a Study Group

Elizabeth R. Saavedra

My journey in transformative learning began as a classroom teacher and eventually led me to the University of New Mexico as researcher and educational activist. Through the years, I have been working with groups of teachers at their school sites, learning a great deal about the process of teacher transformation through study groups. In this chapter I will be describing one of these, the Davis Teacher Study Group. But first, a bit about the beginnings of my own transformative journey.

A Bit of History

In the summer of 1980, I had just finished my fourth year as a classroom teacher, and had made a critical discovery. I found that I knew precious little of how children learn, and more specifically how they learn to read and write. I knew how to follow teachers' manuals and how to use textbooks and reading basals. I had assumed that the materials and activities I used in the classroom were based on sound ideas about learning and literacy processes, and therefore if I diligently used these materials I was sure to be an effective teacher. In other words, I had swallowed—hook, line, and sinker—the concept of "teacher-proof materials." And no wonder. In my undergraduate preservice teaching program and then in the District inservice workshops during my first four years of teaching, I had been presented with a transmission view of learning and a skills orientation toward literacy development—viewpoints I dutifully applied. But the more I worked and

Reprinted from Chapter 15 of *Making Justice Our Project,* edited by Carole Edelsky.

applied what I had been taught to do, the more I realized that my students, who were linguistically, ethnically, and socioeconomically diverse, were barely progressing in their learning and literacy development. Frustrated with the present and disillusioned with the future (i.e., with my own potential as a teacher), I came to a critical insight: Studying was going to help. I simply had to learn more about learning and literacy development. Little did I know that studying (goal-driven questioning, serious investigating, and critiquing) and study groups were going to become such constants in my professional life.

That summer I took a class entitled "The Reading Process," taught by Claudia Dybdahl, a visiting professor who had been a student of Ken and Yetta Goodman. In this class I began to examine my own history as a learner, a reader, and a writer and the schooling I had experienced as a working class Chicana. In that class it started to become clear: Certain educational opportunities had been kept out of my reach. Not just mine, but minorities' in general. Through expectations, pedagogical methods, and content, we had been denied a rigorous education. Eventually, I made the connection between opportunities denied to me as a student and opportunities I was offering (or withholding) as a teacher. I also began to question how, within a female-dominated profession, teachers are situated in a bureaucratical and paternalistic hierarchy and how they/we live a general tradition of disempowerment.

When I returned to school in the fall, I began a new position as a Chapter 1 reading teacher. I was eager to try out my new views. However, I was met with opposition by my peers, students, and parents; others were not charmed by the changes I had made. Still, I kept on studying, talking with others, and reformulating my goals, choosing as my ultimate goal working to eradicate social inequity and injustice, and helping to create an educational system that transforms, rather than reproduces and perpetuates social injustice. The loftiness of that goal felt right for me then; it inspired me. It still does.

The following year, I pulled together the first of what became a series of weekly study groups to explore whole language theory and, with my peers, to pursue some of the questions that had transformed my own thinking and sense of myself as a teacher. I did not presume to be the expert, capable of teaching my peers; instead, we met because we were unable to find experts or even support from the district to learn about whole language. What the district provided were one-shot workshops. What we hungered for was an opportunity for dialogue, reflection, support, and continuity so that we could learn about the things we were interested in and what we then felt was crucial to our own working conditions—namely, whole language.

The Davis Teacher Study Group

Ten years later, as a doctoral student at the University of Arizona, I began a teachers' study group at Davis Bilingual Learning Center in the Tucson Unified School District. For the first time, I was not only participating in a teacher study group; I was studying study groups. I was interested in transformative development—i.e., changes in basic beliefs to be brought about by pursuing one's own questions while maintaining an awareness of power relationships. Our first meeting began with a discussion of the teachers' major concerns—teaching language-minority students and how to effectively facilitate their learning. Throughout the study, two layers wove through our exploration—questions chosen by individual participants and those chosen by the collective group. As the teachers engaged in critical inquiry concerning these questions, my own questions dealt with teachers' emancipatory learning and the transformation process itself. Both of these simultaneous inquiries included an analysis of the internal and external effects of power.

At the heart of the Davis Teacher Study Group was an agenda for emancipatory learning; i.e., for making sure that the major activity was critical reflection and self-reflection for the purpose of facilitating transformations. We were trying, through self-conscious and informed critique, to free ourselves "from forces that limit our options and our control over our lives, forces that have been taken for granted or seen as beyond our control (Cranston, 1994, p. 16)."

As is common for teacher study groups, the Davis study group met weekly with a designated facilitator (a role that alternated among members), for an agreed amount of time (one and a half hours, in our case). Both outside that time and within it, we read, wrote, critiqued, reflected, dialogued, and came to new conclusions. Just as important, we created together a community for our mutual support as learners, one that could (and did) lead to significant personal and professional change.

During the two and a half years we were together, our studies went through cycles. We would begin by establishing a topic and a direction. Then, after lengthy discussion of interests and needs and how these related to the topic, we would discuss various issues and questions we had about the topic. From these questions, the entire group would decide on one or two as focal questions for the group. Additionally, each participant chose questions for individual study. Usually, we spent two or three sessions generating and negotiating topic and question choices.

Next, the Davis Teacher Study Group would determine individual and group goals and plan the directions, activities, and strategies of the investigation. We planned what articles and books we would read, by when, and by whom; what kinds of activities we would undertake (reflective journals, demonstrations, classroom observations, data collection such as students' reading or writing samples); and who we would call upon as expert consultants (often these were our own members), over what length of time. It often took a couple of sessions to work out these plans.

As we met to plan and subsequently to talk about the work we had agreed to do (the reading, classroom observations, journal writing, etc.), we worked at developing collaborative, cooperative, respectful, and nurturing interactions. We were determined not to replicate the social and power structures and ideological stances of the institutional status quo. We had established conditions and activities that helped us to avoid that replication (e.g., settings for dialogue, direct access to sources of knowledge, ownership of topics and processes, a safe space for dissonance and conflict, etc.) But the collaborative interactions were what supported us as we tried to integrate our classroom experience with our investigations and to learn at "deep" enough levels to effect transformations. On the one hand, the transformative conditions were constructed through study group interactions; on the other, they emerged from our growing professional and intellectual strength.

Though we shared our discoveries informally in each session, we also planned a more formal, deliberate presentation of what was learned in order to culminate the investigation. These formal presentations would address what was learned about the topic (including our beliefs about the topic); about students' learning and the implications for our teaching; and about ourselves as teachers, researchers, and educational activists. Each of these cycles (developing questions, planning activities for investigating the questions, presenting our learning) enhanced our professionalism and competence. And each led us toward new directions and helped us to refine new questions.

Facilitating the Process of Emancipatory Learning and Transformations: Some Conditions

As a result of studying (and participating in) the study group at Davis, I have had to rethink my work as a teacher educator—what I know and what I do—vis à vis both my students and my colleagues.

The Need for Dedicated Space

I now understand more about the need to create a specific space for collaborative, transformative learning. It is always difficult to meet with peers during the regular teaching day. Without specific space in our week being set aside for the study group, we could not have experienced the same kind of learning. We needed those study-group sessions in order to push the edges of what we knew and what we experienced. We needed the regularity of the time and at least that amount of uninterrupted time to sustain a problem-posing stance, to keep focused on the topic we had chosen and the quality of our interactions. There was always the lure of letting immediate business and what was occurring in our day-to-day lives intrude into our study group sessions. We had to challenge ourselves about how we spent our time together. That we were able to keep to our intention during the space/time we had set aside can be seen in the coherence of the topics and activities we engaged in during the two and a half years of the study group (see Figure 1).

Being able to work seriously on these topics would not have been possible without the time we had carved out and the space we had created by temporarily moving aside the demands of our daily lives in school.

Critical Questioning

I am now even more convinced of the importance of the inquiry process in transformative learning. That inquiry process was central to our personal and professional changes as well as the changes in how we worked as a group. It enabled us to explore, shift, change, and develop. It pushed us to ask questions of importance to us. It let us venture far beyond the typical learning of methodology and practice that we were accustomed to. It helped us to learn about the content we teach, the contexts in which we teach, and the reasoning and beliefs which ground both the content and contexts we were responsible for. It also helped us to learn about ourselves and each other, about the experiences that have shaped our thinking and actions, about the knowledge and expertise we have, and the ways our interactions shape our learning and teaching.

More than that, through inquiry, we grew into a collaborative and reflective collective. Learning how to learn together and to work together was a major transformation. It did not happen quickly, smoothly, or easily. We experienced dissonance and frustration as we struggled to understand what we were learning and sharing with each other. We tended to want to find ideal solutions, to try to resolve hard issues and lay them to rest once and for all. It took considerable work before we achieved mutual trust and before we were able to welcome ambiguities. But as we persisted in the inquiry process to which we had committed ourselves, we began to experience some profound and exhilarating changes. The examples that follow concern only two teachers, Ellen and Maria. It is important to note, however, that transformative development also occurred for the other participants.

> In the first year, when the study group began, Ellen (and the other teachers) came to the study group expecting to be handed ideas, knowledge, and direction. Over time, Ellen realized that she must construct and shape her own learning—in her classroom and in the study group. In her written reflection on students becoming writers in both Spanish and English, she noted:
>
> We started out in study group examining the process children go through in developing the ability to write for various purposes. Elizabeth began bringing us, over the next few months, articles about both the writing process and the teaching of writing . . . we commenced talking, we did discuss, and discuss, but that discussion lit a fire; it served as a catalyst for me, in that it inspired me with new knowledge, both theoretical and practical, that I was able to translate into action. I set out to try these ideas in my own classroom, to try to replicate the successes I read about, and finding that some worked better than others (of course), for a variety of reasons—which reasons I was encouraged to identify, to reflect on, to use as a basis for adaptation of classroom events to this particular group of students and to my own personal style of teaching.

At about the time of this writing, Ellen began to deliberately take a more active role in facilitating the activity of the group. It was through the inquiry process that she became conscious of her beliefs about learning. When she realized that she saw learning as a passive process, she began to make changes in how she approached her own learning and in how she facilitated her students' learning. Later, she broadened her focus to include the content (the "what" of her learning and teaching); the underlying ideological and theoretical premises of that content; the structure, goals, and methods within the institution of schooling and their effects on teachers and students (especially minority learners); and her theories, beliefs, and goals concerning all of the above.

Our inquiry process was not one of questioning for questioning's sake. We questioned with a critical eye toward systems of power, and we

Davis Study Group Themes

Issues/questions about biliteracy; Davis goals/objectives

Collecting unassisted student writing samples in Spanish

Transforming deficit myths (Flores, et al.)

Involving parents of students learning Spanish as L2

Analysis of students' bilingual reading/writing; development of appropriate evaluations for Davis students

Teacher demonstration v. teacher intervention

Writing program components

Management of writing workshop

Getting kids to edit

Sharing student writing

Influence of reading on writing

Theme cycles introduced

Students as researchers

Writing process: from multiple drafts to publication

Children helping children

Designing instructional strategies that really address the objective

Writing conferences

Groupings in the classroom

Writing to learn

Tracking students' writing progress while at Davis

E. Saavedra works with small group of students

Daily writing time

Process writing

Cumulative writing folders

Generativeness in writing

Importance of demonstration by a more knowledgeable person

Introducing different types of writing

Using literature to help students develop their writing

Theme cycles introduced; process discussed

Communicating with other teachers (other grade levels)

Revisiting students' work: marking for reference to peer comments

continued on next page

Figure 1. Topics and Activities Engaged in During the Study-Group Period.

Figure 1 *continued*

Planning for next year:
   biliteracy development (different disciplines)
   portfolios/assessment
   faculty-meeting study groups once a month
   facilitating development of writing in both languages
   developing ourselves as writers/teachers with literature study
   student research (documenting with audio/video)

Brainstormed study-group topics (integrating curriculum, biliteracy development, writing process/developing children's writing, literature studies,
   developing reading and writing in the content areas)

Using the study-group experience for personal development

Elizabeth as a resource in the classroom

Portfolios

Writing/reading samples from bilingual students

Miscue analysis (choose a child; set up analysis schedule; review reading
   selections)

Research skills; check out library for teachers

Teacher's role in theme cycle studies

Getting to the heart of the matter: a search for origins (Steven Levy)

Practicing the first step of the theme cycle (brainstorm/web)

Teaching kids to do research: what is research?

Practicing miscue analysis: Luis M [student] (silent reading/retelling)

Learning through experiencing the theme cycle process in study group

Asking students to help define research by describing what they do when
   they want to find out about something

questioned in collaboration; i.e., we had a conceptual frame combined with
an interactional context that pushed us to discover, learn, and transform. We
recognized that most of our professional learning had occurred through staff
development activities which had provided little more than new ideas for
current practice. Almost never did staff development activities lead to
substantial changes in our knowledge and beliefs.

   Our study group provided a very different result. For instance, during one
of the study group sessions, when Ellen was relating that her daughter had

been tested on cultural knowledge as defined by E. D. Hirsch, she began to realize that what is to be taught and therefore what knowledge is privileged are "handed down" to teachers from the powers that be. "Obviously," she said, "there's been a lot of handing down for a lot of years, and here we are in the middle of the system." Ellen was changing her beliefs and ideologies about learning and teaching, but she was aware that the ideologies that govern the system stayed the same. She went on to talk about this tension as it would emerge in the community: "I'm wondering how this [the changes she was making] is all going to come out, and how it's going to be accepted by parents." She also pointed out that she wanted to talk with the principal about the paradox of administrators supporting her for her innovative teaching but also pressuring her to get high test results by focusing on specific skills. Finally, she juxtaposed her work in helping children develop into critically conscious learners with what she called "putting our print on them," preparing them to be well-trained vessels of standard knowledge. Through inquiry with the study group, Ellen became more conscious of the conflicting voices of the different positions she needed to reconcile in order to teach according to her new beliefs. She came to see more clearly that as a subordinate within a hierarchical system, she had to consider the vision, expectations, and goals of her supervisor and also of the parent community in trying to negotiate change. Indeed, a major consistent thread throughout our study group sessions was not only to reconcile the space between our ideological beliefs and our practice, but also to figure out how to navigate the space between what was best for the students and ourselves and the requirements and mandates of the institution.

Ellen was not the only one who shifted paradigms, found herself faced with new dilemmas, but faced them knowing she had come to them through traveling a considerable professional and personal distance. Maria, another participant, talked about her own shifts. She remembered how she had taken her plans and agendas and imposed them on her students, but then through her own critical inquiry realized that students had "their own minds" and experiences that they could draw from, their own abilities and knowledge that could be extended through an inquiry process. This was an important statement for Maria. Until that time, she had held back, abstaining from making definite statements about her own beliefs. In a subsequent meeting, she began to talk about how, in previous times, when she heard teachers talking negatively about students and their learning abilities, she would quietly listen. Now, however, "I can no longer sit in silence—when I hear these teachers talking about their students' shortcomings, I have to speak up.

I have to ask them about their teaching and how they think about the way students learn. I can't keep quiet anymore. I won't be quiet anymore."

Acting on What We Had Learned

From the beginning of the Davis Teacher Study Group, I had understood, to some extent, the history and experiences that get teachers to devalue their own knowledge. Participating in the study group showed me how important it is for teachers who are devoting themselves to critical inquiry—inquiry that is likely to contradict accepted knowledge in the system—to learn to value their learning and to help others to see it as legitimate. Our study group's new knowledge resulted from reflection and empirical investigation, and we had to learn to trust it. And we did—by acting on it in our classrooms and by sharing it. Acting on it in our teaching led us back into further inquiry that deepened our understanding and our confidence in what we knew. Sharing (indeed, building) our new knowledge with each other led us, eventually, to want to tell others about what we were experiencing and discovering. Toward the end of the second year of the Davis study group, we returned to questions that we had raised at the very beginning, questions about teaching linguistic-minority students in ways that would draw on their strengths and knowledge and extend their intellectual abilities.

As we began to reconsider these questions in light of what we had come to know and understand, we felt compelled to encourage the other teachers at Davis to deal with these issues. Perhaps, if the other teachers couldn't come to the study group, the study group could go to the other teachers. The study group teachers approached the principal, who consented enthusiastically, and plans were made to conduct the first schoolwide study group. I asked the teachers why they felt so strongly about taking an action such as this. Maria said,

> I am learning a lot. I have changed my thinking. I am aware of how much we affect children, how our teaching affects them. The way we think about and talk about children has an effect. I can't just sit and watch this school keep on doing the things I have discovered are not good for children. I have to do something. Before, I wouldn't have. But now I have to.

Ellen added,

> We have goals concerning biliteracy, and our practice is not achiev-ing those goals with our students, and from the research that I have

> read and from our discussions, and from maybe smaller pieces of
> . . . what other people have done in other places, I BELIEVE that we
> can make this goal happen, that we can work toward biliteracy. . . .
> There is a way. I really believe this. It's not an unfounded belief,
> entirely on faith. In reading about what other people have done, I've
> said, "Yeah, this is what we could do." We could. It's going to take
> some sacrifice; it is going to take a lot of learning and change. But
> we will do it."

In that first meeting with the staff, the discussion was lively and engaging.
The focus was on ways to determine schoolwide development of
bilingualism and biliteracy, and on how to examine the social and political
learning contexts for linguistic-minority students. The core participants had
found that their peers supported their growth and ideas. The entire staff felt
that these issues were important to them as well and decided at the end of
that first meeting to begin a biweekly study group composed of the entire
staff.

Conclusion

The Davis Teacher Study Group was based on a major premise: If teachers
are to transform learning contexts for their students, then the learning
contexts for teachers must be transformed. This premise is, in turn, based on
the assumption that teachers need to work together in order to develop
knowledge and practice that will affirm themselves and their students. The
Davis study group provided a radically different professional culture for the
participants. Not only did it offer a space for participants to determine the
direction of their own personal and professional development, and not only
did it provide a context for creating a collaborative, collegial learning
community, it also opened up a critical space. It gave us all opportunities to
confront our own situatedness, as male or female, and as members of
diverse racial, ethnic, cultural, and economic groups. It helped us to use a
framework of relations of power to analyze (not just to complain about or to
feel oppressed by) our own interactions and intersections with institutional
structures—all as part of a process of transforming ourselves and our schools.

Reference

Cranston, P. (1994). *Understanding and promoting transformative learning: A guide for educators of adults.* San Francisco, CA: Jossey-Bass.

12 Rights, Respect, and Responsibility: Toward a Theory of Action in Two Bilingual (Spanish/English) Classrooms[1]

Beth Yeager, Irene Pattenaude, María E. Fránquiz, and Louise B. Jennings

> To look is one thing.
> To see what you look at is another.
> To learn from what you understand is still something else.
> But to act on what you learn is all that really matters.
>
> The Talmud

Introduction

This quote from the Talmud provides a snapshot of life in two fifth-grade bilingual (Spanish/English) classes in Southern California. In these classes, tolerant and intolerant actions are central for understanding how to construct and be responsible members of communities. In order to construct opportunities for differentiating between tolerant and intolerant actions, the two teachers, Beth and Irene, share a common view in which teacher and students are members of a community of learners (Glover 1986). In practices of inquiry that echo the quotation from the Talmud, these learners learn to

Reprinted from Chapter 11 of *Teaching for a Tolerant World, Grades K–6*, edited by Judith P. Robertson.

see and make visible certain phenomena, to understand and learn from what is made visible, and to take action individually and collectively on what is learned. How these practices affect studentsí learning is reflected in a student essay:

> In the beginning of the year we discussed responsibility. We all signed a piece of paper that said what our responsibilities were. Some of the things were respect for each other and to listen to each other. Most of us have tried really hard to follow what we signed. Some of the most common words in the community of Room 18 were why?, to observe, to be historians, to look for evidence, to think, to investigate, to interpret, and to make theories. Almost all of the time, whenever we do something, at least one of these words come up. . . .
>
> Our community also studied the subject of tolerance. Most of the time we talked about the Holocaust, but we also talked about tolerance and intolerance. We talked about a lot of things that were tolerant and about things that were not. Some of the things we talked about . . . were helping each other, sharing with each other, respecting each other, being nice to each other, being cooperative with each other, working together, listening to each other, respecting all languages, all of us having rights, and finally, but not least being tolerant with each other. (Karen Ramirez 1996)[2]

Karen's essay captures many actions taken up in classroom life, including actions of tolerance (e.g., helping, sharing, respecting, listening to each other) and actions of inquiry (e.g., asking why, observing, looking for evidence, interpreting, making theories). In what follows we demonstrate how particular literate and inquiry processes provided opportunities for students living in these bilingual classes to make visible, understand, and take up responsible actions within multiple communities. Such actions across the academic year have potential for contributing to the growth of a generation "where learning is an outcome of inquiry, initiative, construction and responsible action toward justice and equity" (LeVesque and Prosser 1996, 332).

Our intention is to trace the journey Karen experienced in fifth grade that led to the text cited above. First, we describe the theoretical constructs that framed the fifth-grade journey. Then we introduce the ethnographic method and theory of action guiding the teacher's conceptualizations of inquiry[3] used for planning the tolerance focus that influenced student learning. Next, we describe the initiation of the journey during the first days of school when opportunities were made available for students to identify and integrate understandings about responsibility into a classroom "Bill of Rights." Then an illustrative case demonstrates how teacher and students take up particular literate and inquiry actions to examine a range of topics across content areas. Following the case is a description of how students bring literate and inquiry practices negotiated early in the year to a mid-year, literature-based, interdisciplinary study of the Holocaust.[4] This study focuses on expanding understandings of the constitutive nature of tolerant and intolerant actions for both individuals and groups. The study also makes visible how inquiry practices draw from intertextual[5] connections made available to classroom members throughout the year. These connections support students' growth in applying new understandings of tolerant actions to their own lives in the classroom, the school, and the neighborhood. Finally, we provide ideas for engaging students in writing for social action. The goal is to show how social action becomes a critical component of the tolerance focus. Examples of personal and community actions taken over the years by students living in and beyond these classrooms provide not a "one size fits all" prescription for bilingual writing process classrooms (Reyes 1992, 431), but snapshots of the journey undertaken by communities of inquirers.

Constructing Communities of Inquirers: A Historical Context

Many educators informed by a humanizing pedagogy (Bartolomé 1996) face constraints of time and a predefined curriculum. Yet, they struggle to find a place for teaching substantive issues such as tolerance and intolerance that offer potential for improving the quality of everyday life for all. Beth and Irene know this struggle well, and have worked and reworked the framework of their school year in order to integrate a focused study of tolerance within the ongoing literate and inquiry practices that support learning in their classrooms. Both initiated the tolerance focus in 1987. Six years ago, Irene joined the faculty at McKinley Elementary School and has worked with Beth in developing ways for linking inquiry processes and responsibility. They encouraged reflection from their students regarding individual and group understanding of tolerant and intolerant actions.

This particular school is a community school recognized by the district for redesigning the curriculum to fit the special linguistic needs of the majority of the school population. The ethic/racial designations for the school are 85 percent Latina/Latino, 11 percent White, 2 percent African American, 1.5 percent Native American, and 0.2 percent Pacific Islander (Santa Barbara School District 1995). Of the 520 students attending grades K–5, 63 percent are native speakers of Spanish predominantly representing immigrant and American-born Mexican families. By the fifth grade many students demonstrate some degree of competence in Spanish and in English even if bilingual fluency is not yet stable (Durán 1994).

Louise and María collected data in Irene and Beth's fifth-grade classrooms for three years. The data is a part of a series of linked ethnographic studies in K–12 classrooms conducted by the Santa Barbara Classroom Discourse Group, a collaboration of teacher-researchers and university researchers. The data is comprised of participant observations, videotapes, transcriptions, field notes, artifacts (e.g., student written work, student art work, family stories, and parent letters), structuration maps, slides, photos, and formal and informal interviews with the teacher and with small groups of students.[6] For this essay, the teacher-researcher team worked collaboratively to make visible the social construction of literacy (Cook-Gumperz 1986) through actions (literate, inquiry, and social) molded and taken up in Irene and Beth's fifth-grade classrooms that promote the ethical dimensions of learning.

During the six years in which Beth and Irene have collaborated, other researchers from the Santa Barbara Classroom Discourse Group have participated in the endeavor. This group uses the tools of the ethnographer (e.g., video camera and field notebook) to study how members construct classroom culture (Collins and Green 1992). The ethnographic method involves studying how members' actions and interactions shape and are shaped by particular classroom practices (Bloome and Bailey 1992), as well as by the language of the classroom (Lin 1993). The highly interactive methodology involves teacher-researchers, students, and university researchers in the collection, analysis, interpretation, presentation, and publication of classroom ethnographies. Fifth-grade students in the "Tower" community (Beth's classroom in the tower of the school) and in Room 18 (Irene's classroom) were able to take up the role of student ethnographers. Teachers expanded students' learning by teaching them to differentiate between notetaking (observing) and note-making (interpreting) in the study of their own classroom communities. These field methods helped members of the two bilingual classrooms to better understand how communities of inquirers are constructed from responsible actions (individual and collective) recorded across time.

Throughout their years of collaboration, Beth and Irene have worked to make visible and to articulate—for themselves, their students, and their studentsí families—the premises that underlie their vision for life in classrooms, a vision which bridges the gap between theory and practice.

Following are the premises that underlie their pedagogical decisions for fifth grade:

- Classrooms are cultures (Collins and Green 1992).
- Communities of learners are co-constructed by members (Santa Barbara Classroom Discourse Group 1992a,b).
- As learners, students with the teacher and other adults co-construct ways of being students, including ways of being that are culturally responsible (Ladson-Billings 1995).
- The native languages of students are resources for co-constructing a common language of the classroom for learning (Fránquiz 1995; Lin 1993).
- Children need to be privy to the hidden curriculum (Aronowitz and Giroux 1985; Giroux and Purpel, 1983) as well as to their own knowledge-making processes and practices. "They should become the keepers of the windows of their souls," says Beth Yeager.
- Inquiry is a sound basis for instruction across the curriculum.
- Content is linked to a particular context (Rutherford and Ahlgren 1990) rather than to the performance of techniques; there is a discipline-based reflective way of knowing (Saxe 1988).
- These premises identify key principles, practices, and participatory actions (linguistic, academic, social) fundamental to learning in these fifth-grade classroom communities.

Rights, Respect, and Responsibility as a Foundation for the Academic Year

Now we describe how the fifth-grade journey initiated during the first days of school integrates the aforementioned premises. We show how particular opportunities assisted students in identifying and demonstrating their understandings about individual and collective rights, respect, and responsibility within a particular classroom community. If tolerance means taking responsibility to respect the rights of other community members, then to begin to understand and enact tolerance, students need multiple opportunities for understanding how responsibility relates to respect and rights. Opportunities for making these connections have become a year-long process in Beth and Irene's fifth-grade bilingual classrooms. The teachers take an explicit approach by helping students make visible what they think community and the 3R's (rights, respect, and responsibility) look and sound like. Students begin by explaining their understandings of the interrelatedness of these concepts. Then they take up opportunities for demonstrating responsible actions in order to improve the quality of life of the communities in which they are involved (i.e., classroom, school, and neighborhood).

Prior research shows that the first days of school are instrumental in shaping patterns of classroom life and defining what it means to be a student in this class in this year (Fernie, Davies, Kantor, and McMurry 1993; Fránquiz 1995; Jennings 1996; Lin 1993; Santa Barbara Classroom Discourse Group 1992a). Accordingly, we identify the particular social actions, inquiry actions, and literate actions that supported classroom members as they began their journey of learning and enacting tolerance.

In order to ground themselves in responsible actions, students and teachers begin on the first day of school to inquire into the range of meanings for community. First, students write their thoughts regarding the meaning of community. Students thus have an opportunity to reflect from prior experience before coming up with a shared classroom concept. After the first entry, students share their writing with others in a whole-class discussion, revising or adding to their own ideas. Thus, they learn to consider othersí points of view. The list of shared ideas generated by classroom members is long and inclusive. It reflects family, school, neighborhood, and global understandings of what constitutes community. One list included "people, barrio (neighborhood), *familias* (families), together, same interests, helping each other, caring." What becomes evident is that once students have generated a "classroom" sense of what community means to them as individuals, they begin to see the cornerstone for understanding the responsibilities they each have for supporting the classroom community.

Next, students engage in a process to generate definitions of rights, respect, and responsibility. We feel it is important that students know, from the beginning, that the 3R's will be the foundation for all work accomplished together throughout the year. Additionally, the teachers create conditions for students to understand that each "R" cannot stand alone. We want students to understand that for every right there is a responsibility and that both are grounded in a basic notion of respect. In other words, the 3 R's are interdependent.

Students also write their definition of responsibility. These early definitions indicate that, at the beginning of the school year, they generally have an underdeveloped understanding of responsibility. Most students initially write

that classroom responsibilities include "doing homework" and "listening to the teacher." These comments do not show students seeing themselves as having a responsibility to the classroom community. Instead, students see themselves as having an individual sense of what they need to do to be successful in the classroom. This finding across the years is surprising because the majority of students entering fifth grade at this school share a history of working with others in cooperative groups, relying on each other for their learning, and using conflict-resolution strategies to resolve problems.[7] It suggests that it is important to provide multiple opportunities to make explicit connections between these strategies and the concept of responsibility.

A similar process entails having students write personal definitions for each of the 3 R's. Group sharing then prompts students to revise personal definitions as influenced by others' points of view. Next, students interview parents for their understandings of the words *rights* (*derechos*), *respect* (*respeto*), and *responsibility* (*responsabilidad*). In this way, the journey toward a shared and comprehensive understanding of the 3R's becomes an inquiry process which involves parents.

After writing, sharing, discussing, and revising their understandings of rights, respect, and responsibility, students engage in a lengthy process of small-group work and whole-class negotiation in order to develop a classroom Bill of Rights and Responsibilities, whose format aligns with the goals of the fifth-grade United States history curriculum. Large chart paper records this class-constructed Bill in both Spanish and English. All members of the classroom community, children and adults, sign the Bill before it is hung on the classroom wall. Students and parents sign individual copies, one of which is kept at home, the other at school. These rights and responsibilities become constant reference points throughout the year, material for discussion and reminders of the ways members of classroom communities expect to live and work together. The English version of the Tower's Bill of Rights in 1995–96 stated:

1. We have the right to feel safe in our classroom. We have the responsibility to walk and behave in a safe way without hurting anyone.

2. We have the right to study and to learn. We have the responsibility to let others study without bothering anyone.

3. We have the right to be respected and to feel that we are equal in our class. We have the responsibility to help each other and to respect each other, without saying bad words and without laughing at each other.

4. We have the right to be listened to by others. We have the responsibility to listen when others are speaking.

5. We have the right to have our own things and have the class respect our things. We have the responsibility to take care of the property of all.

As part of the construction of their understanding of responsibility, students also draw themselves demonstrating respect and taking action in the larger school setting. During the first week of school, then, two important events occur: the construction of a shared definition and the formation of a classroom text, the Bill of Rights and Responsibilities. Through these events, students not only examine personal definitions of what constitutes community, rights, respect, and responsibility, but they identify actions needed to carry them out. Students also experience the others' points of view, including their respective families, as they negotiate and construct a working, viable set of guidelines from which their classroom community can evolve. Thus, the establishment of a Bill of Rights and Responsibilities can be seen as the first "action" step in the construction of individual and collective responsibility.

The processes of the first week also introduce students to particular actions of inquiry (observing, writing, interviewing, interpreting) that will support learning throughout all content areas. We believe that the action of constructing a common textual reference for classroom rights and responsibilities and the concomitant actions of inquiry required to produce an inclusive text are central to initiating particular ways of action that serve as a resource for present and future classroom communities.

Inquiry as Action

We ask students not only to take up the social actions they have defined in their Bill of Rights and Responsibilities, but also to understand and enact processes of inquiry that cross disciplines. The theory of action we propose examines the interrelatedness between social actions (3R's), actions of inquiry (e.g., observing, interviewing, interpreting from evidence), and literate actions (e.g., constructing and reconstructing texts). We now illustrate how a set of inquiry actions (observing, describing, interpreting, reflecting from multiple points of view), and a set of literate actions (notetaking and note-making) accomplish the fifth-grade curriculum.

As seen previously, from the first day of school we teach observation defined as an ordinary practice. Besides observing overlap in each others' definitions of both community and the 3R's, during the first week of school students observe watermelons in order to solve a problem as mathematicians (for an analysis of this event, see Brilliant-Mills 1993). They also observe themselves as artists for painting self portraits. Thus, the action of observation becomes a common practice that crosses content areas, although the observational actions may look and feel different depending on the purpose for the observation—a purpose most often grounded in the actions particular to each discipline. Additionally, observation as a tool aids in the development of students' understanding of point of view, evidence, and interpretation. Understanding how evidence can be interpreted from different points of view becomes integral to Beth and Irene's goals for the development and understanding of empathy and tolerance and the construction of responsibility. Students in their classrooms learn to base their interpretations in evidence. This practice encourages critical thinking as students consider evidence, not just emotional reactions, to support their own point of view while, at the same time, considering others' perspectives.

The inquiry actions of observing, interpreting from evidence, and considering point of view occur over the year in and through a variety of literate actions. One of the literate actions used frequently is notetaking/notemaking, often called "double-entry journals" when used for other purposes. In this case, the left side is for notetaking—for recording what is observable. The right side, the notemaking side, is for interpretation of what has been observed and described. Students begin to understand observation and the gathering of data for different purposes across the disciplines early in the school year. They are introduced to notetaking as one of the actions of writers through "saturation observations" in a variety of school and community settings. The researchers then introduce the students to notetaking as an action of ethnographers. In this activity, the researchers encourage students to notice where they are physically positioned in relation to others, and to differentiate between their own descriptions and those of their peers. Students engage in these inquiry and literate actions in all of the disciplines at this time of the year in order to understand how these actions may differ depending on purpose and point of view.

It is critical for students to understand how evidence is interpreted from different points of view and for different purposes. It is at this point that teachers make explicit to students the relationship between notemaking and interpretation. Students observe and interpret a picture from the story of the

"Three Little Pigs" from a particular character's point of view (e.g., that of the wolf, of the stick salesman) in the notetaking/notemaking format. Students then write or draw the history of this event using evidence from the witness whose perspective they took in the observation activity. They come to understand the actions of historians as well as the limitations of having only one point of view before drawing conclusions. In reflecting on the project, Jared shows his understanding of the actions of historians, the interpretation of data, and point of view:

> I learned that when you look at different points of view, they're all very different than each other. I think historians look at data the way itís shown and they interpret the data how they think it is. I also learned that there are different points of view even when youíre looking at the same thing.

Students such as Jared continue to use the action of notetaking/ notemaking as an inquiry tool for understanding ethnography (see Yeager, Floriani, and Green 1998), as well as in curricular areas such as literature and social science. Thus, notetaking/notemaking are literate actions which are made available for different purposes across the year. By mid-year, these literate actions and actions of inquiry become ordinary practices to classroom members. After winter break, this foundation of social actions (the 3 R's), literate actions (notetaking/notemaking), and inquiry actions (observing, describing, interpreting) are brought into a literature-based study of the constitutive nature of tolerance and intolerance.

The Tolerance Focus

The tolerance focus begins in January with a study of the Holocaust because it is an obvious example of atrocity in the twentieth century which continues to have an impact on our lives and decisions today. The tolerance focus is carefully crafted and always evolving. This transformational character is due to the ongoing dialogue among Irene, Beth, and their colleagues. It is also affected by current events, local and global. Unfortunately, there are always new events which provide "teachable moments" within this focus of study. The cycle of activity[8] is interdisciplinary and literature-based and includes nonfiction. The tolerance focus also involves viewing videos, drawing and writing literature responses, and visiting museum displays.

We now describe events across the cycle of activity, where students critically assess actions of tolerance and intolerance from multiple points of view using the inquiry actions that have become ordinary practices within the classroom. The students learn from characters, plot, and setting in literature as well as from past and present interpretations of historical texts. They then use this information to examine the actions of individuals and groups in local and global contexts.

The context of the focus on the Holocaust is set with three introductory events. First, students read a picture book allegory of the Holocaust called *The Terrible Things* by Eve Bunting (1980). Teachers do not disclose in advance the historical context for the book, which shows the removal of specific groups by another strong, though invisible, group force. The setting is a forest and the characters are forest animals. The story allows students to speculate as to what the "terrible things" are that take away specific groups of animals from the forest and to think about why other groups of animals do not reach out to help. After listening to the story, students respond through pencil drawings that reflect their feelings and interpretations of the story. They then interpret their thoughts, questions, and concerns through a quickwrite format. The ensuing class discussion is grounded in what was happening in the allegory so that everyone has an opportunity to voice concerns about how the animals treated each other and to offer alternative endings or solutions to the problems the animals faced. In this way, students can consider a range of perspectives for comprehending the actions of characters in the story. This text becomes a referential point throughout the tolerance focus cycle of activity and after. Thus, inquiry actions (observing and interpreting events in the story) accomplished through literate actions (drawing and writing responses in literature log) produce opportunities for students' refinement of what constitutes responsible social actions (providing concrete alternatives for dealing with the intolerant actions of the terrible things).

The second literate event in the tolerance focus is the reading and viewing of a photo essay representing Jewish children of the Holocaust, titled *The Children We Remember* (Abells 1983). Again, after a class reading of this text, students draw representations of their thoughts and feelings with black markers. Across the years students have drawn people crying, while others have expressed their feelings of anger through crossed out swastikas and Nazi soldiers being shot in retaliation. These visceral responses become important throughout the cycle of activity because we are constantly looking for ways to "touch" students and make the kind of inant actions addressed in texts real to them. This challenge is difficult in the face of the desensitization to pain and violence that is so prevalent among media references available to children today.

Next, students engage in actions of inquiry by interviewing family members for information about World War II and recording their points of view. After sharing and discussing the various points of view reflected in the family interviews, the students have an opportunity to learn about the broader historical context of the war by listening to a teacher or guest "lecture." Students take notes using the same literate action of notetaking/notemaking that has been used across the curriculum since the beginning of the school year. As a homework assignment, students read over the notetaking side of their "lecture" itself. At this point, students' interpretations often include dismay at how a person like Adolf Hitler could gain so much power over others. Many students also say they cannot understand how so many people could go along with Hitler and commit such intolerant acts against other groups of human beings. They also begin to see through this lecture that some people banded together to take responsible actions against intolerant acts (i.e., resistance movements, people who hid Jews, Catholics, Gypsies, and others).

In the following excerpt, Sergio, a student making the transition from Spanish reading and writing to English, describes (in the notemaking list) what he heard in the lecture. He writes in a shorthand, "listing" style that was recommended for taking lecture notes. In the notemaking example, Sergio draws on the literate and inquiry actions he has been developing during the first half of the year to interpret and draw conclusions from the information given. Thus, he uses the literate action of notetaking and the inquiry action of interpreting from evidence in order to declare the type of social actions he would take if he had been there.

Notetaking

There aren't that many jobs they were worrying about WWII and the countrys that want to change how they live are Germany and Italy.

The Nazi party, Adolf Hitler had the master race.

Adolf Hitler wanted all races to be destroyed, except the Master race the German race.

Notemaking

I think Adolf Hitler was a powerful man but at the same time he was a tyrant. I don't think he could have tooken over the world. there would have been a lot of people fight. I I were [there] I would fought back. I wouldn't let him taker over the world.

Sergio (1995)

After working with the historical context, students share a second reading of *The Children We Remember* (Abells 1983). Since the students now have a broader understanding of social issues during World War II, they are able to demonstrate in their second quick-write a more profound understanding of why these events occurred. By this time students have also seen maps and tables of the locations of death camps and numbers of persons killed. They have also seen that some countries, such as Denmark, lost fewer Jews than other countries. Students begin to question why there is a difference.

Literature grounds the study of the Holocaust itself, although many other resources are used. In addition to the two picture books mentioned above, the central focus is a shared reading of a historical novel, *Number the Stars/¿Quién Cuenta las Estrellas?* (Lowry 1989a, 1989b). The novel is set in Denmark during World War II and relates one Danish family's efforts to help their Jewish neighbors escape to freedom in Sweden. Beth and Irene selected the text because it is appropriate for the ages and reading levels of fifth graders, is on the list of approved literature for California elementary schools, is available in Spanish and English, and has potential for expanding understandings of what the students have been talking about throughout the year (taking responsible social actions against actions of intolerance). During the shared reading of the novel, students also read excerpts from Anne Frank's *The Diary of a Young Girl* (1995), and *Zlata's Diary: A Child's Life in Sarajevo* (Filipovic 1994). Through the reading of personal narratives, students have an opportunity to compare past and present historical contexts and to increase understanding of the effects that actions of tolerance and intolerance can have on an individual child's life. This understanding can be further advanced when students have opportunities to make connections between excerpts from personal narratives and the novel they are studying in depth. Irene and Beth provide this opportunity by asking students to write diary entries from the four different main characters' points of view in *Number the Stars*. Through the juxtation of identities and through making entries in a diary, students try to imagine what it means to be walking in someone else's shoes.

The shared novel provides one perspective of the Holocaust, in essence a very positive one, in that people reach out to help others. The lecture that students received helps them begin to understand the competing political, economic, and philosophical circumstances that led to genocide. Students also view powerful videos, such as *Children Remember the Holocaust* (Gordon 1995), which does not have such a positive perspective. What touches many students in the video is the realization that they are viewing actual photographs and video footage of real people experiencing real cruelty and real intolerance. As mentioned earlier, the constant struggle for the teachers is making the past real and helping students believe that they can make a difference in addressing the intolerant actions which often are treated as normal, everyday, acceptable behavior in their lives.

Throughout the tolerance focus, students experience and respond to a wide variety of texts (lecture, literature, video, and picture books that extend their understanding of history as well as of current "ethnic cleansings"). Students also experience the personal stories of people around them, such as other teachers whose relatives were affected by intolerant actions of individuals, groups, and governments. One of the most significant events of the tolerance focus in 1995–96 was a visit from Judith Meisel, a Holocaust survivor, who brought the reality of her life into the students' lives. Thus, during the tolerance focus students are constantly asked to try to imagine being there, to reflect on what it feels like to be a victim of intolerance, to make intertextual connections between past and present actions of tolerance and intolerance by thinking in terms of "what if?" and "why?" In other words, there is a continuous focus on the implications of remaining silent and not taking action.

Significantly, the Holocaust is not taught in a vacuum, but is embedded in what has gone on before and what will come after the cycle of activity. The tolerance focus is grounded in practices of meaningful inquiry into the actions, interactions, and lack of intervention into the suffering of both real and fictionalized people. From the beginning of the academic year, students are provided with multiple opportunities for making meaningful connections within their own lives and for coming to understand their place within an ongoing and ever-changing history. As intertextual connections occur across the year, the students construct a referential system that helps them expand understanding of historical contexts, character actions, and mature responses to intolerance.

One location the teachers see for intertextual connections comes from the approved California social studies curriculum. Study of the Iroquois Confederacy is exemplary for teaching about nonviolent actions involved in the peacemaking process. For example, students explore the actions of the legendary Hiawatha and the Peacemaker. In this inquiry of actions toward peace, they make "peace belts" on which they superimpose the pine tree, the Iroquois symbol of peace, over conflicting points of view as experienced in their lives (two arguing parents, two gangs, two warring nations— whatever is important to them at the time). Throughout the study of American

Indians and other groups, students must make connections and investigate the actions of individuals living with conflict. Concurrently, students have opportunities to observe, describe, and interpret parallel actions of tolerance and intolerance toward individuals living during World War II (e.g., Holocaust victims or Japanese Americans in U.S. internment camps). In this way, intertextual connections are made available through the tolerance focus in the social studies curriculum.

Below is an excerpt from a student essay which demonstrates how he made intertextual links across the social science curriculum and tied these to inquiry practices that had become familiar within his classroom community:

> When we do our projects, like our newest one on the colonies, we don't just go too a book and write a report. We get information from a lot of different places and we use skills from other projects. . . . We always have to use evidence and we have to know the answer to the Tower's famous questions: So what? (What does it mean?), How do you know?, and Why? . . . All through our projects, we have to look at these points of view. When we did the colonies, we saw who was missing from some things, like Native Americans. Also when we share a book in class, we write letters and diaries from characters' points of view. When you're in the Tower, you have to look at different points of view. (Chris 1994)

Chris describes his classroom as one where students make meanings of a range of topics across disciplines through inquiry and literate actions and by considering different points of view. During the activity cycle focusing on tolerance, students brought practices of literate and inquiry actions into a study of the "whys" of acts of intolerance and genocide across time and in different settings. Students also examined and reflected upon responsible and tolerant responses. Thus, the nature of both intolerant and tolerant acts becomes more visible to students, who are able to make meaning of these acts through particular literate (notetaking/notemaking, making intertextual connections) and inquiry practices (observing, describing, interpreting from evidence, taking different "angles of vision"). Students, like Chris, then begin a process of acting upon these understandings through both individual and collective social action steps.

Up to this point, students have worked with some sights, sounds, words, and pictures that are evidence of humankind's capacity and potential for cruelty. At the same time, they have also uncovered individuals and movements that demonstrate human aptitude for strength, resistance, resilience, and care for others. Since some children begin to feel overwhelmed by all they have seen and heard, it becomes important to focus more explicitly on social actions for change. As we have demonstrated, in the beginning of the school year the fifth graders defined a particular set of social actions in terms of rights, respect, and responsibility within the classroom community. Toward the end of the tolerance cycle of activity, students broaden those understandings by addressing issues within their school, neighborhood, and world communities. Thus, students move into the action phase of the tolerance cycle by identifying particular social issues within the various communities that influence their lives.

Expanding the Meaning of the 3 R's: Responsibility

Students begin the process of focusing upon tolerant and intolerant actions through four events. First, they draw upon their daily lives to develop a list of tolerant actions (e.g., talking through conflicts, helping classmates) and intolerant actions (e.g., name calling, fighting), which they later prioritize and graph according to degree of positive or negative impact. This literate action of graphing results in an effective visual display that develops deeper understandings of responsibility.

The second event is a field trip to the Museum of Tolerance in Los Angeles, California.[9] The museum comprises several parts, two of the largest being the Holocaust Museum and the Tolance Center. The latter is an interactive center where visitors explore issues of stereotyping, prejudice, name calling, tolerance, and intolerance. Here, visitors can also view a brief but powerful movie on genocide. The museum visit is an overpowering experience that brings everything home. The key question asked in graphics throughout the museum is "Who is responsible?" We start asking that question ourselves early in the year at school, and it makes an impact on the children when they visit the museum. It becomes an important reference point.

Following this trip, students reflect on what they have seen and heard, personally and in terms of their own lives and community, as well as on what they have learned about tolerance and responsibility throughout the year. Their "tolerance essays" become a mechanism for moving students to an action focus, as demonstrated in this student essay:

> I think that it is all of our responsibility for what happened. The people who didn't speak up are also very responsible for what happened, because everything that people do, or what you do, in the past can affect what is happening today (right now) or in the future.

Irene and Beth seek the construction of responsibility alongside the construction of empathy. Oscarís essay reflects empathy while naming ways to deal with what has been learned (translated from Spanish):

> Here in the Museum, we have engraved for us the bad things we do and this is always going to remind us, what it is to suffer. We have to change. We have to do tolerant things. It's our responsibility to change with respect to other people, because if we don't change, we can commit the same mistake as the Nazis and some day we will have to remember. That's why we will change (Oscar 1996).

Students then move to the fourth event, constructing a new definition of responsibility. Classes brainstorm and negotiate actions which reflect actions of community and personal responsibility. In the 1996 class, they were defined as:

1. Speaking up   Decir algo—Hablar en público
2. Having respect   Tener respeto
3. Taking action   Hacer algo—Tomar acción
4. Walking the talk   Siguiendo con lo que dice
5. Walking in someone else's shoes   Caminar en los zapatos de otra persona

Whereas students' early perceptions of responsibility centered on individual actions to be successful in the classroom, this list reflects how students' understandings broadened to include responsibility to act in order to maintain a just, respectful community. The important challenge is living up to the expanded definition.

Through events, students begin to take up individual and collective actions. The first opportunity for action involves the construction of a wall/mural outside of the school office. The inspiration for constructing the wall in the main entrance of the school community comes from the Wall of Remembrance in the United States Holocaust Memorial Museum in Washington, D.C. The wall is made up of individual inscriptions, each one sending a message from one child (or adult) to other children and adults. The messages convey what the sender considers important to remember and what the sender desires for the world.

Another opportunity for action occurs when each child is asked to draw a picture showing himself or herself taking a responsible action within the context of everyday life (usually at school). This action must be something that the student believes is realistically possible. Each student makes a public affirmation of action beginning with a positive "I will" statement. In this way, students take up the literate action of drawing in order to make a public statement of commitment toward responsible social action.

Finally, the students begin a process that involves them in collectively taking responsible action within the local community, action that reflects their understanding of tolerance and intolerance. Through a brainstorming process that involves parent interviews, individual writing, and small and large group conversations, students begin to define their concerns about their neighborhood and local community. Collectively, the class prioritizes problems to address. Each year, the students take a different set of actions.

In 1994–95, the issues of neighborhood safety and the pressure to join gangs were discussed throughout the year. Since these issues were very much a part of their lives, the students brainstormed actions that could be taken to spread the message of tolerance, respect for differences, and nonviolence toward others in the community. Students took action by writing pen pal letters to a school located in a so-called "rival territory"—the East Side. These individual letters attempted to explain a point of view regarding tolerance and respect for difference that reflected understandings from the tolerance cycle of activity. Collectively, the students wrote an open letter in Spanish and English that was sent to local newspapers, public agencies, local middle schools, and high schools. The letter expressed their desire for nonviolence and peace between Eastsiders and Westsiders. For the students this was a risky undertaking, for they feared that older students, including their siblings, would perceive that they had somehow "sold out." Thus, this letter involved both actions of commitment and actions of perceived risk taking. A nice turn of events occurred when a teacher in a nearby district (another "rival" area) shared the letter in the newspaper with her fifth-grade students. These students wrote to McKinley's fifth graders, expressing their admiration of their public act and asking for advice and support. Their responses validated the actions taken personally and collectively by fifth-grade students at McKinley.

The following year, four fifth-grade classes participated in taking up community actions. Because students were unable to narrow down the number of actions they wanted to take, four action committees emerged, composed of children from each fifth-grade class. These representatives planned the following actions, in which all students participated: (1) an open letter to the public about the need for positive action that was published in three newspapers, two English and one Spanish, (2) a campaign through skits to educate younger McKinley students about tolerant and intolerant actions, (3) a neighborhood campaign to distribute literature against drunk driving, and (4) a neighborhood cleanup held on the opening day of a new community park. Many of these actions encouraged participation from the larger community: local high school students responded to the open letter, and twelve community members joined in the neighborhood cleanup. Although positive action in the larger community often goes unsung, these students had the opportunity to learn that the actions of responsible human beings in a community can make a difference. Furthermore, these experiences provided a foundation for students to analyze, reflect, and broaden understandings regarding the actions necessary to realize the 3 R's (rights, respect, and responsibility) in the many contexts which influence their lives.

The Journey Continues

The journey that we have represented shows how students make the 3 R's meaningful by taking up a set of particular actions: literate actions, inquiry actions, and social actions. This theory of action offers teachers an approach to teaching that is multidimensional (integrating social and academic actions) and multidisciplinary (integrating concepts across content areas). This framework for action allows teachers and students to expand the selected school curricula in order to fit the needs of the local classroom community that is interested in engaging in a critical literacy as a form of ethical address (Giroux 1993). As the year advances, members learn to use literate actions (e.g., notetaking and notemaking, writing and drawing responses to literature) to discover and problematize a wide range of disciplinary knowledge. As these literate and inquiry actions become familiar in the fifth-grade classroom, students are directed into real-world situations that have an impact on their lives.

It is this "situatedness" that provides the context for taking up individual and/or collective social action. This evolving process has been referred to as the development of a critical social consciousness (Freire 1970, 1978), because students name, reflect critically, and act on their world (Wink 1997). The process of constructing responsibility can be seen as analogous with a definition of critical pedagogy, one that "challenges teachers and students to empower themselves for social change, to advance democracy and equality as they advance their literacy and knowledge" (Shor 1993, 25).

This essay demonstrates how literate actions and inquiry actions can create conditions for establishing critical consciousness. It suggests that learning to take tolerant and responsible actions requires the ability to observe, describe, pose questions, analyze, and interpret. Above all, this transformative process involves students moving from writing insightful literate responses to taking responsible actions. Thus, the dialogue between members of the classroom community and the wider community in which members live infuses a humanizing pedagogy (Bartolomé 1996) where actions for social justice become possible. The transformative power of this type of pedagogy rests on an understanding that all students are treated as knowers and active participants in learning for improvement of self and the world in which all selves live (Shor 1992).

For teachers like Beth and Irene who consciously use historical incidences of tolerance, intolerance, and genocide to help students produce work that demonstrates depth of feeling and imaginative visions of a more just world, the struggle is an enduring journey. This living, dynamic, and evolving curriculum is constantly constructed and revised to help students learn what it means to be a responsible member of a global community. For students in these classrooms, the theory of action realized in fifth grade becomes a point of departure rather than a destination.

Acknowledgments

The tolerance focus has evolved over the years so that it includes all fifth grades at McKinley School. We wish to acknowledge and extend our appreciation to our colleague Phoebe Hirsch-Dubin for her contributions to the Tolerance Project as a member of the fifth-grade team. We also want to thank María Rey and Nancy Morris for sharing in this effort during their year as fifth-grade teachers. Special thanks go to Judith Green and Carol Dixon, and members of the Santa Barbara Classroom Discourse Group for ongoing support. Additionally, we are grateful to Jules Zimmerman, Bob Ream, and contributors from the wider community toward the UCSB Tolerance Project. Finally, we thank several granting agencies who provided financial support for the study: The California Writing Project and South Coast Writing Projects (SCWriP), The American Educational Research Association Minority Program, the Inter-University Program for Latino Research and the Social Science Research Council, the University of California Institute for Mexico and the United States, and the Graduate Research Mentorship Program at UCSB.

Notes

1. Authorship of this essay reflects the equal contribution of all named authors. Beth Yeager and Irene Pattenaude are fifth-grade teachers. María Fránquiz and Louise Jennings were researchers in Beth and Irene's classrooms respectively. All

four authors are members of the Santa Barbara Classroom Discourse Group, a group of teachers, administrators, doctoral students, and university faculty engaged in collaborative ethnographic studies of life in K–12 writing process classrooms. The authors are also fellows of the South Coast Writing Project and have presented from the data set represented in this essay at national conferences, including NCTE, AERA, and NABE.

2. Students whose voices have been included in this chapter assisted in writing this project into being. Permission has been obtained to use their real names as authors of their own work as cited in the chapter: Sergio Dueñas, Veronica Galvan, Jared Ingling, Oscar Morales, Chris Nordin, and Karen Ramirez.

3. Inquiry learning has been defined as an approach in which students are guided in their own learning in a stimulating environment that requires them to become examiners, questioning texts in and outside the classroom, and questioning the actions between each other as well as by themselves (see Farris 1997).

4. The authors acknowledge that there have been many holocausts in history which have resulted in the genocide of ethnic and indigenous groups. The capitalization of Holocaust in reference to the horrors inflicted during the Nazi regime indicates that the systematic extermination of European Jews and other groups during World War II was unique in the sense of incorporating methods of slaughter unseen in other genocides (i.e., the death camps). It does not indicate that any one group's victimization is qualitatively any more or less significant than another group's experience of inhumanity.

5. The construct of intertextuality has been discussed by Bloome and Egan-Robertson (1993) and Bloome and Bailey (1992) to mean that people propose intertextual links, and in interaction with each other they recognize, acknowledge, and assign social significance to these intertextual links. Over time, these intertextual processes establish particular ways of being a member of a classroom and contribute to establishing particular ways of engaging in literate action in the classroom (e.g., particular ways of problem solving, learning, and writing). These intertextual connections contribute to a referential system which is a resource for teacher and students across the year (Santa Barbara Classroom Discourse Group 1992b).

6. Informed consent from students, parents, teachers, and administrators was obtained for the three years of data represented in this essay.

7. The faculty members of this school have indicated that they value and use collaborative learning in a variety of ways. Additionally, the principal has arranged for conflict resolution to be induced in all classes. A peer mediation system has been implemented on the playground as well.

8. A cycle of activity (Green and Meyer 1991) is composed of all events that were constructed by members of the classroom as they sought to accomplish a particular aspect of the academic curriculum. In this case, the fifth-grade teachers and students modified activities planned to meet the State of California Framework in both language arts and social studies.

9. One of the early action steps students take during the year is to earn money for this trip through a public dinner. The purpose of this month-long mathematical investigation is to understand how to coordinate estimating, purchasing, and

organizing the dinner in order to make sufficient profit for classroom members to pay for transportation expenses to the Museum of Tolerance.

Works Cited

Abells, Chana B. 1983. *The Children We Remember*. New York: Greenwillow Books.

Aronwitz, Stanley, and Henry A. Giroux. 1985. *Education Under Seige: The Conservative, Liberal, and Radical Debate over Schooling*. South Hadley, MA: Bergin & Garvey.

Bartolomé, Lilia I. 1996. "Beyond the Methods Fetish: Toward a Humanizing Pedagogy." *Harvard Educational Review Reprint Series* 27: 229–52.

Bloome, David, and Frances Bailey. 1992. "Studying Language and Literacy through Events: Particularity and Intertextuality." In *Multidisciplinary Perspectives on Literacy Research*, edited by Richard Beach, Judith L. Green, Michael Kamil, and Timothy Shanahan, 181–210. Urbana, IL: National Council of Teachers for English.

Bloome, David, and Ann Egan-Robertson. 1993. "The Social Construction of Intertextuality in Classroom Reading and Writing Lessons." *Reading Research Quarterly* 28(4): 304–33.

Brilliant-Mills, Heidi. 1993. "Becoming a Mathematician: Building a Situated Definition of Mathics." *Linguistics and Education* 5(3-4): 301–34.

Bunting, Eve. 1980. *The Terrible Things*. New York: Harper & Row.

Collins, Elaine, and Judith L. Green. 1992. "Learning in Classroom Settings: Making or Breaking a Culture." *In Redefining Student Learning: Roots of Educational Change*, edited by Hermine H. Marshall, 59–86. Norwood, NJ: Ablex.

Cook-Gumperz, Jenny. 1986. *The Social Construction of Literacy*. Cambridge, MA: Cambridge University Press.

Durán, Luisa. 1994. "Toward a Better Understanding of Code Switching and Interlanguage in Bilinguality: Implications for Bilingual Instruction." *The Journal of Educational Issues of Language Majority Students* 14: 69–88.

Farris, Pamela J. 1997. *Language Arts: Process, Product and Assessment*, 2nd ed. Iowa: Times Mirror Higher Education Group, Inc.

Fernie, David, Bronwyn Davies, Rebecca Kantor, and Paula McMurry. 1993. "Becoming a Person: Creating Integrated Gender, Peer and Student Positionings in a Preschool Classroom." *International Journal of Qualitative Research in Education* 6 (2): 95–110.

Filipovic, Zlata. 1994. *Zlata's Diary: A Child's Life in Sarajevo*. Translated with notes by Christina Pribicevic-Zoric. New York: Viking.

Frank, Anne. 1995. *The Diary of a Young Girl: The Definitive Edition*. Edited by Otto H. Frank and Mirjam Pressler. Translated by Susan Massotty. New York: Doubleday.

Fránquiz, María E. 1995. *Transformations in Bilingual Classrooms: Understanding Opportunity to Learn within the Change Process.* Ph.D. diss., University of California, Santa Barbara.

Freire, Paulo. 1970. *Pedagogy of the Oppressed.* Translated by Myra Bergman Ramos. New York: Seabury Press.

———. 1978. *Education for Critical Consciousness.* New York: Seabury Press.

Giroux, Henry. 1993. "Literacy and The Politics of Difference." In *Critical Literacy: Politics, Praxis, and the Postmodern*, edited by Colin Lankshear and Peter L. McLaren, 367–78. New York: State University of New York Press.

Giroux, Henry, and David Purpel. 1983. *The Hidden Curriculum and Moral Education: Deception or Discovery?* Berkeley, CA: McCutchan.

Glover, Mary Kenner. 1986. *A Community Of Learners: An Insider's View of Whole Language.* Tempe, AZ: Awakening Seed Press.

Gordon, Mark. 1995. *Children Remember the Holocaust.* Produced by Frank Doelger and Howard Meltzer. CBS Schoolbreak Special.

Green, Judith L., and Lois A. Meyer. 1991. "The Embeddedness of Reading in Classroom Life: Reading as a Situated Process." In *Towards a Critical Sociology of Reading Pedagogy*, edited by Carolyn Baker and Allan Luke, 141–46. Philadelphia, PA: John Benjamins.

Jennings, Louise. 1996. *Multiple Contexts for Learning Social Justice: An Ethnographic and Sociolinguistic Study of a Fifth Grade Bilingual Class.* Ph.D. diss., University of California, Santa Barbara.

Ladson-Billings, Gloria. 1995. "Toward a Theory of Cultural Relevant Pedagogy." *American Educational Research Journal* 32(3): 465–91.

LeVesque, J., and T. Prosser. 1996. "Service Learning Connection." *Journal of Teacher Education* 47(5): 325–34.

Lin, Lichu. 1993. "Language of and in the Classroom: Constructing the Patterns of Social Life." *Linguistics and Education* 5(3-4): 367–409.

Lowry, Lois. 1989a. *Number the Stars.* Boston: Houghton Mifflin Co.

———. 1989b. *¿Quien Cuenta las Estrellas?* Translated by Juan Lucke. Boston: Houghton Mufflin Co.

Reyes, María de la Luz. 1992. "Challenging Venerable Assumptions: Literacy Instruction for Linguistically Different Students." *Harvard Educational Review* 62(4): 427–46.

Rutherford, James, and Andrew Ahlgren. 1990. *Science for All Americans.* New York: Oxford University Press.

Santa Barbara Classroom Discourse Group (Green, Dixon, Lin, Floriani, and Bailey). 1992a. "Constructing Literacy in Classrooms: Literate Action as Social Accomplishment." In *Redefining Student Learning: Roots of Educational Change*, edited by Hermine H. Marshall, 119–50. Norwood, NJ: Ablex.

Santa Barbara Classroom Discourse Group (Dixon, de la Cruz, Green, Lin, and Brandts). 1992b. "Do You See What I See? The Referential and Intertextual Nature of Classroom Life." *Journal of Classroom Interaction* 27(2): 29–36.

Saxe, Geoffrey B. 1988. "Candy Selling and Math Learning." *Educational Researcher* 17(6): 14–21.

Shor, Ira. 1992. *Empowering Education: Critical Teaching for Social Change*. University of Chicago Press.

———. 1993. "Education Is Politics: Paulo Friere's Critical Pedagogy." In *Paulo Freire: A Critical Encounter*, edited by Peter McLaren and Peter Leonard, 25–35. New York: Routledge.

Wink, Joan. 1997. *Critical Pedagogy: Notes from the Real World*. New York: Longman.

Yeager, Beth, Ana Florriani, and Judith L. Green. (1998). "Learning to See Learning in the Classroom: Developing an Ethnographic Perspective." In *Students as Researchers of Culture and Community in Their Own Community*, edited by Ann Egan-Robertson and David Bloome, 115–39. Cresskill, NJ: Hampton Press.

13 Exploring Critical Literacy: You Can Hear a Pin Drop

Christine Leland, Jerome Harste,
Anne Ociepka, Mitzi Lewison,
and Vivian Vasquez

"One thing about these books is that I can hear a pin drop when I'm reading them to my class," reports Lee Heffernan, who teaches third grade at the Childs School in Bloomington, Indiana. The "pin drop" description is supported by a videotape shared with us by Sheilah Lyles, a first-grade teacher from Indianapolis. Although the children were noisy and inattentive as their teacher began to read aloud, the change in their demeanor was dramatic as she got further into the book *White Wash* (Shange, 1997). Within a few minutes, the wiggling had stopped and the children were clearly focused on the pictures and their teacher's voice. This was surprising to Ms. Lyles, who later commented that showing such rapt attention during a read aloud is a rare occurrence for these children.

In both cases, the teachers were reading books from an evolving text set that provides a framework for a new kind of "critical literacy" curriculum which focuses on building students' awareness of how systems of meaning and power affect people and the lives they lead. These books invite conversations about fairness and justice; they encourage children to ask why some groups of people are positioned as "others." According to the definition we developed, critical books meet one or more of the following criteria:

Reprinted from *Language Arts,* September 1999.

They don't make difference invisible, but rather explore what differences *make a difference*;

They enrich our understanding of history and life by giving voice to those who traditionally have been silenced or marginalized;

They show how people can begin to take action on important social issues;

They explore dominant systems of meaning that operate in our society to position people and groups of people;

They don't provide "happily ever after" endings for complex social problems.

Among teachers, we have found mixed reaction to the critical literacy text set. We recently introduced *Voices in the Park* (Browne, 1998) to a group of teachers and found a wide range of opinions. This book shows how the same events can be viewed from different perspectives. The four gorilla (dressed as human) characters take turns telling their own unique versions of what transpired in the park that day. For instance, the first voice, a wealthy, over-protective mother, observes that her son is talking to "a very rough-looking child" and decides that it's time to go home. From the illustration, however, it can be inferred that the children are too far away for her to see them in any detail. One might conclude that the real problem is the other child's shabbily dressed father, who glumly reads the want-ads as he sits on a nearby bench.

After this book had been shared, several teachers said that they thought it would be a good vehicle for promoting classroom discussions. Others disagreed, however, and commented that the book was "too sad for young children." One teacher said that as a parent, she would object to having her child exposed to the book. "My daughter doesn't have ideas like this and I don't want someone putting them into her head. We don't talk about stuff like that at home." Another teacher agreed, claiming that "We don't have problems like this at our school. Everyone in my class plays with everyone else, older or younger, boys or girls." When the accuracy of this statement was questioned by one of the university interns, the teacher insisted that "there might be isolated problems, but these are the exceptions." As in *Voices in the Park* (Browne, 1998), this incident shows that indeed, people often see what they want to see.

Conceptually, our investigation of critical literacy is anchored in Luke and Freebody's (1997) model of reading as social practice. Arguing that literacy is never neutral, the authors lay out a grid showing four different constructions or views of literacy. According to the first view, reading is decoding and the function of reading instruction is to help children break the code. The second view was introduced during the 1970s and 1980s when psycholinguistics and schematheoretical notions of reading emphasized reader-text interactions. This approach drew attention to "text-meaning practices" and the development of a reader who understood how to use the textual and personal resources at hand to coproduce a meaningful reading. The third view evolved during the late 1980s and early 1990s, when sociolinguistic and socio-semiotic theory focused attention on language in use. During this period, reading came to be viewed in terms of what it did or could accomplish, pragmatically, in the real world. More recently, Luke and Freebody (1997) suggest that reading should be seen as a non-neutral form of cultural practice—one that positions readers and obscures as much as it illuminates. They argue that in the 21st century, readers need to be able to interrogate the assumptions that are embedded in text as well as the assumptions which they, as culturally indoctrinated beings, bring to the text. Questions such as "Whose story is this?" "Who benefits from this story?" and "What voices are not being heard?" invite children to interrogate the systems of meaning that operate both consciously and unconsciously in text, as well as in society. In a later communication, Luke (personal communication, 1998) suggests that rather than looking at the four categories individually, researchers should study programs that emphasize various combinations and aspects of them.

While critical literacy involves critical thinking, it also entails more. Part of that "more" is social action built upon an understanding that literacy positions individuals and, in so doing, serves some more than others. As literate beings, it behooves us not only to know how to decode and make meaning but also to understand how language works and to what ends, so that we can better see ourselves in light of the kind of world we wish to create and the kind of people we wish to become. We have observed a movement toward social action in two classrooms where teachers or interns have been reading critical books.

In one classroom, third and fourth graders listened as their student teacher read aloud *Making up Megaboy* (Walter, 1998). The story is presented through the voices of various community members as they try to explain why Robbie Jones, on his 13th birthday, walked into Mr. Koh's convenience store and shot the elderly Korean proprietor with his father's gun. As we try to figure out why this horrible killing happened, we hear from his disbelieving mother, a glib TV news reporter, Robbie's disapproving father, a Vietnam vet, the local barber, his classmates, the girl he had a crush on, Robbie's teacher, his best friend, a correctional officer, and many more. This book reads like a TV drama and brings us face-to-face with real world issues like teen violence and the proliferation of guns. After lengthy discussions of this book and the different social problems it raised, the students felt the need to take some sort of action—they wanted to do something to stop things like this from happening in their neighborhoods. Their social-action piece involved making posters about the dangers of firearms and sharing these posters with the rest of the school.

In another instance, fifth and sixth graders who had read a number of critical books began to interrogate the assumptions embedded in a school rule that forbids student conversation in the lunchroom. In this case, their social action took the form of an editorial in the class newspaper. Although the principal had already agreed to give the older students their own area for lunch so that they could talk, these students immediately launched into a crusade to win the same privilege for the younger children.

> Now that we get our own lunchroom, we can talk, but I think that everyone should be able to talk in the lunchrooms without the teachers and the janitor yelling and griping at us! We should be able to talk in a whisper, a six-inch voice for goodness sake! They can close the lunchroom doors when we're being too loud. The teachers talk and they can disturb other classes, too! When they yell, they're louder than us. We were born with mouths and tongues and we intend to use them!

What's particularly interesting about this example is how the author moves from "we" (the fifth and sixth graders) to "everyone" (students in the other grades) to "us" (both groups combined) in the first sentence. It would be easier for these students to enjoy their new freedom to talk in the lunchroom and not give a second thought to the others in the school, but instead they have positioned themselves as advocates for what they see as an oppressed group. In addition, they question the power structure in the school that makes lunchtime conversation permissible for some (teachers), but not for others (children).

From several perspectives, then, these books are of crucial importance to educators and how we view curriculum. While they invite specific conversations around specific topics, they function as a whole to create a curriculum which honors diversity and invites students and teachers alike to explore a new kind of literacy curriculum—one built upon the premise that a model of difference is a model of learning for individuals as well as for society. One of the implicit arguments being tested by our use of these books in classrooms is that a diversity-and-difference model of education serves a multilingual and multicultural society such as our own far better than the conformity-and-consensus model of learning that currently permeates the whole of our educational system.

According to Arthur Applebee (1997), the best teachers think about curriculum in terms of what conversations they want their students to be engaged in, not in terms of what concepts they want to introduce through reading or through direct instruction. Concepts, he argues, will be developed as learners engage in conversations which address the real issues that exist in the world in which they are living and the disciplines they are studying. While many of the books we review can be seen as controversial, they reflect life in a way that most school curricula do not. It is this relevancy and the potential to explore new curricular possibilities that make discussions about these books so important. The topic of critical literacy supports the kind of conversations we cannot aford to ignore.

Our expanded view of curricular possibilities for critical books encouraged us to develop an expanded format for reviewing them. While we still provide a summary of each text, we also highlight potential conversations that the reading of the text makes possible, and we share actual conversations that have accompanied the reading of these books in classrooms. We hope that this format will help teachers who wish to invite students to engage in critical conversations, given events that have transpired in their classroom or community, to locate texts that fit the bill. Others, who have already started these conversations with their students and wish to continue, will find it useful to refer to the themes and alternative perspectives identified for each book. Although there are a number of different ways to categorize these books, our primary purpose here is to share books that focus on the theme of "understanding how systems of meaning in society position us."

Reviews

Your Move

Bunting, Eve. (1998). Illus. James Ransome. New York: Harcourt Brace & Co. Unpaged. ISBN: 0-15-200181-6. *Genre:* contemporary realistic fiction. *Primary Topics:* coming-of-age-in-difficult times; sibling relationships; gangs. *Picture Book.*

James is ten, and his six-year-old brother Isaac likes to do whatever he does. One evening, after their mother goes to work, James sneaks out to meet the K-Bones and brings Isaac with him. The K-Bones, led by Kris and Bones, say that they're not a gang, just kids who hang out together. When James wants to join them, they give him the task of spray painting the K-Bones' name over the Snakes' name way up on a sign over the highway. Although James is scared, he feels he must prove himself to the K-Bones.

After the mission is accomplished, James feels "suddenly so cool," but the feeling is short-lived. As they flee the scene, James pulls Isaac by the hand and thinks,

"I'm not feeling too great about getting him mixed up in this. I should have known the kind of stuff the K-Bones do. I'm not that dumb" (Unpaged).

That's when they run into the Snakes, who have a gun. James hears a shot, and little Isaac drops to his knees.

In the end, Isaac ends up with just two skinned knees, but *Your Move* does much more than scratch the surface of the issues it raises. Bunting explores the reasons why James and even six-year-old Isaac are attracted to the K-Bones—both seek not only to connect with peers, but also to find older males to look up to, especially since their father left. The reasons why they both decide not to join the K-Bones, when Kris offers them the chance, are even more compelling. Exploring with kids how they would deal with similar situations is crucial, since (as the book reminds us) very young children may need to make such difficult and important decisions.

Whirligig

Fleischman, Paul. (1998). New York: Henry Holt. 133 pp. ISBN: 0-8050-5582-7. *Genre:* Fiction. *Primary Topics:* coming-of-age; social responsibility; human interconnectedness. *Chapter Book.*

The premise of this book is deceptively simple. The thoughtless act of an unhappy teenager has tragic results that set in motion a series of surprising events. As the story opens, the main character, Brent, is charged with the task of designing, constructing, and placing four memorial whirligigs at various locations throughout the United States. Although Brent's story is engaging in its own right, it is here that Fleischman subtly and without warning inserts four completely independent narratives about other characters with varying backgrounds and social positions. The single connector between these stories are Brent's whirligigs. In each of these parallel stories, a character has a unique encounter with one of the whirligigs. As a result, each character has to rethink his or her own life. These concurrent story layers provide the reader with a broad perspective of the impact Brent and the whirligigs have on very different individuals. The compilation of events shows the impact one individual can have on many others, regardless of time or space.

Flying Solo

Fletcher, Ralph. (1998). New York: Clarion Books. 144 pp. ISBN: 0-395-87323-1. *Genre:* Fiction. *Primary Topics:* social responsibility; multiple perspectives; child/adult relationships; peer pressure; ethics. *Chapter Book.*

Told from the perspective of different students in Mr. Fabiano's sixth-grade class, this is the story of what happens when a substitute teacher doesn't show up and the class decides they'll run things by themselves for the day No one discovers their secret as they maintain most of the usual routine, bringing the attendance sheet to the office, walking to music class in straight rows. But there's a lot going on, even as they stick to most of "Mr. Fab's" lesson plan. Rachel, who hasn't spoken since the death of their classmate Tommy six months ago, confronts Bastian about his cruelty to Tommy while he was alive. The conflict and emotions that ensue make Karen, who masterminded a few lies to keep their day of self-governance secret, wish that Mr. Fab were there after all. But at the same time, the class talks and writes about things they probably wouldn't have with the teacher there. It's only at the end of the day that the principal discovers the deception.

When Mr. Fab does appear, it's easy to see why the class loves him and his structured routines. Like the other adults, he's concerned and dead serious when he brings up what the class did. But he also wants to know what each of them thinks, and asks each student to write to him with his or her version of what happened that day. The varying responses allow for great discussions on taking responsibility and on how school practices can both inhibit and empower kids.

Just Juice

Hesse, Karen. (1998). Illus. Robert Andrew Parker. New York: Scholastic Press. 138 pp. ISBN: 0-590-03382-4. *Genre:* Fiction. *Primary Topics:* literacy as power; poverty; marginalization; intergenerational relationships. Chapter *Book.*

This multi-layered story is told from the point of view of nine-year-old Juice Faulstich, a chronically truant child who is happier at home with her unsuccessful father and pregnant mother than at school where she is constantly reminded of her inability to read. As the story unfolds, Juice comes to realize that her father is also a non-reader and that his lack of reading proficiency has brought the family to the brink of disaster in the form of eviction from their home. Juice begins to understand that although both she and her father are skilled in many ways, their illiteracy greatly affects their acceptance by society and even by other family members. The book ends on a hopeful note as the family finds a way to avert the eviction and makes literacy a goal for all of them.

The critical issues embedded in this story begin to surface as the reader considers how learning and literacy position individuals as successes or failures, both personally and socially, in school and in everyday life. The story of the Faulstich family shows how other ways of knowing are seldom valued as highly as literacy skills. In addition, the story illustrates how the efforts of well-meaning social service professionals can negatively affect the people they are attempting to help if the voices of those individuals are not being heard. When extended to these critical levels, the story of Juice and the Faulstich family invites readers to consider how some people are marginalized not only by their poverty, but also by their illiteracy

The Circuit: Stories from the Life of a Migrant Child

Jimenez, Francisco. (1998). Albuquerque NM: University of New Mexico Press. 134 pp. ISBN: 0-8263-1797-9. *Genre:* memoir/historical fiction. *Primary Topics:* migrant farm workers; Mexican American immigrant experience; poverty; institutional dehumanization. *Chapter Book.*

In this powerful collection of short stories, Franciso Jimenez presents a brilliant, close-up view into the lives of Mexican immigrant farm workers. We see the humanity of this usually faceless group that brings food to our tables while continually being subjected to various types of political and media degradation. The book begins with the authors' parents risking all to come to the promised land of California to escape the poverty in Mexico. What they find instead of good jobs is the backbreaking life of migrant workers. As they continually follow the ripening of the crops on "the circuit," they live in tents, don't earn enough money to feed their children or provide them with medical care, and constantly worry about being deported.

The twelve stories in this book are told from the perspective of young Panchito, whose voice lets us feel both the joy and despair of migrant life. The memoirs of school experiences and the frustration his father feels when he is unable to feed or protect his family are especially poignant. This book would be a marvelous way to begin class discussions on a variety of critical issues including poverty in the United States, the working conditions of farm laborers, how schools position students whose primary language is not English, and health care issues. The book is an inspirational tale of personal courage and growth.

Sweet Dried Apples: A Vietnamese Wartime Childhood

Breckler, Rosemary. (1996). Illus. Deborah Kogan Ray. Boston, MA: Houghton Mifflin Co. Unpaged. ISBN: 0-395-73570-X. *Genre:* historical memoir. *Primary Topics:* war; social responsibility; child/adult relationships; social action. *Picture Book.*

This story is told from the point of view of a young Vietnamese girl whose life is changed by the encroaching war that surrounds her. What starts out as a distant threat gradually comes to encompass her family and her life. A major figure in the book is Ong Noi, the girl's grandfather, a "revered elder" who has been the herb doctor in his village for many years. When his son becomes a soldier, he comes to help look after his two grandchildren. With him, Ong Noi brings baskets of medicinal herbs and sweet dried apples to cover their bitter taste. When their grandfather leaves to tend wounded soldiers in a distant area, the children continue to gather herbs as he taught them to do. In the end, Ong Noi uses his position as the herb doctor to sacrifice his own life so that others can have relief from pain and suffering. He gives all of his medicines to others and saves nothing to heal his own wounds. This book invites conversations about the different forms that social action can take and how this action affects people's lives.

One More Border: The True Story of One Family's Escape from War-Torn Europe

Kaplan, William. (1998). Illus. Shelley Tanaka. Toronto, Ont., Canada: Groundwood Books. 61 p. ISBN: 0-88899-332-3. *Genre:* historical nonfiction. *Primary Topics:* Holocaust; segregation; marginalization; cultural differences; power and control; cultural persecution; social action. *Picture Book.*

In this powerful example of historical nonfiction, William Kaplan shares the story of the struggle experienced by his father's family as they escaped war-torn Europe during the late 1930s to avoid persecution for being Jewish. Through the story of the Kaplan family's escape, the reader learns about the oppression and marginalization of the Jews during the war. Inclusion of authentic artifacts such as photographs, maps, and the visa that allowed the Kaplans to leave Europe reinforce that this is true story.

The story reveals the social repositioning of the Kaplan family from living in comfort and luxury to being penniless. It raises issues regarding how some systems of meaning manage to oppress certain groups or individuals. When partnered with *Passage to Freedom: The Sugihara Story* (Mochizuki, 1998), this text set offers a rich demonstration of how people taking social action can make a difference in the lives of the oppressed. Through the support of others, the Kaplans were able to escape Nazi persecution and rewrite their lives back into existence. A glimpse of their new home in Canada provides a sense of closure for readers. Both books encourage conversation about the Holocaust and why such terrible oppression was allowed to happen. After hearing *Passage to Freedom: The Sugihara Story*, a group of second and third graders got into a heated discussion of how someone like Hitler had been able to get away with doing the horrible things he did. When the student teacher asked if the way the Germans followed Hitler was similar to the way kids some times follow clothing fads, Caryn responded by saying, "It's like monkey see, monkey do. They copied off him instead of going against him."

Sister Anne's Hands

Lorbiecki, Marybeth. (1998). Illus. K. Wendy Popp. New York: Dial Books. Unpaged. ISBN: 0-80-372038-6. *Genre:* historical fiction. *Primary Topics:* African American culture; civil rights; creative response to racism & prejudice; school life. *Picture Book.*

Set within the context of the racially torn 60s, this is the story of Anna Zabrocky and her first encounter with an African American teacher. Anna's new second grade teacher, Sister Anne, believes in story, the power of example, and hands-on learning. Anna never loved school so much nor were Sister Anne's lessons ever more meaningful than the day when a paper airplane crashed into the blackboard with a note that read:

Roses are Red
Violets are Blue
Don't let Sister Anne
Get any black on you!

Like good teachers everywhere, Sister Anne transformed this incident into a curricular invitation to learn about Black Americans and understand the systems of oppression and opposition in our society. Hands, both Sister Anne's and the multi-colored ones that Anna Zabrocky drew, become the metaphor for what we can give and learn. *Sister Anne's Hands* is a gentle way to invite conversations about difference which teachers in both public and private school settings will find uplifting. Popp's illustrations are "tonal" both in terms of the period in which the story is set as well as in terms of the mood which the story evokes. When we asked Robert, a second grader, what he thought of the story, he said, "It's important. You learn to be fair and get along with people." In several primary classrooms, the part of the text where Sister Anne showed pictures of signs that said Blacks should go back to Africa generated much discussion. Jordan, a first grader, said that he didn't like that part: "Even though they are Black, they belong here. They are my sisters and brothers." Samantha, a second grader, said, "I don't want that to happen because I have plenty of Black friends." Later, as illustrated in Figure 1, Samantha chose to follow up on the book by doing a "Written Conversation" (Short, Harste, & Burke, 1996) with her friend Colleen.

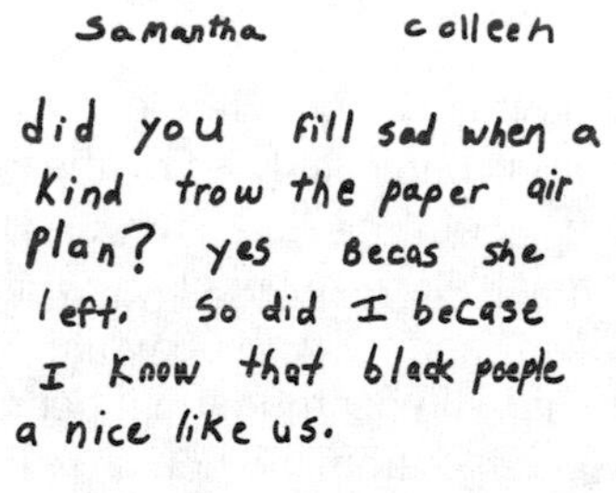

Samantha   colleen

did you fill sad when a
kind trow the paper air
plan? yes Becas she
left. So did I becase
I know that black poeple
a nice like us.

Figure 1. A "Written Conversation" by Samantha and Colleen. (Translation: Samantha: Did you feel sad when a kid threw the paper airplane? Colleen: Yes, because she left. Samantha: So did I because I know that Black people are nice like us.)

Tomas and the Library Lady

Mora, Pat. (1997). Illus. Raul Colon. New York: Alfred A. Knopf. Unpaged.
ISBN: 0-679-80401-3. *Genre:* biography. *Primary Topics:* literacy as power;
marginalization; migrant farm workers. *Picture Book.*

Based on the life of Tomas Rivera, a migrant farm worker who became a
national education leader and University of California chancellor, this story
shows how literacy and access to good books can work together to give
voice to people who historically have been marginalized. With the help of a
caring librarian and lots of books, Tomas is able to forge a new identity as the
next-generation storyteller in his family. This book shows how libraries and
literacy have the power to help all of us escape the mundane and explore
new worlds. The seemingly textured illustrations add an almost surrealistic
quality to the story.

On another level, *Tomas and the Library Lady* can be seen as a story that
can help raise children's consciousness about migrant workers and what
they and their families endure to survive. This book would be a good
addition to a text set dealing with inequities and harsh working conditions.

Whitewash

Shange, Ntozake. (1997). Illus. Michael Sporn. New York: Walker and
Company. Unpaged. ISBN: 0-8027-8490-9. *Genre:* Contemporary realistic
fiction; *Primary Topics:* African American culture; racism & prejudice; social
action. *Picture Book.*

Helene-Angel, an African American preschooler, walks home from school
with her brother, who doesn't particularly enjoy the task of walking his little
sister home. One day, a gang of White kids surrounds them, blackening
Mauricio's eye and painting Helene-Angel's face white as they show her
how to be a "true American" and "how to be white." Helene-Angel is, of
course, traumatized; she hides in her room until her grandmother convinces
her to come out. As she emerges from the house, her classmates greet her
and promise to stick together so that events like this won't happen again.

Based on a series of true incidents, *Whitewash* is a powerful story written
in narrative style by the poet Ntozake Shange, with illustrations from a
Carnegie Medal-winning video. Overall, it gives voice to a little-known
racial incident that became a lesson in tolerance and a child's triumph.
Children need to understand why stories such as this one should never be

forgotten. They should also be encouraged to explore how they might transform the bad things in their own lives into triumphs. While several first graders like Porter said "It made me want to cry," others focused on the positive impact of Helene-Angel's friends. "When I saw how her friends helped her, it made me feel strong" (Desmond) and "Her friends made her happy" (Nia).

Leon's Story

Tillage, Leon Walter. (1997). New York: Farrar, Straus & Giroux. Collage by Susan Roth. 107 pp. ISBN: 0-37434379-9. *Genre:* autobiography. *Primary Topics:* African American culture; racism &: prejudice; civil rights; literacy as power. *Chapter Book.*

Every year, Leon Tillage tells the story of his life to the children at the Baltimore school where he works as a custodian. We're lucky to have his amazing story in print. Remembering his childhood as the son of a sharecropper in North Carolina, Tillage describes his personal experiences of—and profound insights into—segregation, racial violence, and the economic disenfranchisement of Blacks in the South as he was growing up. He tells of joining marches for civil rights as a high school student:

> Our parents would say to us, "We don't understand. Don't you know you're going to get killed for listening to those people? You're going to get beat up. What's wrong with you?" Then we would say to them, "We're getting beat up now. We're getting killed now. So I'd rather get beat up for doing something or trying to change things. I mean, why get beat up for nothing?" (Tillage, 1997, p. 88–89)

When he was fifteen, Tillage witnessed the violent murder of his father by some White boys who were drunk, "just out to have some fun," and who never faced any consequences for their crime. His voice, as he shares his story, is spirited and gentle, rich with wisdom, humor, anger, and pain.

The book covers so much personal, political, and historical ground that critical questions abound. This is truly a book for all ages. Readers can explore American slavery's legacy of racism, racial violence and economic injustice, as it was when Tillage was growing up and as it persists today. The book also generates discussions about the power of literacy and storytelling.

What's the Most Beautiful Thing You Know about Horses?

Van Camp, Richard. (1998). Illus. George Littlechild. San Francisco: Children's Book Press. 30 pp. ISBN: 0-89239-154-5. *Genre:* fiction. *Primary Topics:* multiple perspectives; Native American culture; ethnic differences; inquiry-based learning. *Picture Book.*

The most beautiful thing about this book is that it provides space for us to see the world and ourselves in entirely new ways. Author Richard Van Camp is the main character. In his hometown of Fort Smith in the Northwest Territories of Canada, on a day so cold that he says the ravens refuse to fly, he cannot go outside. He decides to ask his friends and family a question he has been thinking about, "What's the most beautiful thing you know about horses?"

On the surface, the book appears to be a demonstration of what it truly means to be an inquirer. However, the perspectives offered to Van Camp in response to his question set up the possibility for a number of conversations to take place regarding stereotypes, ethnic differences, biracial issues, language and power, animal rights, and cultural perspectives.

His search for responses to his questions appears to be playful, serving as a gentle reminder that critical issues can arise in conversations that are not primarily centered on such issues. George Littlechild's bold and bright illustrations encourage curiosity and support the generation of further inquiries.

References

Applebee, A. N. (1997). Rethinking curriculum in the English language arts. *English Journal, 86* (3), 25–31.

Browne, Anthony (1998). *Voices in the park.* New York: DK Publishing.

Luke, A., & Freebody P (1997). Shaping the social practices of reading. In S. Muspratt, A. Luke, & P Freebody (Eds.), pp. 185–225. *Constructing critical literacies.* Cresskill, NJ: Hampton Press, Inc.

Mochizuki, K. (1998). *Passage to freedom: The Sugihara story.* New York: Lee & Low Books.

Shange, N. (1997). *Whitewash.* New York, NY: Walker and Company.

Short, K., Harste, J., with Burke, C. (1996). *Creating classrooms for authors and inquirers.* Portsmouth, NH: Heinemann.

Walter, V (1998). *Making up megaboy.* New York: DK Publishing.

Chapter Books

Leon's Story (L. Tillage, 1997). Farrar, Straus (Sr Giroux. Hardcover. ISBN: 0374343799.

Bat 6 (V E. Wolff, 1998). Scholastic. Hardcover. ISBN: 0590897993.

My Home Is Over Jordan (S. Forrester, 1997). Lodestar. Hardcover. ISBN: 052567568X.

Follow the Leader (V Winslow, 1997). Yearling Books. Paper. ISBN: 044041296X.

Flying Solo (R. Fletcher, 1998). Clarion Books. Paper. ISBN: 0395873231.

The Circuit (F Jimenez, 1998). University of New Mexico Press. Paper. ISBN: 0826317979.

Just Juice (K. Hesse, 1998). Scholastic. Paper. ISBN: 0590033824.

Wringer (J. Spinelli, 1997). HarperTrophy Paper. ISBN: 064405788.

Slave Day (R. Thomas, 1997). Aladdin. Paper. ISBN: 068982193X.

Old People, Frogs, and Albert (N. H. Wilson, 1997). Farrar, Straus &: Giroux. Hardcover. ISBN: 034356254.

Books for Older Readers

The Buffalo Tree (A. Rapp, 1998). HarperCollins. Paper. ISBN: 006440711X.

Just One Flick of the Finger (M. Loribiecki, 1996). Dial Books. Hardcover. ISBN: 0803719485.

Run for Your Life (M. Levy, 1997). Paper Star Books. Paper. ISBN: 0698116089.

Behaving Bradley (P Nodelman, 1998). Simon &: Schuster. Hardcover. ISBN: 0689814666.

Talk to Me: Stories and a Novella (C. Dines, 1999). Laureleaf. Paper. ISBN: 0440220262.

Making Up Megaboy (V Walter, 1998). DK Publishing. Hardcover. ISBN: 0789424866.

Taking Social Action

We Shall Not Be Moved (J. Dash, 1998). Scholastic. Trade. Paper. ISBN: 0590484109.

Whirligig (P Fleischman, 1998). Henry Holt. Hardcover. ISBN: 0805055827.

Whitewash (N. Shange, 1997). Walker & Co. Hardcover. ISBN: 0802784909.

The Bus Ride (W Miller, 1998). Lee & Low Books. Hardcover. ISBN: 1880000601.

Passage to Freedom: The Sugihara Story (K. Mochizuki, 1997) Lee & Low Books. Hardcover. ISBN: 1880000490.

Seedfolks (P Fleischman, 1999). HarperCollins. Paper. ISBN: 0064472078.

Sweet Dried Apples (R. Breckler, 1996). Houghton Mifflin. Hardcover. ISBN: 039573570X.

14 Critical Literacy in a Fourth-Grade Classroom

Maria Sweeney

June 13, 1994. A fourth-grade class in an upper-middle-class, predominantly white New Jersey suburb takes its bows to enthusiastic applause from parents and fellow students. A familiar scene? Not quite. These children created "No Easy Road to Freedom: A Play about South Africa" from scratch. They researched, wrote, staged, directed, acted in, and produced this play and provided background materials for their audience. It was the students' idea to create the play. In the process, they learned far more than most educated adults know about South Africa and the injustices of apartheid, and they experienced the power of working collectively to take a stand on an issue they grew to care about deeply. They also learned what it's like to grow something from the seed stage to a plant in full bloom. Every student, regardless of academic ability, played a critical role. The children experienced their power to make a positive difference in the world.

In reflecting on the experience, one of the students, Maia, wrote:

> I think that everyone in the audience learned something new today. I believe that our play was a form of protest. I am very proud that our class worked together and we made an important statement. I think we should put on the play a bunch more times to really get the message into many people's minds. I wish we could show our message to all racists. Most people would never think that a group of fourth graders could ever understand what's going on and send out a strong message like we did, but we did!

Maia's feelings of empowerment and commitment to social justice, feelings I believe were shared by all students in my classroom, evolved

---

Reprinted from Chapter 5 of *Making Justice Our Project*, edited by Carole Edelsky.

during an entire school year of a critical-literacy curriculum which prompted students to confront social inequities and assume responsibility to forge a more just society. I asked students to consider alternative views of events past and present. I asked them to look for missing or silenced voices in the materials we read, and to consistently ask of what they read, heard, or witnessed: Is this fair? Is this right? Does this hurt anyone? Is this the whole story? Who benefits and who suffers? Why is it like this? How could it be different, more just? Through these questions I sought "to give students the tools to critique every idea that legitimates social inequality, every idea that teaches them they are incapable of imagining and building a fundamentally equal and just society" (Christensen, 1994, p. 8).

I strive to create a classroom atmosphere and curriculum that prepares my students to build and participate in a critical democracy. I help my students gain the necessary skills and knowledge to critique their world, unveil injustices and needless suffering, and work for social change. I nurture a strong sense of compassion and equity, and I urge children to get angry and do something.

I don't pretend that my teaching is neutral or objective; education never is. Behind everything taught is a point of view or particular perspective. Value-free education is a myth and, in fact, an impossibility. As Ira Shor states in *Empowering Education*:

> Critical education is not more political than the curriculum which emphasizes taking in and fitting in. Not encouraging students to question knowledge, society, and experience tacitly endorses and supports the status quo. . . . As Freire said, education that tries to be neutral supports the dominant ideology in society. (1992, p.12)

Year after year across the United States, most young children still learn the traditional story of "Columbus the hero who discovered the New World" taught by teachers who consider themselves objective and fair. But this approach to the story actually legitimizes the invasion and theft of another people's (Tainos) land, and it ignores the perspective of those who were "discovered." This is just one, by now obvious, example of the biased way that history and other subjects are taught everywhere.

The radical historian Howard Zinn opens his courses with the following disclaimer:

> This is not an objective course. . . . I am not a neutral teacher. I have a point of view about war, about racial and sexual equality, about

economic justice—and this point of view will affect my choice of
subject, and the way I discuss it. (1993, p. 29)

Zinn openly reveals his biases. He teaches history that values peace, justice,
equality, and freedom and this approach necessarily urges students to look
critically at this nation's past.

Those who fault critical educators for imposing our values on children
ignore the fact that education which doesn't ask children to pose critical
questions, search for alternative perspectives, and uncover untold stories
helps reproduce an unjust society. Certain people benefit while most others
suffer from current social arrangements. Education which claims to be
neutral trains children to take the world for granted and to never imagine a
more just society. Therefore, I openly approach all aspects of my teaching
with my bias for social justice.

In this article I will attempt to illustrate the possibilities of critical literacy
in a whole language elementary classroom by discussing a project my
students and I undertook to follow the events leading up to the South African
elections in April, 1994. Before describing the project, I will briefly
characterize my curriculum.

I use a whole language approach to teaching literacy and infuse issues of
justice and equity throughout the curriculum. My students develop their
skills and strategies as readers and writers through authentic literacy events.
They read whole texts which they have chosen, and they write for their own
purposes for a genuine audience in a reading and writing workshop (Atwell,
1987; Calkins, 1994). During the year we do a few inquiry units (theme
cycles) in which topics of study are collectively chosen, guiding research
questions are generated by all, and we engage in an open-ended,
meaningful inquiry project such as the one described in this article
(Altwerger & Flores, 1994; Short, Harste, & Burke, 1996). I begin each year
with a general idea of my social studies time line, which includes topics
sufficiently open-ended to become theme cycles. For example, my tentative
time line this year is Building Our Classroom Community; Understanding
the "Isms"; Oral History; Labor History and Current Issues; Critical Media
Literacy and Women's Suffrage. I chose these units because they all relate to
New Jersey (the official fourth-grade theme), are potent topics for sparking
questions of interest to the children, and relate to justice and equality. The
length of time devoted to each unit depends on the students' interest. I also
allow space for a topic to be chosen by the students.

Human Suffering and Injustice: So Many Questions

Several weeks before the South African elections, my students viewed the filmstrip *Apartheid Is Wrong* (1986). In this filmstrip the children saw signs like "Europeans Only" on a public bench; "Servant's Entrance" above a railway waiting room; and "Peaceful Demonstration: Don't Shoot" at a squatters' demonstration. They saw contrasting pictures of a black shantytown and a white woman being served a cool drink by a black servant. They also saw pictures of mass demonstrations, funerals, and a chart which presented them with the relative populations of white and black South Africans and the percentage of land owned by each group. (Whites made up 13 percent of the South African population, but reserved 85 percent of the land for their own use.)

The children, shocked and angered by what they had seen, responded with questions like "Why do most white South Africans treat people of color so badly? Don't they realize we're all the same inside?" "Why did black men and women have to work so far from their families?" "How could black people be forced to live on horrible lands when this was their country to begin with?" "Who made the laws, and why were the whites in charge of everything if there were so few of them?" and "Why would the government kill people protesting peacefully?"

As we discussed these questions, several children drew on information learned earlier that year to compare the civil rights movement with the anti-apartheid movement and to make a connection between racism in the United States and in South Africa. One child recalled examples of peaceful civil rights protests crushed by state force in this country. Although the brutal racism of South Africa was still confusing for them, previous class discussions gave them a mental framework for thinking about issues of oppression, racism, and resistance. A single discussion, however, was insufficient to satisfy their questions, so we agreed to follow closely the South African elections.

This group of children was particularly sensitive to human suffering and injustice. Time and time again that year, they seized upon a social-justice issue I had introduced and expressed such sincere concern that we stayed with the topic longer than I had planned. They were curious and caring, always anxious to understand injustice and respond. This topic would, in fact, stir up their strongest passions and inspire them to take on a project to which we devoted the last two months of our school year. But none of us knew this at the time of the filmstrip.

Learning about South Africa

Soon after we viewed the filmstrip, Bob Krist, a student's father who is a professional photographer, came to speak with our class. He had just returned from a month-long tour of South Africa sponsored by the African National Congress. Mr. Krist showed slides depicting stark contrasts in living conditions between whites and blacks. Sharing several compelling anecdotes of incidents he had witnessed, he told of racist behavior and talk as the norm among most of the whites he had met. Again, the children were appalled and deeply concerned. "Did you tell those people who said that stuff they were racist?" Jeremy asked. Another challenged, "Did you do anything?" Mr. Krist explained that what he witnessed was so profoundly woven into the behavior and thinking of most white South Africans that there was little he could have said or done to change anything. Knowing Mr. Krist personally made his accounts of racial oppression in South Africa even more real for the children and heightened their curiosity about the upcoming elections.

To follow the elections, I clipped articles from the daily papers, printed the hourly news from America Online, and plastered our current events wall with photos. Some students videotaped nightly news reports showing mass demonstrations, views of life in shantytowns and homelands, and the fiery enthusiasm among blacks who were anticipating their first opportunity to vote. Each morning I summarized the news and read quotes from black South Africans reacting to the impending elections.

I was passionate and joyful about events in South Africa and openly shared my feelings with the class. I wanted the children to understand that we were living through an extremely momentous event. At one point one of the students said, "I think this is one of those things that we're going to tell our own kids about someday if we're doing our own oral histories." (Earlier in the year, we had studied oral history and the children had gathered stories of older family members, most of which included memories of important historical events.)

Students began spontaneously writing raps, songs, poems, and opinion pieces on South Africa, both during writing workshop and at home. The following rap written by three boys was eventually included in our class play.

> CHORUS: Mandela's free! Yeah! Yeah! Mandela's free! Yeah!
>   Yeah!

We just brought Mandela free! Yeah! Yeah!
He used to be a prison resident,
And soon he'll be our nation's president.

CHORUS: They used to live in fighty towns
          And soon they'll live in mighty towns!

CHORUS: They fought for their freedom,
          They fought for their rights.
          They fought for equality with all their might.

As the children shared their writings, I realized that the strength of their
work and the intense energy behind it merited, even demanded, an
audience beyond the classroom. Most social-justice units we do culminate
with a "real-world" project, something that takes the students' learning and
work beyond the classroom. For example, when we studied the "isms," the
students made posters condemning racism, sexism, ageism, and classism
and celebrating social equality. These posters were hung around the school
and later in store windows downtown. After studying Columbus from the
perspective of those who inhabited the islands he "discovered," the children
wrote picture books telling this alternative view of the story and gave these to
our school library. This study of South Africa called for a project that would
allow the children to extend their strong thoughts and feelings past our
classroom walls. I encouraged the children to begin thinking about an
effective project for this issue.

I showed the film *A World Apart* (Menges, 1988), a poignant story, about
a white anti-apartheid journalist persecuted by the South African government
for her organizing efforts, told from the point of view of her twelve-year-old
daughter. The film made a powerful impression on the children and gave
them a clearer understanding of the history of apartheid and the resistance
movement. Again they were both saddened and outraged by the brutality of
the South African government. Several cried at the site of nonviolent
protestors being crushed by the South African police, an anti-apartheid
leader who was tortured and killed in prison, and the film's star being
arbitrarily arrested and torn from her three young children. I reminded the
children several times that this was a true story and that much of what they
saw was still true today. I wanted to guard against their thinking that the
impending elections meant that all problems would be solved in South
Africa.

The film helped my students to understand that the upcoming elections were the result of years of struggle and not simply the white ruling elite suddenly coming to their senses. Social protest was a theme we had discussed several times earlier when we studied the labor movement, the civil rights movement, and the suffragist movement. I place a strong emphasis on history as a social process, a process involving real people making moral choices and forging their future. This also includes looking at situations in which people "chose" not to take a stand, where passivity determined historical outcomes.

Critical Literacy Across the Curriculum

Just before the elections, a parent with a son in another class at our school complained to me that the elections hadn't even been mentioned in his class. She suggested that my class prepare something to share with other classes. I brought this back to the students, who decided that we should improve the writings they had already done, write more, and create a series of mini-performances based on those writings.

My students assumed that they were already expert enough to create these performances, but I knew that they weren't. I told them that to do this responsibly, we had to do further research and continue our discussions. I decided to devote a substantial part of the curriculum for the following few weeks to this project. In math we studied statistics reflecting differences in wealth, living conditions, and access to power between white and black South Africans. I drew information from a curriculum written by Bill Bigelow (1985) and an excellent booklet prepared by COSATU (1992). Earlier in the year we had done an extensive unit on statistics through which the children learned to gather, represent, and interpret simple and familiar statistical data (e.g., typical family size in our class, school, town). They then studied what I called "statistics for social justice"—U.S. social statistics showing differentials in salaries between women and men and among various racial groups, and contrasting infant mortality rates among various social groups. These experiences had prepared the children to understand the South African statistics.

They restated the South African statistics in their own language, generated new information, wrote problems, and posed questions on the basis of the basic information sheet I had prepared. They then made beautiful posters presenting some of these statistics in words and drawings or graphs, which we later used in a multimedia exhibit supporting the play.

In reading we formed literature groups and read two novels about South Africa: *The Middle of Somewhere* (Gordon, 1992), the story of a family that resists government relocation intended to make way for a whites-only town, and *Journey to Jo'burg* (Naidoo, 1985), the story of a brother and sister's search for their mother, who works far away in the home of a white family. Both books brought my students closer to the thoughts and feelings of typical black South African children and their daily experience with apartheid.

To help my students approach the daily experience of most black South Africans on a more intimate level, I asked each of them to write an interior monologue, a writing device which "prompts students to empathize with other human beings" (Bigelow & Christensen, 1994). It supports students in developing the social imagination necessary to genuinely connect with distant and different others. It puts students inside the experience of another and challenges them to describe a situation from that person's point of view.

Given the vast differences between my students' perceptions of social reality as viewed from a relatively affluent, mostly white suburb and those, for example, of a black South African child of a domestic servant living in a township, writing interior monologues was invaluable in helping my students identify with the people we presumed to teach others about. Because I place a high value on asking children to write only for genuine purposes, I explained that this "exercise" would help them better imagine the thoughts and feelings of the characters they would later portray in our skits.

After reading each book, we brainstormed critical moments in the stories and all major characters. Each child then chose to describe a given situation in a first-person narrative from a particular character's perspective. A few children wrote about various characters' resolve to resist, and I highlighted these for the rest of class in order to ensure that they would not see black South Africans as passive and pathetic. I was impressed by the children's ability to enter into the experiences of others and to capture the pain, confusion, and humiliation felt by so many black South African children.

My students also wrote poems, questions, and personal responses to those novels in their writer's notebooks. My aim was to saturate their thoughts and creative imaginations with the black South African experience. I felt that before we could be qualified to teach others about apartheid and the upcoming elections, we had to work rigorously to understand it ourselves.

We set up a series of charts to keep track of the many questions generated as well as the research gathered to answer them, adding questions and answers each day. Some of the questions recorded were "What is the length of the presidency in South Africa and who will take over after Mandela (assuming he would win)?" "What would Ruth First be doing now if she hadn't been killed by the government and what is her husband, Joe Slovo, doing [the couple featured in the film *A World Apart*]?" "Why didn't Reagan and Bush want sanctions against South Africa?" During this research process we continued following the news and having daily discussions of events leading up to the elections.

At about this time, I showed *Cry Freedom* (Attenborough, 1987), a film about black activist Steve Biko and Donald Woods, the white journalist who brought Biko's message to the world. Both this film and *A World Apart*, shown at the beginning of our study, are long, complex films which were difficult for fourth graders and required extensive mediation on my part. I frequently paused each video to answer questions, clarify situations, and discuss content. The children clearly would not have been able to comprehend either film on their own, but in the context of our research and with my support, they learned a great deal from these films, which contained images of life under apartheid that could not have been conveyed through text alone.

The children were particularly disturbed by the scenes of police brutality, arbitrary arrests, and total absence of justice. Grappling with why "the state" (military and police) might not always protect the people was difficult for the children but important. In an effort to connect racism in South Africa with racism and injustice in the United States, I talked with my students about examples of police brutality in the United States, including the Rodney King incident. I also revealed that I personally had never even considered that the police or military could work against justice and freedom until college, that I had never learned the "underside of history" as a child. I often compared my own sanitized and patriotic education with the way we were learning so that the children would not take for granted a critical view of history and current events. I wanted to ensure that they were somewhat prepared for the years of uncritical teaching they were sure to experience in the future. And, of course, I again wanted to connect the South African reality of racism and injustice with that reality here in the United States. I continually brought our discussions back home and drew analogies between the two countries whenever possible.

"No Easy Road to Freedom": A Play

By this time the children were becoming "experts" on South Africa—
informed and articulate. I asked the class to consider how we might expand
the project to create something that would have more impact than the series
of mini-performances we had planned to do. One student, who recalled a
play my class had done for the school on the Montgomery bus boycott two
years earlier, suggested we write and produce a play about the conditions of
apartheid, the history of resistance, and the upcoming South African
elections. The class agreed.

I have no formal background in guiding play writing or drama with
children. However, I find myself using this medium regularly to bring
historical events, literature, and contemporary issues to life. I use drama to
help children take on the perspectives of others, understand different
historical periods, and devise solutions to their own everyday problems.
Since the children are engaged in informal drama throughout the year and
across the curriculum—in role-plays, simulations, and open-ended skits—
they were already comfortable with the medium.

Once the decision was made, I sent a letter to parents which described
what we were doing and why, and requested their help. I wanted them to be
aware that most of our remaining school days would be taken over by this
project and to understand my rationale for this. Fortunately, my teaching
situation affords me the flexibility to take on a project that replaces what had
been my original curricular time line, but I could never do this successfully
without informing and involving parents. Seven parents responded to my
letter by offering fairly substantial assistance. A few worked on scenery with
a group of children after school for several days; others helped with props,
costumes, and a range of other tasks.

The students wanted to show footage from the films they had seen in
order to give the audience images of the living conditions of black South
Africans, of mass protests, and of other scenes that our play couldn't possibly
depict. They thought we could choose a series of short scenes from each
film, which we would show during our play's scene changes. I thought their
idea was brilliant, but I considered the technical aspects to be daunting.
Ultimately, I had a parent and child manage this. They rented the videos
again, viewed them at home, and recorded the sections the class decided to
show. Later, a few children went to our high school and worked with our
district's "video expert" to create a video with these scenes in the order to
use them. The three children who worked on this became our technical crew

for the play. All three were responsible and intelligent, but too shy to perform. They were thoroughly involved with the play, but truly did not want to appear on stage. They managed these film clips, the sound system, and the lights for our play.

The children were bursting with great ideas, and I realized we needed a system for gathering and responding to their suggestions. I placed a notebook in our discussion area, where the children wrote their ideas whenever they occurred to them. Each day we read through the ideas as a class and decided which to use and how to use them. This was a way of honoring everyone's ideas and saving my sanity, because otherwise children were constantly grabbing me to share their latest brainchild.

The process we used for writing the play was simple, efficient, and drew significant input from every child. The class brainstormed about six scenes on chart paper and discussed generally what each scene would look like. Then the children signed up to write different scenes. I gave each group a work folder, a place to work, and encouragement. They worked for an hour that first day discussing and writing, then brought their drafts back to the class for feedback. We continued this way for a week. When we weren't writing we were gathering more research as the process of writing generated more questions. We called the Africa Fund in New York, the ANC, and the South African Embassy, and had many questions answered. During this process we also referred back to the interior monologues written earlier in order to assist the children in writing more plausible dialogue and action.

Although we had had many discussions linking racism in the United States and in South Africa, I realized that the children were not weaving these concepts into the play, so I decided to directly suggest that this connection be made in the play. I asked the children to brainstorm all the analogous situations here that we had considered during earlier discussions. The list included the following: Jim Crow laws in the South and actual segregation in most places now; police arresting peaceful picketers during a local labor strike; Reagan's refusal to support divestment; the anti-apartheid movement here; statistics revealing a significant differential in the living conditions of blacks and whites in the United States with regard to infant mortality, wealth, and income and education levels. We divided these issues among the playwriting groups, who then went back to find ways of working the information into the play.

One example of this is a dialogue in our last scene between an American visitor to South Africa and a South African—"The ANC Victory Celebration." The American shares an article which refers to the New Jersey system of public education as apartheid. (This was an article that had actually appeared recently in our local paper.) The American goes on to explain that rich suburban districts have far more resources for their schools than urban areas, and given that students in urban schools are predominantly children of color while those in suburban schools are mostly white, this creates an educational system of apartheid.

At the end of one week of scriptwriting, I typed and revised the script and made sure there were parts for everyone, apart from the technical crew. The groups went over the copies of the revised draft and made revisions which were then discussed with the entire class. This process of going through the entire play and soliciting input from all children was tedious, but the children stayed focused and engaged. The children then chose their parts, and auditions were held for the most sought-after roles. The class voted on who would play those roles. Once everyone had a part they were satisfied with, the children set out to learn their lines. For one week their homework was to study their lines and cues every day and read the entire script several times. I wanted to be sure that every child had a strong working idea of the entire play in order to ensure smooth transitions and so that they could all help each other with their lines and staging. We practiced in the classroom every day for about an hour. All the children were directors, giving feedback and suggesting revisions.

During this process, our class was also learning songs for the play, including the new South African national anthem "N'kosi Sikelel'i Africa" and "Sing Mandela Free." The music teacher helped the class learn two of the children's own raps, including the one mentioned above. I also taught these songs to the other fourth-grade classes during our social studies sessions so that they could sing with us during the play.

The scenery for the play included a huge backdrop of a crowd scene, painted by children and parents after school under the guidance of our art teacher. We also hung all of the children's posters which illustrated the statistics we had studied in math and the numerous posters from the Africa Fund. The costumes were black T-shirts with anti-apartheid slogans, made one afternoon with the help of a parent.

The technical crew, with the help of Bob Krist, made a series of slides of South Africa which we used between scenes, alternating with the film clips. They made slides of newspaper photographs showing the long lines for voting, elderly and sick black South Africans being carried and wheeled to voting places, and celebrations during the elections.

This crew also thought we should attempt to make a high-quality video of the play. They suggested that we ask the district's "video expert," with whom they had worked earlier, to bring in his high school students to videotape the play. Once we arranged for the high school students to do the taping, my students became even more serious and committed to creating a high-quality production. There wasn't a single child who wasn't engaged and enthusiastic. No one grew bored, lazy, or disruptive. Students had a strong sense that they were involved in something big and important and so had a responsibility to do it well. I overheard several conversations among the children, discussing how our play was going to make a difference.

One of my four classified students was particularly committed to the play. Melanie, whose previous year's teacher described her as passive, difficult to motivate, and "not interested in ideas," could think of nothing but the play, according to her mother. Melanie played the part of a black servant in a white home, and she decided to refer back to relevant sections in the novels we had read and the film *A World Apart*, in order to get a better idea of how to play the part. She was so serious about her role that she assigned herself this bit of research to ensure that she acted with authenticity. Melanie also stayed after school numerous afternoons to work on scenery, and she involved her mother in organizing props for most of the play. The day after the play she wrote the following:

> I think that we were second hand freedom fighters because we don't go to protests and rallies, but we did a play and showed seventy people what happened in South Africa. I think if everyone chips in we could make South Africa a great place to be and we could end racism everywhere.

Melanie clearly felt effective as a student and an agent for social change. School made sense to her while participating in this project, and therefore motivation came naturally.

The week before the play, my students went in groups of five to all the classes that would be attending the play (grades 3–5), to review background information and leave fact sheets for teachers to use with their classes. We also circulated the book *At the Crossroads* by Rachel Isadora (1991), a beautifully written and illustrated story about children living in a South African township awaiting the return of their fathers, who work as miners and are away for months at a time. The teachers all read this book to their classes and led discussions about it, and reviewed the fact sheets we had prepared. This preparation for the play was critical for our audience to really absorb all that we covered. We also encouraged the teachers to have their students view the posters that were up on stage a few days before the play. Although none of these teachers had devoted much time to following the elections, they all seemed quite willing to spend class time on the preparation and follow-up to the play.

June 13: Performance Day

The play went incredibly well. The children knew their lines and delivered them powerfully. There were no major problems despite the complicated technical aspects of our production—video crew, slide show, films projected onto a large screen during scene changes. The audience loved the performance. It was obvious they were not only well informed, but well entertained, too. After the play, one of my students spoke to the audience about what they could do to fight racism; for example, give money to the Africa Fund, keep learning about and paying attention to South Africa, join anti-racist groups, take a stand against racism whenever they witness it personally. We also prepared and distributed a set of sheets with this information to all the classes.

The day after the play, Naoko, a student from one of the other two fourth-grade classes, said to me, "What Matt said in the play was right; we do have apartheid in New Jersey. We have apartheid right here in Ridgewood." She then showed me a diagram she had drawn which fairly accurately depicted the racial segregation in our town with Blacks, Whites, and Asians living in distinct neighborhoods. Obviously, there are huge differences in degree between racism and segregation in South Africa and the United States, and the children were aware of this. However, I also think it was significant that children, such as Naoko, made such connections.

The parent of one of my students wrote me a letter after this project, expressing her understanding of and appreciation for its effect on her daughter:

> Throughout the year, you helped the children understand issues of participatory democracy and allowed them to experience it in the classroom. The questions raised by the South Africa project went beyond race issues into broader understandings about the power of each individual's participation in community decisions, the essence of participatory democracy. Experiencing how democracy works, how people can form intelligent and critical opinions and make responsible decisions were at the core of what my daughter learned this year.

This parent was one among five extremely progressive, vocal, and supportive parents who set an unusually welcome tone for a critical-literacy program that year. They loved it, encouraged it, and managed to bring along the rest of the parents. In *A Pedagogy for Liberation*, Ira Shor (Shor & Freire, 1987) discusses the importance of keeping your finger on the political pulse of your workplace and making tactful decisions about what that climate can tolerate. He cautions that to ignore this is to be irresponsible and risk losing one's job and thus an opportunity to make progressive change. Each year I try to get a measure of the politics of my students' parents. I need to know just to what extent I can safely pursue a social-justice curriculum. This is not to say that I ever "sell out" or neutralize my curriculum. I do not. I always approach my teaching from a social justice, critical-literacy perspective. However, some years I must modify and slightly tone down the program.

My work climate during the school year of the South Africa project was more fertile for radical teaching than at any time in my ten years of teaching, so I therefore pulled out all the stops. Other years have been different, and so I have had to adjust my program in response to more conservative pressures. For example, during a unit on prejudice and stereotypes and the history of intolerance in the United States, I was accused of being too negative and "not showing all the good things about this country." This prompted me to seek out current examples from the newspaper of people fighting discrimination and to highlight historical examples of successful social-justice campaigns and individual activists. I have also been accused of not showing "the other side of the story." To this I did not respond that, in fact, the children are drilled daily with the official and status-quo supporting version of the past and present. Instead, when teaching about exploitative working conditions in Nike and Disney overseas plants, I had the children read documents from those companies' public relations departments. The documents were written in response to criticisms from labor-advocacy groups. In reading these documents, the children gained skills in critically analyzing various points of view, considering the interests and perspectives behind texts, and forming their own opinions. Teaching for social justice requires that you find that delicate balance between taking risks and pushing the limits of your particular work world, and maintaining your job for future years of transformative teaching. To be a teacher for social justice, one must also be brave and willing to not always be popular.

When viewed in the larger context of an ongoing struggle for social justice, the impact of our play was modest. But when I consider the effect it had on my students, the strength of the project is heartening. My students felt empowered as social activists and believed they had a mandate and the ability to make a difference. The project was successful because it nurtured the children's sense of their own power to build a more just world. I believe that such an experience can propel children forward as future activists—hopeful, committed, critical, and with concrete skills to effect social change.

References

Apartheid is wrong: A curriculum for young people. (1986). Trenton, NJ: Educators Against Racism and Apartheid. Filmstrip.

Altwerger, B., & Flores, B. (1994). Theme cycles: Creating communities of learners. *Primary Voices, 2*(1), 2–6.

Attenborough, R. (Dir.). (1987). *Cry freedom.* 157 min. Universal City, CA: MCA/Universal. Videocassette.

Atwell, N. (1987). *In the middle: Writing, reading, and learning with adolescents.* Upper Montclair, NJ: Boynton/Cook.

Bigelow, B. (1985). *Strangers in their own country: A curriculum guide on South Africa.* Trenton, NJ: Africa World.

Bigelow, B., & Christensen, L. (1994). Promoting social imagination through interior monologues. In B. Bigelow, et al. (Eds.), *Rethinking our classrooms: Teaching for equity and justice* (pp. 110–111. Milwaukee: Rethinking Schools.

Calkins, L. M. (1994). *The art of teaching writing.* New ed. Portsmouth, NH: Heinemann.

Christensen, L. (1994). Unlearning the myths that bind us. In B. Bigelow, et al. (Eds.), *Rethinking our classrooms: Teaching for equity and justice* (pp. 8–10). Milwaukee: Rethinking Schools.

COSATU. (1992). *Our political economy: Understanding the problems.* Johannesburg, South Africa.

Gordon, S. (1992). *The middle of somewhere: A story of South Africa.* New York: Bantam.

Goggenheim, C. (Dir.). (1991). *A time for justice: America's civil rights movement.* 38 min. Santa Monica, CA: Direct Cinema. Videocassette.

Isadora, R. (1991). *At the crossroads.* New York: Greenwillow.

Menges, C. (Dir.). (1988). *A world apart.* 114 min. Los Angeles: Media Home Entertainment. Videocassette.

Naidoo, B. (1985). *Journey to Jo'burg: A South African story.* New York: Harper & Row.

Shor, I. (1992). *Empowering education: Critical teaching for social change.* Chicago: University of Chicago Press.

Shor, I., & Freire, P. (1987). *A pedagogy for liberation: Dialogues on transforming education.* South Hadley, MA: Bergin & Garvey.

Short, K. G., and Harste, J. C., with Burke, C. (1996). *Creating classrooms for authors and inquirers.* 2nd ed. Portsmouth, NH: Heinemann.

Zinn, H. (1993). *Failure to quit: Reflections of an optimistic historian.* Monroe, ME: Common Courage.

This book was set in Optima and Trajan by
City Desktop Productions.
The typeface used on the cover was Trajan.
The book was printed by IPC Communication Services.